REVISION WORKBOOK

Constitutional Law:
THE MACHINERY OF GOVERNMENT

Second Edition

CONSULTANT EDITOR: LORD TEMPLEMAN

OLD BAILEY PRESS

OLD BAILEY PRESS
200 Greyhound Road, London W14 9RY

First published 1997
Second edition 1999
Reprinted 2001

© The HLT Group Ltd 1999

All Old Bailey Press publications enjoy copyright protection and the copyright belongs to the HLT Group Ltd.

All rights reserved. No part of this publication may be reproduced or transmitted in any form or by any means, electronic, mechanical, photocopying, recording or otherwise, or stored in any retrieval system of any nature without either the written permission of the copyright holder, application for which should be made to the Old Bailey Press, or a licence permitting restricted copying in the United Kingdom issued by the Copyright Licensing Agency.

Any person who infringes the above in relation to this publication may be liable to criminal prosecution and civil claims for damages.

ISBN 1 85836 340 3

British Library Cataloguing-in-Publication.

A CIP Catalogue record for this book is available from the British Library.

Printed and bound in Great Britain.

Contents

Acknowledgements

Some questions used are taken or adapted from past University of London LLB (External) Degree and the University of Wolverhampton examination papers and our thanks are extended to the universities of London and Wolverhampton for their kind permission to use and publish the questions.

Caveat

The LLB answers given are not approved or sanctioned by the University of London or the University of Wolverhampton and are entirely our responsibility.

They are not intended as 'Model Answers', but rather as Suggested Solutions.

The answers have two fundamental purposes, namely:

a) To provide a detailed example of a suggested solution to an examination question, and

b) To assist students with their research into the subject and to further their understanding and appreciation of the subject of Law.

Introduction

This Revision WorkBook is aimed to be of help to those studying constitutional law. Its coverage is not restricted to any one syllabus but embraces all the core topics which can be found in university level examinations.

Students will hopefully find it useful not only at examination time but also as a helpful summary of and introduction to the subject when studying it for the first time.

The WorkBook has been designed specifically to address common problems suffered by students when studying any legal subject. All examination based courses consist of four main processes, all of which may cause problems for some students. The WorkBook can be of help with each of these processes.

a) *Acquisition of knowledge*

   This is achieved by individual work – attending lectures and reading the relevant textbooks and source materials such as cases and articles. The WorkBook is not intended to be a textbook and is in no way a substitute for one. However, the 'key points' and 'recent cases and statutes' sections will help students to direct their study to the important areas within each topic.

b) *Understanding*

   Whilst difficulties in understanding a topic or particular point are best solved by a teacher's explanation. The WorkBook offers a summary of the essential points together with cases. This is the key to understanding for many students.

c) *Learning*

   The process of learning is also a highly individual one. As a rule, however, students find it much easier to learn within a clear structure. The WorkBook will be an aid to those who find learning a problem.

d) *Applying the knowledge to the question*

   This is, perhaps, the most common problem of all. The WorkBook includes examination questions and answers covering many possible question variations within each topic.

The final chapter contains the complete June 1997 University of London LLB (External) Constitutional Law question paper, followed by suggested solutions to each question. Thus the student will have the opportunity to review a recent examination paper in its entirety, and can, if desired, use this chapter as a mock examination – referring to the suggested solutions only after first having attempted the questions. Note that some questions will be on administrative law, and for these reference should be made to the *Administrative Law Revision WorkBook* also published by Old Bailey Press. For the June 1997 paper the relevant question is Q8.

How to Study Constitutional Law

Constitutional law is a vast subject covering a variety of topics ranging from the structure and organisation of government to civil liberties. Examiners must be selective in the areas they choose to examine and students should pay regard to their particular syllabus and the emphasis placed on each topic. By and large however the subject divides into two areas – the characteristics of the British Constitution and civil liberties. If your syllabus includes judicial review of administrative action you should also refer to the *Administrative Law Revision WorkBook*, published by Old Bailey Press.

The first part of any syllabus – usually the characteristics of the British Constitution – demands a background knowledge of British history and politics. This can cause problems for students who do not have any interest or knowledge of this area and overseas students in particular can experience difficulty here. To place the subject in its proper context requires some background reading – Maitland's *A Constitutional History of England* is authoritative – and knowledge gleaned from keeping abreast of current affairs is vital. In addition there are several good introductory works which help students. In terms of the examination this area can unsettle students simply because there is an absence of legal authority for the points they make. The questions are often discursive demanding the discussion of an issue and the presentation of a point of view. A well-read student who can present the salient points with authority will achieve good marks – the student who 'waffles' will not. Examples are important eg answer to a question on conventions demands an explanation of the part played by convention in our constitution backed by examples of conventions in operation.

The second part of the syllabus will deal with civil liberties. Again this is an extensive area and examiners are often selective. Police powers may appear in some syllabuses, citizenship and immigration in others. It is important to appreciate that what liberties are enjoyed in the United Kingdom are residual and the part played by the European Convention on Human Rights as enacted in the Human Rights Act 1998 must be understood. The subject matter is topical, statute and case law are important. Questions can be either essay or problem. Problem questions, for example on public order or police powers, require students to apply the relevant statute and case law to the facts given, remembering again to take care to advise the client.

In essence constitutional law, like all legal subjects, requires students to present arguments in a precise, reasoned and authoritative manner.

Revision and Examination Technique

(A) REVISION TECHNIQUE

Planning a revision timetable

In planning your revision timetable make sure you don't finish the syllabus too early. You should avoid leaving revision so late that you have to 'cram' – but constant revision of the same topic leads to stagnation.

Plan ahead, however, and try to make your plans increasingly detailed as you approach the examination date.

Allocate enough time for each topic to be studied. But note that it is better to devise a realistic timetable, to which you have a reasonable chance of keeping, rather than a wildly optimistic schedule which you will probably abandon at the first opportunity!

The syllabus and its topics

One of your first tasks when you began your course was to ensure that you thoroughly understood your **syllabus**. Check now to see if you can write down the **topics** it comprises from memory. You will see that the chapters of this WorkBook are each devoted to a topic. This will help you decide which are the key chapters relative to your revision programme. Though you should allow some time for glancing through the other chapters.

The topic and its key points

Again working from memory, analyse what you consider to be the key points of any topic that you have selected for particular revision. Seeing what you can recall, unaided, will help you to understand and firmly memorise the concepts involved.

Using the WorkBook

Relevant questions are provided for each topic in this book. Naturally, as typical examples of examination questions, they do not normally relate to one topic only. But the questions in each chapter *will* relate to the subject matter of the chapter to a degree. You can choose your method of consulting the questions and solutions, but here are some suggestions (strategies 1–3). Each of them pre-supposes that you have read through the author's notes on key points and question analysis, and any other preliminary matter, at the beginning of the chapter. Once again, you now need to practise working from *memory*, for that is the challenge you are preparing yourself for. As a rule of procedure constantly test yourself once revision starts, both orally and in writing.

Strategy 1

Strategy 1 is planned for the purpose of *quick revision*. First read your chosen question carefully and then jot down in abbreviated notes what you consider to be the main points at issue. Similarly, note the cases and statutes that occur to you as being relevant for citation purposes. Allow yourself sufficient time to cover what you feel to be relevant. Then study the author's *skeleton solution* and skim-read the *suggested solution* to see how they compare with your notes. When comparing consider carefully what the author has included (and concluded) and see whether that agrees with what you have written. Consider the points of variation also. Have you recognised the key issues? How relevant have you been? It is possible, of course, that you have referred to a recent case that *is* relevant, but which had not been reported when the WorkBook was prepared.

Strategy 2

Strategy 2 requires a nucleus of *three hours* in which to practise writing a set of examination answers in a limited time-span.

Select a number of questions (as many as are normally set in your subject in the examination you are studying for), each from a different chapter in the WorkBook, without consulting the solutions. Find a place to write where you will not be disturbed and try to arrange not to be interrupted for three hours. Write your solutions in the time allowed, noting any time needed to make up if you *are* interrupted.

After a rest, compare your answers with the *suggested solutions* in the WorkBook. There will be considerable variation in style, of course, but the bare facts should not be too dissimilar. Evaluate your answer critically. Be 'searching', but develop a positive approach to deciding how you would tackle each question on another occasion.

Strategy 3

You are unlikely to be able to do more than one three hour examination, but occasionally set yourself a single question. Vary the 'time allowed' by imagining it to be one of the questions that you must answer in three hours and allow yourself a limited preparation and writing time. Try one question that you feel to be difficult and an easier question on another occasion, for example.

Mis-use of suggested solutions

Don't try to learn by rote. In particular, don't try to reproduce the *suggested solutions* by heart. Learn to express the basic concepts in your own words.

Keeping up-to-date

Keep up-to-date. While examiners do not require familiarity with changes in the law during the three months prior to the examination, it obviously creates a good impression if you can show you are acquainted with any recent changes. Make a habit of looking through one of the leading journals – *Modern Law Review, Law Quarterly Review* or the *New Law Journal*, for example – and cumulative indices to law reports, such as the *All England Law Reports* or *Weekly Law Reports*, or indeed the daily law reports in *The Times*. Specialist journal(s) for the subject eg *Public Law* are also helpful sources.

(B) EXAMINATION SKILLS

Examiners are human too!

The process of answering an examination question involves a *communication* between you and the person who set it. If you were speaking face to face with the person, you would choose your verbal points and arguments carefully in your reply. When writing, it is all too easy to forget *the human being who is awaiting the reply* and simply write out what one knows in the area of the subject! Bear in mind it is a person whose question you are responding to, throughout your essay. This will help you to avoid being irrelevant or long-winded.

The essay question

Candidates are sometimes tempted to choose to answer essay questions because they 'seem' easier. But the examiner is looking for thoughtful work and will not give good marks for superficial answers.

The essay-type of question may be either purely factual, in asking you to *explain the meaning* of a certain doctrine or principle, or it may ask you to *discuss* a certain proposition, usually derived from a quotation. In either case, the approach to the answer is the same. A clear programme must be devised to give the examiner the meaning or significance of the doctrine, principle or proposition and its origin in common law, equity or statute, and cases which illustrate its application to the branch of law concerned.

The problem question

The problem-type question requires a different approach. You may well be asked to advise a client or merely discuss the problems raised in the question. In either case, the most important factor is to take great care in reading the question. By its nature, the question will be longer than the essay-type question and you will have a number of facts to digest. Time spent in analysing the question may well save time later, when you are endeavouring to impress on the examiner the considerable extent of your basic legal knowledge. The quantity of knowledge is itself a trap and you must always keep within the boundaries of the question in hand. It is very tempting to show the examiner the extent of your knowledge of your subject, but if this is outside the question, it is time lost and no marks earned. It it inevitable that some areas which you have studied and revised will not be the subject of questions, but under no circumstances attempt to adapt a question to a stronger area of knowledge at the expense of relevance.

When you are satisfied that you have grasped the full significance of the problem-type question, set out the fundamental principles involved. You may well be asked to advise one party, but there is no reason why you should not introduce your answer by:

> 'I would advise A on the following matters ...'

and then continue the answer in a normal impersonal form. This is a much better technique than answering the question as an imaginary conversation.

You will then go on to identify the fundamental problem, or problems posed by the question. This should be followed by a consideration of the law which is relevant to the problem. The source of the law, together with the cases which will be of assistance in solving the problem, must then be considered in detail.

Very good problem questions are quite likely to have alternative answers, and in advising A you should be aware that alternative arguments may be available. Each stage of your answer, in this case, will be based on the argument or arguments considered in the previous stage, forming a conditional sequence.

If, however, you only identify one fundamental problem, do not waste time worrying that you cannot think of an alternative – there may very well be only that one answer.

The examiner will then wish to see how you use your legal knowledge to formulate a case and how you apply that formula to the problem which is the subject of the question. It is this positive approach which can make answering a problem question a high mark earner for the student who has fully understood the question and clearly argued his case on the established law.

Examination checklist

1 Read the instructions at the head of the examination carefully. While last-minute changes are unlikely – such as the introduction of a *compulsory question* or *an increase in the number of questions asked* – it has been known to happen.

2 Read the questions carefully. Analyse problem questions – work out what the examiner wants.

3 Plan your answer *before* you start to write. You can divide your time as follows:

a) working out the question (5 per cent of time);

b) working out how to answer the question (5 to 10 per cent of time);

c) writing your answer.

Do not overlook (a) and (b).

4 Check that you understand the rubric *before* you start to write. Do not 'discuss', for example, if you are specifically asked to 'compare and contrast'.

5 Answer the correct number of questions. If you fail to answer one out of four questions set you lose 25 per cent of your marks!

Style and structure

Try to be clear and concise. Basically this amounts to using paragraphs to denote the sections of your essay, and writing simple, straightforward sentences as much as possible. The sentence you have just read has 22 words – when a sentence reaches 50 words it becomes difficult for a reader to follow.

Do not be inhibited by the word 'structure' (traditionally defined as giving an essay a beginning, a middle and an end). A good structure will be the natural consequence of setting out your arguments and the supporting evidence in a logical order. Set the scene briefly in your opening paragraph. Provide a clear conclusion in your final paragraph.

Table of Cases

Table of Statutes

From the European Union

1 The Nature of Constitutional Law

1.1 Introduction

Constitutions define political authority and the basis for the exercise of political authority. They regulate the relationships of the principal organs of government – legislature, executive and judiciary – to each other and define their functions. A constitution is essentially a framework of rules which make up the system whereby a state is governed.

In most modern states these rules are contained in a single document and usually include a Bill of Rights which provides citizens of that state with guarantees regarding the protection of certain civil liberties. Such constitutions are subject to judicial interpretation in the sense that the courts can assess the legality of legislative measures by reference to the constitutional document. The United Kingdom has no written constitution as such. The sources of the constitution are to be found in statute, the common law, custom and convention. Whilst conventions undoubtedly play an important part in the United Kingdom they cannot be enforced in the courts.

The constitution of the United Kingdom has evolved over centuries and the 'rules' of constitutional behaviour are not contained in any single document. A point of comparison can be made with the USA where, following the American War of Independence, a written document was prepared, which established fundamental constitutional principles and safeguarded the rights of citizens.

1.2 Key points

a) *Written and unwritten constitutions*

The term 'written constitution' is used in relation to those countries with a single document (or a group of documents) that contains the basic rules and to which reference can be made to test whether or not the organs of government are acting 'constitutionally'. By contrast, under an 'unwritten constitution' no such document exists and the rules have to be established from the ordinary laws of the land.

b) *Flexible and rigid constitutions*

Most countries with a written constitution require some special procedure before constitutional changes can be effected – for example a referendum or a two-thirds majority of the elected chamber. In this sense the constitution is 'entrenched'. Flexible constitutions are so described because constitutional change can be achieved by the same procedure as changes in laws generally. This is the position in the United Kingdom.

c) *Other classifications*

A system of government which is accountable to the people is described as democratic government. constitutions define the way in which a government is to be responsible and the way in which it is elected.

Federal states are those states in which regions enjoy autonomous law-making power – such as the United States. Unitary states are those in which power is focused on central government. The United Kingdom has a unitary system of government in that the United Kingdom Parliament at Westminster is the supreme law-making body. Under the Scotland Act 1998 the Scottish Parliament will have sovereignty in devolved areas, but the Westminster Parliament will retain ultimate power.

The head of state can vary in form. It may be a monarch, a president or a chairman. The extent of their powers is defined by the constitution so that, for example, while the President of the USA enjoys significant powers, the President of the Republic of Ireland enjoys a position analogous to our own Monarch – that is to say most of their executive powers are exercised by ministers.

A constitution is in a sense a 'higher' form of law. It is the basis upon which all other laws derive their validity and force. However, it remains valid only for as long as those subject to it accept its rules as binding.

d) *Aspects of the United Kingdom constitution*

The United Kingdom Parliament is sovereign. There is no limit on the competence of Parliament to enact legislation (subject to the constitutional implications of membership of the European Union). Furthermore, constitutional changes can be achieved by ordinary legislation, ie a simple majority in each house of Parliament and the Royal Assent.

The legislature of the United Kingdom comprises the House of Lords and the House of Commons – a bi-cameral system. The House of Lords is, at present, an unelected chamber, a politically controversial feature of the legislature.

The Head of State is the Queen but the role of the monarch is largely ceremonial and circumscribed by convention. Residual powers of the Crown are in fact exercised by the government.

Government is democratic, ie membership of the House of Commons is dependent on elections and the government is ultimately accountable to the electorate. The electoral system used for general elections in the UK – 'first past the post' – as opposed to any form of proportional representation arouses occasional political controversy.

In the absence of a written constitution there is a greater dependence on the government's respect for the rule of law as there is no clear line on what is constitutionally legitimate.

Some argue that the United Kingdom needs a written constitution in order to more effectively protect the individual rights of citizens. There is also support for reforming the House of Lords, reforming the the electoral system by moving over to proportional representation, improving the accountability of the executive to Parliament, and moving towards a more open system of government.

e) *Sources of the constitution*

Because the United Kingdom has an unwritten constitution its sources are to be found in the general law, ie statute and precedent, and in practices that have become firmly established over time, ie conventions. In addition, the United Kingdom's membership of the European Union has important constitutional implications.

i) Statute

There are many statutes which relate either to the system of government or to the rights of the citizens. Identifying statutes of constitutional significance can be difficult. Major examples are: the Bill of Rights 1689 which laid down the foundations of the modern constitution; the Act of Settlement 1700 which provided for the succession to the throne; the Act of Union 1706 which united the Parliaments of England and Scotland; the European Communities Act 1972 by which the United Kingdom acceded to the Treaty of Rome; and the Human Rights Act 1998 which effected the incorporation of the European Convention on Human Rights into domestic law.

ii) Case law

Through the development of the common law the courts can establish important rules relating to the powers of the various organs of government: *Entick* v *Carrington* (1765) 19 St Tr 1030; *Council for Civil Service Unions* v *Minister for the Civil Service* [1984] 3 All ER 935. Similarly, through the interpretation of statutory provisions.

iii) Community law

The United Kingdom became a member of the European Communities from 1 January 1973: see European Communities Act 1972. As a consequence Community law takes precedence over domestic law: see *Costa* v *ENEL* [1964] ECR 585. The main sources of Community law are:

- The treaties – provisions directly applicable in United Kingdom courts.
- Regulations – these are directly applicable in United Kingdom courts.
- Directives – Community objectives which must be complied with.
- Decisions of the European Court of Justice on European law – these will be applied by the courts in the United Kingdom.

iv) The Royal Prerogative

These are residual powers, privileges and immunities belonging to the Crown, such as the power to: declare war, enter into treaty obligations, issue passports, recognise foreign governments, and maintain domestic law and order. The courts will review the exercise of these powers to the extent that the subject matter is 'justiciable'.

v) The European Convention on Human Rights

With the enactment of the Human Rights Act 1998 the European Convention on Human Rights has (in part) been incorporated into the domestic law of the United Kingdom. The Act will come into effect fully in the year 2000. Decisions of the European Court of Human Rights will be binding on domestic courts as regards the interpretation of relevant Convention provisions.

vi) Conventions

Definition: Conventions are 'rules of constitutional behaviour which are considered to be binding by and upon those who operate the constitution but which are not enforced by the law courts – nor by the presiding officers of the Houses of Parliament.' (Dicey)

Some examples of conventions relating to the monarchy:

- The Sovereign should act on the advice of her ministers.
- The Sovereign should ask the leader who commands a majority in the House of Commons to form a government.
- The Sovereign should dissolve Parliament at the request of the Prime Minister.
- The Sovereign should not refuse the Royal Assent.

Some examples of conventions relating to the executive:

- Ministers are collectively and individually responsible to Parliament.
- Ministers must be members of the House of Commons or House of Lords.
- The government must resign if it loses the confidence of the Commons.

Some examples of conventions relating to Parliament:

- Public expenditure measures must originate in the House of Commons.
- The House of Lords ought ultimately to defer to the will of the House of Commons.

Some examples of conventions relating to the judiciary:

- A judge's professional conduct should not be questioned in either House except on a motion for dismissal.
- A judge should not be active in party politics.

vii) The importance of conventions

The aim of conventional rules is the smooth working of government. See Sir Ivor Jennings who suggested a three-part text for recognising a valid convention: Is there a precedent?; Do those who operate the constitution accept that the convention is binding? Is there a good political reason for the convention?

The conventional wisdom is that the conventions of ministerial and collective responsibility help to ensure the accountability of the executive – the extent to which this theory is matched by reality is considered further in Chapter 8. The failure to observe constitutional conventions can have significant political repercussions, eg the refusal of a government to resign on losing the confidence of the House of Commons. Such repercussions are dependent on the perceived importance of the conventional rule. Rules of political practice do change and conventions can change accordingly. This gives the constitution flexibility.

viii) Conventions and the courts

Conventions are not enforceable in the courts because they are not rules of law: see *Madzimbamuto* v *Lardner-Burke* [1969] 1 AC 645. The courts do, however, recognise the existence of conventions: see *Attorney-General* v *Jonathan Cape* [1976] QB 752 and *Re Amendment of the Constitution of Canada* (1982) 125 DLR (3d) 1.

1.3 Recent developments

An up-to-date knowledge of recent political debate and legislative changes is important for any student of constitutional law. Issues to be aware of include:

The effect of devolution in Scotland and Wales, particularly the possible conflicts between

Parliament at Westminster and the Scottish Parliament. There may also be a re-examination of the role of Scottish MPs at Westminster.

Reform of the House of Lords is clearly going to occur between 1999 and 2000 – the debate will centre around the composition of the second chamber following the removal of its hereditary membership.

In 2000 the Human Rights Act 1998 will start to take effect – there are likely to be numerous legal challenges that will place the constitutional role of the judges under the spotlight.

Proportional representation will be used for electing MEPs in 1999, and for the election of some members of the Scottish Parliament and Welsh Assembly.

Moves towards joining a single European currency will again intensify debates over sovereignty in areas of fiscal and monetary policy.

1.4 Analysis of questions

Examiners frequently set questions on the nature of the United Kingdom constitution or on the sources of that constitution. Care must be taken to answer the question asked and not simply provide the examiner with a list of points. Ensure that you have a clear idea of what you want to say before you attempt any such question. In this area there area few 'right' or 'wrong' answers. You are entitled to express your view on the desirability of a written constitution or on the desirability of retaining flexible conventions provided your case is cogently argued and supported by authorities. One of the most common mistakes students make is that of referring to examples from case law or statute without explaining to the examiner why the example has been cited, or indeed how it advances the student's argument.

1.5 Questions

QUESTION ONE

To what extent, if any, do you agree with the statement that 'conventions constitute probably the most discussed and least definable source of the constitution' (Norton).

University of London LLB Examination
(for External Students) Constitutional Law June 1987 Q1

General Comment

A relatively difficult question. Unless you can deal with the specific point raised concerning the definition of conventions you should not attempt this question. The danger with such a question is that your answer becomes too general and there is the temptation to fill it out by simply producing a list of conventions.

Skeleton Solution

- Introduction – what are conventions of the constitution?
- The difficulty of defining conventions. The lack of written form; their political nature; lack of legal form; effect of disagreement; absence of pre-existing usage; flexibility.
- Why conventions are discussed. Distinction between law and convention; why conventions are obeyed; the advantage of conventions over legal rules.

Suggested Solution

A great many of the rules of the British constitution, which are observed by the Sovereign, the Prime Minister, ministers, Members of Parliament, the judiciary and civil servants, are not contained in Acts of Parliament or judicial decisions, but are to be found in those rules of conduct called constitutional conventions. These have been described as 'rules of constitutional behaviour which are considered to be binding by and upon those who operate the constitution but which are not enforced by the law courts ... nor by the presiding officers in the Houses of Parliament': Marshall & Moodie, *Some Problems of the Constitution,* 5th ed 1971 pp22–23. These conventions of the constitution are obeyed by those to whom they apply not because of the threat of any legal sanction in case of breach, but because of the political difficulties which may follow if they are not obeyed.

Some conventional rules are very well known and have great authority but many others have been developed on a very informal basis so as to avoid the sort of strictness one usually associates with changes in the law. This informality associated with conventions of the constitution often means that, while some may be publicly recorded, others are not formulated in writing, having simply evolved as practice over a period of time. It is for this reason that at a given moment in time it may be impossible to ascertain whether practice on a certain matter has crystallised into a conventional rule. This, together with the fact that they operate in a political context, often means that disputes may arise about the existence and content of conventional rules. Whereas disputes about the existence and content of legal rules are settled by judicial decisions, no formal judicial mechanism exists to settle disputes concerning conventional rules.

Problems may arise therefore when attempting to identify conventional rules. By their definition conventions of the constitution are forms of political behaviour based upon usage and regarded as obligatory, but at the same time lacking legal sanction. But when or how does such a non-binding usage become binding? One answer is of course that usage becomes binding because those to whom the usage applies consider that there is an obligation on their part to continue to behave in that way. But the dominant motive is not always apparent. Is the usage obeyed out of a sense of obligation or for some other reason? Also, what if there is substantial disagreement as to the existence or content of a convention. Political expediency or personal prejudice may result in divided interpretations of the obligation, if any, to be assumed. Certainly the opinions of politicians may differ as to the scope of the conventions they should observe. The fact that conventions may be created without any evidence of pre-existing usage also results in problems of identification.

Their non-legal nature also means that conventions are very flexible in the sense that they may lose their binding force or undergo a change in content without the need for any formal mechanism being followed. Conventions established by express agreement may be superseded or changed by agreement. Decisions taken by the Prime Minister or the Cabinet about the way Cabinet is to operate, for example, may be superseded by new decisions. Changes in circumstance may result in a convention losing its force, or indeed, the fact that a convention has been disregarded with impunity. Other conventions disappear with general acquiescence.

It is therefore probably true to say that conventions constitute the least definable source of the constitution. They are also probably the most discussed source especially as regards their interrelationship with the legal rules of the constitution. The differences between law and convention, the reasons why conventions are obeyed, whether or not conventions should be codified as law and the attitudes of the courts towards conventions are all matters which have occupied constitutional writers for many years and no doubt will continue to do so into the future.

QUESTION TWO

A written constitution for the United Kingdom would preserve the best of the existing constitutional practices and would remove the major defects.

Discuss.

University of London LLB Examination
(for External Students) Constitutional Law June 1986 Q2

General Comment

A difficult question which should only be attempted as a last resort. It is, however, currently a very topical issue.

Skeleton Solution

- Introduction: What is a constitution?: The unwritten nature of the United Kingdom constitution.
- The defects of our constitutional system: the absence of a higher form of law; the sovereignty of Parliament.
- The benefits of our constitutional system: the flexible nature of the constitution; the process of evolution.
- Conclusion: adoption of a written constitution need not result in rigidity, but even if desirable is change necessary?

Suggested Solution

The constitution of a state may be defined as the body of rules relating to the structure, functions and powers of the organs of state, their relationship to one another, and to the private citizen. The word 'constitution' is also used to refer to a document having a special legal sanctity which sets out the framework and the principal functions of the organs of government within the state, and declares the principles by which those organs must operate. This document has usually been enacted by the legislature or adopted by some other constituent body, for example a constituent assembly. In this sense of the word, as de Tocqueville observed, the United Kingdom has no constitution. There is no single document from which is derived the authority of the main organs of government, such as the Crown, the Cabinet, Parliament and the courts of law. No single document lays down the relationship of the primary organs of government one with another, or with the people.

Within the United Kingdom therefore there is no written constitution which can serve as fundamental law. This can create certain difficulties. In most states the constitution is a higher form of law in the sense that other laws must conform with it. The constitution imposes limits on what may be done by ordinary legislation and the courts may declare certain legislative acts void. But in the United Kingdom, in the absence of a written constitution to serve as the foundation of the legal system, the vacuum is filled by the legal doctrine of the legislative supremacy of Parliament. The result is that formal restraints upon the exercise of power which exist in other states do not exist in the United Kingdom. Parliament may make or unmake any law. There is no limit to its competence to legislate. No Parliament may bind its successors or be bound by its predecessors and the courts cannot question the validity of an Act of Parliament. Note, however, that since our membership of the European Union and the developing jurisprudence of the European Court of Justice, it has been established that our courts can grant an injunction suspending part of a statute which is inconsistent with European law: see *R* v *Secretary of State for Transport, ex parte Factortame (No 2)* (1991).

Historically, a major defect therefore of the United Kingdom constitution is that the absence of any higher form of law makes it virtually impossible to ensure that the rights of minorities and individual citizens are protected against legislative infringement by Parliament. Moreover, the absence of a written constitution means that there is no special procedure prescribed for legislation of constitutional importance. For example, before the Republic of Ireland could join the EC, a constitutional amendment to the Irish constitution had to be approved by a referendum of the people. In the United Kingdom, however, while the European Communities Act 1972 was debated at length in Parliament, the Act was passed by essentially the same procedure as would apply to any legislation of purely domestic concern. The absence of a written constitution means that in practice the British constitution depends far less on legal rules and safeguards and relies much more upon political and democratic principles. But can the politicians be trusted to observe these informal restraints on their power?

These problems could, it is argued, be overcome if the United Kingdom adopted a formal written constitution which defined the scope, and set out the legal limitations on, the functions and powers of the organs of government. But it must be remembered that no written document alone can ensure the smooth working of a system of government. A written document has no greater force than that which persons in authority are willing to attribute to it. Also our present unwritten constitution founded as it is partly on Acts of Parliament and judicial decisions, partly upon political practice, and partly upon detailed procedures established by the various organs of government for carrying their own tasks, provides a complex and comprehensive system of government which has served the United Kingdom well. In particular, as all law in the United Kingdom, including laws relating to the constitution, may be enacted, repealed or amended by the Queen in Parliament using the same legislative procedure, our constitution is highly flexible and can adapt to meet changes in social, moral and political circumstances. Indeed this facility for gradual evolution has been one of the major contributions to the political and social stability of the United Kingdom.

But the adoption of a written constitution need not necessarily destroy this flexibility altogether. A written constitution cannot contain all the detailed rules upon which government depends and accordingly a written constitution usually evolves a wide variety of customary rules and practices which attune the operation of the constitution to changing conditions. These customary rules and practices will usually be more easily changed than the constitution itself and their constant evolution will reduce the need for formal amendment of the written constitution. For example the rules for electing the legislature are usually found not in the written constitution but in ordinary statutes enacted by the legislature within the limits laid down by the constitution. Such statutes can when necessary be amended by the ordinary process of legislation whereas amendments to the constitution may require a more elaborate process, such as a special majority in the legislature or approval by a referendum.

Therefore it may well be the case that a written constitution for the United Kingdom would preserve the best of the existing constitutional practices and would remove the major defects. But, in spite of the defects, so long as our present constitutional system works so well, why change?

QUESTION THREE

'Conventions are unlike legal rules because they are not the true product of a legislative or judicial process' (Geoffrey Marshall *Constitutional Conventions*).

The University of Wolverhampton
Constitutional Law June 1990 Q10

General Comment

A question that requires students to explain the part played by conventions in the British constitution, distinguish law and convention and examine both the consequences of breach and the court's approach to conventions.

Skeleton Solution

- An outline of the sources of the British constitution emphasising its unwritten character.
- Definition of conventions followed by examples of the part they play.
- Distinguish law and examine the court's approach to conventions.

Suggested Solution

The constitution of the United Kingdom is described as unwritten – that is to say there is no single document to which reference can be made to establish constitutional principles of government or the safeguards that exist to ensure government is accountable and that individual liberties are safeguarded. To describe the United Kingdom constitution as unwritten is a little misleading, however, because of course much of the source material is written in the form of statutes and case law or common law. For example many statutes contain important constitutional rules, eg the Bill of Rights 1689, the Parliament Acts 1911 and 1949, the Representation of the People Act 1983 and so on. Many decisions of the courts contain important constitutional 'statements' which form the basis of judicial reasoning, for example, *Entick* v *Carrington* (1765), *Hipperson* v *Electoral Registration Officer for Newbury* (1985). The point of course about both written constitutions and in the case of the United Kingdom statute and case law sources is that the courts can adjudicate directly on the source.

The United Kingdom constitution has been described as the product of evolution rather than revolution. The consequence is that many non-legal rules supplement the legal sources. Described as conventions, these non-legal rules play a significant part in the constitution. Conventions have been defined as 'rules of constitutional behaviour which are considered to be binding by and upon those who operate the constitution but which are not enforced by the law courts ... nor by the presiding officers in the Houses of Parliament'.

Conventions can be seen to operate in all areas of the constitution. The Sovereign's relationship with the executive is significantly defined by convention, ie the Sovereign must act on the advice of her ministers, must not exercise her own initiative in refusing to assent to Bills which have passed through both Houses of Parliament, and must appoint as Prime Minister the person who can command a majority of seats in the Commons.

Conventions relating to the legislature include: the House of Lords ought ultimately to defer to the will of the House of Commons; Parliament must be summoned to meet at least once a year. Conventions relating to the judiciary include: judges shall not be active in party politics; Lords of Appeal who sit in the House of Lords must not participate in the political affairs of the House. In addition, the whole basis of cabinet government is convention – ministers are collectively and individually responsible to Parliament.

Dicey drew a clear distinction between law and convention. Laws are enforceable in the courts, conventions are not. To this extent conventions are unlike legal rules. However, the general values inherent in the constitution, expressed in the rule of law, are interrelated with conventions and sanctions exist for the breach of a convention. Dicey argued that the breach of a convention 'will almost immediately bring the offender into conflict with the courts and the law of the land'. This is palpably not the case and Sir Ivor Jennings suggests that conventions are obeyed because of the political difficulties which follow if they are not. The failure of a minister to abide by the doctrine of collective responsibility will result in dismissal/resignation. The failure of a government to resign on losing the support of the House of Commons would precipitate a political uproar supported by public opinion. Sometimes the failure to follow a convention can result in a change in the law so for example the refusal of the House of Lords to support Liberal reforms in 1909–1910 led to the Parliament Act 1911.

The courts do not recognise conventions as legal rules: see *Madzimbamuto* v *Lardner-Burke* (1969) and *Re Amendment of the Constitution of Canada* (1982) where the Canadian Supreme Court recognised but refused to apply a convention. However, conventions can indirectly influence a decision; in *Liversidge* v *Anderson* (1942) and *R* v *Secretary of State for the Home Department, ex parte Hosenball* (1977) reference was made to the responsibility and accountability of the Home Secretary to Parliament. In *Attorney-General* v *Jonathan Cape* (1976) the government based its case on the convention of Cabinet secrecy. Lord Widgery stated that the convention was relevant to establishing a balance between the public interest and confidentiality. Conventions are, then, unlike legal rules in that the courts cannot give direct effect to them. However, other sanctions can result in adherence to convention in much the same way as adherence to a legal rule, more particularly in respect of those where breach would be fundamentally unconstitutional.

QUESTION FOUR

'When an Englishman speaks of the conduct of a public man being constitutional or unconstitutional, he means something wholly different from what he means by conduct being legal or illegal.'

Discuss.

University of London LLB Examination
(for External Students) Constitutional Law June 1989 Q1

General Comment

A relatively difficult question which requires students to analyse the term 'constitution' as a higher form of law in the context of the United Kingdom.

Skeleton Solution

- Explain the meaning of the quotation setting it in context by showing what would be meant by the words in a system with a written constitution.
- Look at role of convention and statute in British constitution.

Suggested Solution

Today most countries of the world possess a 'constitution' ie a document or series of documents laying down the fundamental rules relating to the organisation of the state. In such countries if a person decries a law or an action as being unconstitutional or illegal what he means is that it offends against the higher law laid down in the constitution, which is normally protected from later legislative changes by the need to follow a more difficult prescribed legislative process, ie the constitution is entrenched. To a degree the two adjectives are in these countries interchangeable.

To discover the fundamental rules governing the constitution in Britain one has to look to various sources – statute, judicial decisions and conventions of the constitution. Conventions of the constitution are rules of political practice regarded as biding by those to whom they apply but which are not enforced by the courts or by Parliament. The important point to grasp is that although statute is the most important source of our constitution and a statute can always override a convention, nevertheless one would not understand how the British constitution operated without an understanding of conventions. For instance, the existence of the Prime Minister, Cabinet and other ministers is dependent on convention and their relationships to each other and to Parliament are regulated by conventions of ministerial responsibility. Furthermore, if one looks strictly at the legal powers of the Monarch those are immense until one appreciates the convention that for the most part the Monarch follows the advice of her government. Conventions are also important in the functioning of the legislature and even of the judiciary.

The quotation in the question is therefore alluding to the difference between statute and convention as a source of the British constitution. If an Englishman spoke of something as 'illegal' he would normally be referring to a breach of a statute or common law rules. If he is talking of something being 'unconstitutional' he would be taken to be referring to a breach of a convention. This is however somewhat of an oversimplification for sometimes in speaking of a breach of a statute or case law rule of constitutional importance the Englishman might at once describe the behaviour as 'unconstitutional' and 'illegal', but what is unconstitutional is not necessarily illegal, although it may be.

Mallory said 'for the Americans anything unconstitutional is illegal, however right or necessary it may seem; for the British, anything unconstitutional is wrong, no matter how legal it may be'.

Some conventions are well known and possess great authority whilst others have developed on an informal basis. This means that some conventions are not even recorded in writing in public documents having evolved informally over a period of time. Indeed, this is one of the reasons why disputes arise as to the existence and content of conventional rules. There is no judicial procedure or mechanism to settle disputes concerning such rules. One of the results of these uncertainties is that the phrase 'unconstitutional' is often used by politicians in circumstances where it may not strictly be appropriate, thus devaluing the term.

For example in 1932 the National government's agreement to differ and the 1975 Labour government waiver of collective responsibility over the EC referendum were both described by some commentators as 'unconstitutional' but these occasions were both without precedent and should, some would argue, merely be seen as developments and glosses on a convention. The twin conventions of collective and individual responsibility (see in particular the 1954 Crichel Down affair on individual responsibility) do give rise to uncertainty as to whether a minister's behaviour merits resignation and whether breach of the convention amounts to action which is unconstitutional. Recent controversy over MPs' personal interests and the tabling of questions for cash in the House of Commons highlight this dilemma.

The courts will not enforce conventions but conventions are taken into account. The Crossman diaries are a good example illustrating the 'grey area' between legal and non-legal rules. In that case the Attorney-General tried to prevent the breach of a conventional rule and to establish the existence of a legal obligation. It was held that former Cabinet ministers could be restrained by injunction from publishing confidential information – there is a legal obligation to respect confidentiality. The court, however, must not be thought to have enforced a convention in this case. Collective responsibility (the convention in question) was no more than one factor taken into account by the judge in establishing the limits of the legal doctrine of confidence. In *Re Amendment of the Constitution of Canada* (1982) the Canadian Supreme Court recognised, but refused to apply, a convention. It could well be argued that what the government was proposing was legal but unconstitutional.

Some jurists take the view that all constitutional rules ought to be enacted as law. To a large degree this is what would happen if the United Kingdom were to entrench a written constitution. If that were done a Supreme Court (or Law Lords in the House of Lords) would interpret constitutional articles. It is true that some areas would be quite difficult. For example, to anticipate every possible eventuality in which the Sovereign might be required to invite a new Prime Minister to form a government. Also it could be argued that even if all present non-legal rules were susceptible to a written code, new conventions could be born at any time. (Note Wade and Bradley say that 'provisions contained in a written constitution' are not all suitable for judicial enforcement. This, however, may not be valid as some constitutional lawyers will maintain that all provisions/articles of a written constitution have equal standing; it is either an article or not.) This argument, however, is not entirely satisfactory – the main point about codification is that all non-legal rules (conventions) are brought under a legal footing, namely, a constitution. Were conventions fully codified then the use in Britain of the phrases 'unconstitutional' and 'illegal' would alter to resemble that in other countries.

QUESTION FIVE

Should all or any of the conventions of the constitution be given statutory force?

University of London LLB Examination
(for External Students) Constitutional and Administrative Law June 1992 Q5

General Comment

This is a standard question on conventions. It is not an opportunity to list every known convention, but obviously examples are needed. This suggested solution adopts the view that conventions need not be given statutory force – but that is not the 'right' answer!

Skeleton Solution

- Definition.
- An example of a convention.
- Problem of scope.
- Difficulty of definition.
- Enactment in case of breach.

- Flexibility.
- Illegality and recognition by the courts.
- Certainty if enacted.
- Conclusion.

Suggested Solution

Conventions have been described as 'rules of constitutional behaviour' (Marshall & Moodie, *Some Problems of the Constitution*). They are unwritten and they are not enforced by the courts. Nevertheless they are considered binding upon those whom they cover. If that is the case, what is to be gained by giving some or all of them statutory force?

A good example of a convention is that the Prime Minister and the Chancellor of the Exchequer should both belong to the House of Commons. The last member of the House of Lords to hold office as Prime Minister was Lord Salisbury in 1902, making this a comparatively recent convention. Yet, in 1963, the 14th Earl of Home felt constrained to renounce his title so that he could enter the House of Commons as Harold Macmillan's successor (although it took four days from his appointment as Prime Minister to the disclaimer!). Thus, an unwritten rule both enforced and reflected the political impossibility of a Prime Minister governing from the House of Lords.

In theory, all conventions could be given statutory force and this has been the practice in several Commonwealth countries. However, there are various reasons why this is unnecessary. Firstly, conventions cover a very wide area, involving executive, judiciary and legislature. No single code could embrace them all.

Secondly, there is the difficulty of definition. For example, ministers are responsible both collectively and individually, and resignation is the appropriate response. It is impossible to define the limits of that responsibility – as much as anything it is a question of political judgment. In 1954, Sir Thomas Dugdale resigned over the Crichel Down affair. In 1982, Lord Carrington resigned over the Falkland Islands occupation. Yet, Kenneth Baker as Home Secretary did not resign over the escape from Brixton Prison of IRA suspects.

The classic view is that a minister must protect a civil servant who has carried out his explicit orders, and must defend a civil servant who acts properly in accordance with policy. Political practice reveals, however, that of the 22 resignations by Cabinet ministers between 1945 and 1995, 13 were resignations because of differences over principle and policy. Only five have resigned because of the way in which they have discharged their ministerial functions. A further erosion of ministerial responsibility has occurred with the growth in the use of executive agencies to run key areas of the administration. A good example is provided by the Prison Service, which was set up as an executive agency to run prisons in the late 1980s. Following a number of high profile prison escapes, including escapes from Parkhurst, there were calls for the then Home Secretary, Michael Howard, to resign. He, however, argued that the running of prisons was now chiefly the responsibility of the Prison Service, and duly sacked its chief executive Derek Lewis, pointing out that the escapes in question were not the direct result of any Home Office policy for which the Home Secretary was responsible.

Thirdly, a breach of convention can always be corrected by statute if necessary. In 1909, the House of Lords rejected the Liberal government's Finance Bill. Until then, the Commons had asserted their authority when it came to the passage of money Bills and the Lords had generally acknowledged this convention. The crisis that followed in 1909 led to the Parliament Act 1911 which – in terms – enacted the convention.

Fourthly, while it may seem questionable to wait for a breach before enactment, conventions are largely followed because they describe how the constitution works. They are also, in their unwritten form, sufficiently flexible to reflect change. By convention, the Queen appoints as Prime Minister the person who can command a majority in the Commons. Until 1965, the death or retirement of a Conservative Prime Minister required the Queen – to some extent – to make a choice, but since then there has been a system within the party for electing a new leader. The convention remains, but it has become a formality.

However, what would happen if the Queen decided to ignore it? That may be a fanciful idea, but at present, while breach of a convention may cause political difficulty – which may also be its strongest restraint – it does not result in illegality. (Dicey argued that if Parliament did not follow the convention of meeting each year it would have to raise taxes illegally, but that is an exception.) Similarly, although recognised by courts (as in *Attorney-General* v *Jonathan Cape* (1976)) they are not legally enforceable. Enactment would alter that, although one might consider whether the present court structure would be adequate for 'trying' resultant breaches of the law.

Another argument in favour of enactment is that of certainty. For example, the Sovereign's conventional power with regard to the dissolution of Parliament and the appointment of ministers is – on paper – considerable but ill-defined. Is it enough to say that in practice it is not a problem?

In conclusion, it is submitted that – despite these arguments – there is no need to give all conventions statutory force. If they are breached then that is the time for enactment. However, they are obeyed because they reflect constitutional practice and, unlike laws, when they are no longer relevant, they simply fade away.

QUESTION SIX

Discuss the nature and effect of the constitutional conventions which regulate the public conduct of the Sovereign as head of state in the United Kingdom.

University of London LLB Examination
(for External Students) Constitutional and Administrative Law June 1992 Q5

General Comment

This is a rather narrow question relating to the role of the sovereign. An understanding of the term 'convention(s)' is required. The candidate should also be able to discuss such issues as the appointment and dismissal of the Prime Minister and the related issue of the dissolution of Parliament. Historical examples are necessary when dealing with the influence of conventions upon the role of the monarchy. Also some knowledge of the 1975 Australian constitutional crisis would be useful.

Skeleton Solution

- Definition of conventions.
- Royal Assent to Bills.
- Apportionment of ministers and the Prime Minister.
- Dissolution of Parliament.
- Conclusion.

Suggested Solution

Constitutional conventions have been described by Dicey (*Law of the Constitution*, 10th edn, 1959) as 'understandings, habits or practices – which are not in reality laws at all since they are not enforced by the courts'. They do, however, make sense of the constitution, and in the words of Sir Ivor Jennings (*The Law and the Constitution*, 1959) 'they provide the flesh which clothes the dry bones of the law; they make the legal constitution work'.

This is particularly true of the role of the Monarch. The powers of the head of state are limited by convention, and in the majority of cases the functions of the Monarch have passed into the hands of other actors of the constitution or else the Monarch has no discretion on how to act. This is correct, for example, at the basic level of how statutes come into existence. When a Bill has passed both House of Parliament (the Parliament Acts notwithstanding) the Monarch is obliged to give it Royal Assent, or so the convention would indicate. The position is, however, slightly clouded when one looks at past events in constitutional history. The classic textbook example is that of Queen Anne in 1708 refusing to give her assent to the Scottish Militia Bill, thus seeming to indicate that the monarch is not obliged by convention to assent to each and every Bill. The facts are, however, somewhat more opaque in that not only did her ministers not object but in fact they rather approved of this course of action. In more recent times the issue was resurrected over the question of Home Rule for Ireland in the period of 1912–14. In April 1912 the Liberal government introduced a Home Rule Bill in the House of Commons and, to avoid the nineteenth-century precedent of the Bill being rejected by the House of Lords, stated that they would, if necessary, utilise the Parliament Act 1911 to by-pass the House of Lords' veto. The proposed legislation aroused strong opposition amongst the Ulster Protestant community and their supporters, the Conservative Unionists. The King (George V) had the theoretical power to thwart the progress of the Bill by insisting that an election be held before the legislation was passed or by refusing to assent to the Bill. A memorandum was in fact prepared by the King to Prime Minister Asquith but it was never sent because the outbreak of the 1914–18 war. The memorandum indicated that there might be occasions on which the King would be justified in refusing to assent to legislation. When this would occur is not completely clear, but the memorandum indicated that the Crown would only adopt this course of action if it would have the effect of diffusing a crisis. It is doubtful whether in today's political climate the Monarch would contemplate such an action, even if proposed legislation would have the effect of abolishing the UK's position as a sovereign state (for instance, proposed legislation to join a federal European Union).

The Sovereign (Queen Elizabeth II) has the theoretical power to appoint whoever she wishes as a minister, and she could in theory appoint somebody outside Parliament. In fact her power is regulated by convention, and ministerial appointments are made on the advice of the Prime Minister in relation to individuals who either sit in Parliament (meaning both Houses) or who it is proposed will sit in Parliament by means of either a successful by-election or an elevation to the peerage. Such a constitutional arrangement does not generate controversy; in greater dispute is the Sovereign's power to appoint a Prime Minister.

The Prime Minister (PM) is appointed from the contestants who are able to command an overall majority in the House of Commons. This does not normally present a problem, since because of the workings of the electoral system one party usually commands an overall majority in the House of Commons and it is usually the leader of that party who then becomes PM.

Problems may arise if, for instance, an incumbent PM resigns. In the two leading political parties, Conservative and Labour, a method of electing the next leader is provided for. This was not always the case, and up to 1964 the Conservative Party leader used to 'emerge', which could theoretically leave the Monarch with an area of discretion. In 1923 when the Conservative PM Bonar Law resigned, the Conservative Lord Curzon was put forward as his successor, but George V thought it appropriate to appoint the Conservative commoner Baldwin as the Labour Party was unrepresented in the Lords and the King was of the opinion that it would be inappropriate to appoint a peer as PM.

Such events are unlikely to be repeated, but in more recent history the question as to who should be PM was raised again. In February 1974 the election result proved inconclusive as no one party had an overall majority. The incumbent PM, Edward Heath (as he then was), only resigned after spending three days trying to construct a coalition government. The Queen waited until the situation sorted itself out and then called for the main opposition leader, Harold Wilson, to form a government. The possibility of such events repeating themselves would, of course, be more likely if electoral reform was introduced and overall majority governments cease to be the norm. The role of the Monarch in this area would be highlighted and the Queen would be able to exercise a discretionary function.

Of more constitutional significance is the role of the Monarch in the dissolution or non-dissolution of Parliament. Whether or not Parliament is dissolved is not in fact governed by convention (contrary to popular belief). The request as to the dissolution of Parliament is made, since November 1918, by the PM. The Queen could in theory refuse to grant a dissolution, although this is not likely, particularly as the PM would probably then resign. The converse is also true, and the Monarch could insist upon a dissolution of Parliament if the government of the day was planning controversial and unprecedented legislation. The example of George V in the decade before the 1914–18 war is a precedent for such action. Before George V would create the required number of Liberal peers to effect the passage of the Parliament Act 1911 he insisted upon the dissolution of Parliament and an election. This power is still vested in the Monarch and it is correct to describe it as a personal prerogative rather than a conventional practice.

A more recent instance of this power of the Monarch, and also the role of the Monarch in appointing a PM, arose in Australia in 1975. The Governor-General of Australia represents the Queen and enjoys the power and privileges of the head of state. As a result of an impasse between the House of Representatives and the Senate, the government was denied its financial support. In order to break the deadlock the Governor-General, Sir John Kerr, dismissed PM Gough Whitlam and called in the opposition leader as PM upon condition that he then requested a dissolution of Parliament. There would appear, however, to be no reason to suppose that the Governor-General, exercising the Royal Prerogative, could not insist upon a dissolution of Parliament.

The public conduct of the Sovereign is largely determined by the operation of conventions. Although they are not laws, conventions are regarded by the sovereign as obligatory. Many matters, particularly relating to foreign affairs, such as the signing of treaties, are done in the name of the Sovereign; they are not, however, associated with the public conduct of the sovereign. Those that are, such as the appointment of the Prime Minister, leave the Sovereign with little discretion as to how to act. If an unpopular, in the eyes of Parliament, individual were to be appointed PM he or she would be unable to obtain a vote of confidence. It is the application of conventions that prevents the Sovereign from becoming embroiled in political controversy and preserves the institution in a symbolic role.

2 Constitutional Principles: The Separation of Powers and the Rule of Law

2.1 Introduction

Whilst the United Kingdom may lack a written constitution in the formal sense, it does display two crucial features associated with constitutionalism, namely some adherence to the doctrine of the separation of powers and a commitment to a culture of the rule of law. The doctrine of the separation of powers provides that there should be three distinct sectors of government: the legislature to make the law; the executive to put it into effect; and the judiciary to adjudicate upon disputes regarding the application of the law. Further, the doctrine provides that there ought to be some system of checks and balances whereby each arm of government can exercise some control over the other. The doctrine of parliamentary sovereignty considered in Chapter 3 means that, in theory, the legislature has ultimate power within the United Kingdom constitution – although this does not mean that they system of checks and balances is fatally flawed. Regard should also be had to the extent to which the legislature is subject to popular democratic control. The doctrine of the rule of law has several facets, but in simple terms it means that no body is above the law, that the law applies to all equally, and that the law is certain and consistent, not arbitrary. Again there are many ways in which the United Kingdom constitution fails to satisfy all of these requirements, but essentially there is a culture of respect for the law. Crucially, the judiciary, through the use of the judicial review procedure, can exercise control over members of the executive and, where necessary, strike down their decisions as unlawful.

2.2 Key points

a) *The separation of powers*

As outlined above, the three basic and essential organs of state are legislative, executive and judicial. With a view to avoiding the potential for an autocratic and tyrannical form of government it has been considered theoretically desirable for the functions to be kept separate. In 1748 the French jurist Montesquieu developed the doctrine of the separation of powers which argues the need for checks and balances to exist between the three. It is a useful concept for analysing the nature of our parliamentary democracy.

i) Legislature and executive

There is a significant overlap. Ministers head departments of state. The government initiates legislation and has the controlling voice in Parliament. Ministers and local authorities have a limited law-making function through delegated legislation.

ii) Executive and judiciary

The Lord Chancellor heads the judiciary, presides in the House of Lords and has a seat in Cabinet. Judges are appointed by the Lord Chancellor or by the Queen on the advice of the Lord Chancellor. The judiciary control the executive authorities from exceeding their powers: see *Associated Provincial Picture Houses Ltd* v *Wednesbury Corporation* [1948] 1 KB 223.

iii) Judiciary and legislature

A degree of separation exists: House of Commons Disqualification Act 1975. Judges do, however, to a certain extent make law: see *Shaw* v *DPP* [1962] AC 220.

Within our constitution Parliament is supreme and the courts cannot challenge an Act of Parliament. In many countries with written constitutions the courts can challenge an act of the legislature as unconstitutional: see *Pickin* v *British Railways Board* [1974] AC 765.

Our membership of the European Union obliges the United Kingdom to legislate in a way that is consistent with European law. In theory, however, Parliament could repeal the European Communities Act 1972, so any loss of sovereignty is limited and partial.

b) *The rule of law*

The rule of law is a somewhat abstract concept based on the principle that government must be seen to be legitimate – in the sense that it is impartial, fair and obeyed even when disagreed with. Dicey expressed this in terms of the following propositions:

No man is punishable except for a distinct breach of the law and then only in the ordinary courts and in the manner prescribed by law. This is contrasted with arbitrary and discretionary power. Governments in the twentieth century do enjoy wide discretionary powers – welfare benefits, public health, sentencing policy etc. Wide arbitrary powers are avoided and attempts made to ensure accountability.

No one is above the law and everyone should be subject to the jurisdiction of the ordinary courts: *Entick* v *Carrington* (1765) 19 St Tr 1030. Disputes between government and citizen are settled in the ordinary courts. But note the part played by administrative tribunals. Whilst the courts cannot challenge an Act of Parliament, they will review administrative action. Note also the fact of parliamentary supremacy and the wide powers of governmental officials. See *R* v *Inland Revenue Commissioners, ex parte Rossminster Ltd* [1980] 1 All ER 80.

Principles of constitutional law are contained in judicial decisions that serve to ensure that individual liberties are protected. This is contrasted with the position in countries with a written constitution where a single document seeks to establish citizens' rights and places reliance on the judiciary to develop laws that protect liberties. The extent to which civil liberties in the United Kingdom are protected in the absence of an entrenched Bill of Rights remains a matter of debate, although the incorporation of the European Convention on Human Rights by means of the Human Rights Act 1998 goes some way to meeting these concerns.

2.3 Recent developments

The enactment of the Human Rights Act 1998 raises some interesting issues relevant to the consideration of the separation of powers and the rule of law. Whilst the courts will not have the power to declare legislation unconstitutional on the basis that it does not comply with the terms of the European Convention on Human Rights as enacted, the higher courts will be empowered to grant declarations of incompatibility. The relevant minister will then be able to use powers granted under the 1998 Act to introduce remedial legislation. This represents a clever compromise that retains the distinct roles of the judiciary and the legislature whilst exploiting the conventions of responsible government to help ensure that any necessary changes are made. Again it is assumed that any government committed to the concept of the rule of law will want to be seen to be acting in compliance with any declaration of incompatibility, or will at least feel compelled to explain why remedial action is not being taken.

2.4 Analysis of questions

Examination papers frequently contain questions on the separation of powers and/or the doctrine of the rule of law. As ever a thoughtful approach will be rewarded. With the separation of powers questions you will normally be required to give some explanation of what the doctrine involves, but additionally you should be prepared to examine the extent to which the United Kingdom complies with the doctrine, the significance of any shortfall, and the extent to which this is remedied by the existence of an effective system of checks and balances between the various branches of government. When dealing with questions relating to the rule of law try to give examples of compliance and non-compliance. It may be appropriate to consider the extent to which there is a conflict between the doctrine of the rule of law and the doctrine of parliamentary sovereignty. To the extent that there is a conflict which doctrine do you think should prevail and why?

2.5 Questions

QUESTION ONE

'It must be conceded that the constitution of the United Kingdom deviates from a pure concept of separation of powers. Nevertheless the concept is respected and adequate safeguards exist to prevent abuse of power.'

Discuss.

University of London LLB Examination
(for External Students) Constitutional Law June 1993 Q1

General Comment

A straightforward question that calls for a clear narrative of the workings of the British constitution and the ways in which the democratic principle is upheld in a system without a rigid constitutional separation of powers. The challenge is to present the material in an original and lively way, because many average students will simply regurgitate large sections of traditional textbooks on this topic. Hence the suggested solution concentrates on a particular theme (the separation between law and politics) and very specialised illustrations, with no attempt to cover the entire (very wide) field of the distribution of power in modern British society. It is one approach; there are many others. It is a useful reminder that, for law exams, there are no 'model' answers, merely suggested approaches to solutions.

Skeleton Solution

- Definition of Montesquieu's 'pure' concept of separation of powers.

- The British constitution and the overlapping of organs and functions.
- Safeguards, illustrated by detailed discussion of one area: the separation of law and politics through constitutional conventions.
- Application to the office of Lord Chancellor.
- Do the particular conventions work?
- The decision in *Pepper* v *Hart* and Lord Mackay's significant dissent.
- The courts and Parliament: Speaker Boothroyd's views and those of Lord Donaldson MR.
- Alternatives to the conventional approach.
- Difficulties in the American system of government.

Suggested Solution

The 'pure' concept of the separation of powers is that propounded by Montesquieu:

'The three main powers of government, namely, the legislative, executive and judicial, should be organically and functionally separated in order to avoid the risk of too much power being accumulated in one person or institution, ie the risk of tyranny': from *L'Esprit des Lois* (1748).

The theory proved of great influence in the drafting of the American Constitution in 1787, but is clearly not strictly followed by the British constitution, which has developed in an unwritten, pragmatic fashion since the Norman Conquest of 1066. Today the three main organs of government can be found in one institution: Parliament. The functions of government are also shared, to take the most famous and obvious example: the Lord Chancellor, who combines the functions of judge, Cabinet minister and legislator in the House of Lords (where he also acts as Speaker).

Yet, as the assertion in question points out, respect is paid to the spirit of Montesquieu's theory, if not the letter of it. Safeguards have developed to minimise the risks of abuse of power from institutions such as Parliament and the Lord Chancellor. Whether they are adequate, however, is another matter, and one that has generated controversy among lawyers and politicians for generations.

Conventions of the constitution have assumed great importance in checking the exercise of power. Conventions are 'unwritten' guidelines designed to persuade decision makers to act fairly, responsibly, democratically and morally. For example, the holder of the office of Lord Chancellor will be expected, by convention, to separate his party political views from the views he must take when acting in the capacity as head of the judiciary, whether he is appointing judges or himself sitting as a judge to hear an appeal taken to the House of Lords.

It has been argued that conventions such as these are followed either because of the integrity and sense of honour of the office holder (an 'internal' limit) or because of the fear of the adverse political consequences of a breach of a fundamental convention (loss of reputation, removal from office, etc: an 'external' limit). A person who is appointed as Lord Chancellor is expected to command the confidence of the judiciary, the legal profession and the public generally when exercising judicial functions and hence the internal limit is more likely to operate in his case than with any other politician. Even the most passionate kinds of politician, eg Lord Hailsham, have been able to exercise dispassionate judgment when exercising those functions of the office of Lord Chancellor that require impartiality and independence from the executive.

Nevertheless the fear remains that, as a member of the Cabinet, the Lord Chancellor may be unable to separate his functions in the sophisticated and subtle manner which may be required. To take a recent example (and one is not questioning the integrity of Lord Mackay on this point) in the case of *Pepper* v *Hart* (1993) six of the seven Law Lords (Lord Mackay LC dissenting) were prepared to allow access to Hansard for lawyers and judges when considering issues of statutory construction. Lord Mackay dissented solely on the ground that to permit such access would add greatly to the costs of litigation. One must be tempted to wonder whether his responsibility for public spending on the legal aid scheme (an executive, political responsibility) may have proved decisive in reaching this particular judgment, since none of the other Law Lords considered costs to be a major problem. If the Lord Chancellor were not permitted to sit as an appeal judge would the decision in this case have been unanimous if one of the other Law Lords had taken his place?

The curious point that emerges from the decision is that, in practical terms, Lord Mackay may be proved right, since use of Hansard has increased dramatically since that landmark decision and the impact on the costs of litigation is likely to be significant. This shows how a merger of powers and functions can be useful in (perhaps) influencing a decision and making it better informed than it otherwise would have been. Lord Mackay's judgment in *Pepper* v *Hart* reveals experience of empirical research that is lacking in the other judgments, which tend to rely heavily on abstract issues of principle.

The separation between law and politics is certainly regarded as a desirable objective in the British constitution, even if the two areas are not organically and functionally separated by rigid written rules. In the recent controversy over the legality of ratification of the Maastricht Treaty, the Commons Speaker, Betty Boothroyd, took the unusual step of reminding the courts not to get involved in politics when they came to exercise judicial review on the issue. In return, she said, Parliament and politicians respect the independence of the judiciary. This echoes part of a judgment given by Lord Donaldson MR in *R* v *HM Treasury, ex parte Smedley* (1985) to the effect that, notwithstanding that the United Kingdom has no written constitution, it is a constitutional convention of the highest importance that the legislature and judiciary are separate and independent of one another. As he observed: 'It therefore behoves the courts to be ever sensitive to the paramount need to refrain from trespassing upon the province of Parliament ... I would hope and expect that Parliament would be similarly sensitive to the need to refrain from trespassing upon the province of the courts.'

What if the British pragmatic approach, based on convention, fails to work? The answer is probably a written constitution, with a Bill of Rights, providing for a compartmentalisation of organs and functions and a system of American style checks and balances. But the price may be high: less well informed decision-making and less efficient and effective government. The American experience of 'gridlock' between President and Congress in recent years is testimony to that risk.

QUESTION TWO

'The Rule of Law is too vague a concept to be of practical relevance to an evaluation of the actions of Government.'

Discuss.

University of London LLB Examination
(for External Students) Constitutional Law June 1993 Q3

General Comment

This is a straightforward question largely requiring descriptive analysis. The challenge must be to make it as original and as critical as possible, with as many useful illustrations as possible, especially any of topical interest. It is important to give equal emphasis to each of Dicey's components of the Rule of Law; it is a common mistake, for example, to concentrate overmuch on equality under the law.

Skeleton Solution

- Modern versions of the Rule of Law.
- The Declaration of Delhi 1959.
- Contrast with Dicey's 19th century formula.
- The three elements and objectives of Dicey's Rule of Law.
- Their influence in establishing safeguards against abuse of power.
- Delegated legislation and tribunals.
- Trades unions and security services.
- Ministers of the Crown and *M* v *Home Office*.
- Judicial review.
- Conclusion.

Suggested Solution

Modern versions of the Rule of Law tend to be formulated in broad political language embracing concepts such as 'justice', the rights of man, fundamental freedoms etc. They tend to be too vague to serve as quality tests for the democratic behaviour of governments. An example is the Declaration of Delhi 1959:

'The Rule of Law means the principles, institutions and procedures, not always identical, but broadly similar, which the experience and tradition of lawyers in different countries of the world, often having themselves varying political structures and economic backgrounds, have shown to be important to protect the individual from arbitrary government and to enable him to enjoy the dignity of man.'

The absence of precise legalistic analysis from this Declaration probably allows various dictatorships around the world to claim that the Declaration has been transplanted, with modifications, into the soil of their constitution and legal system. The Rule of Law becomes a political concept made of clay to be moulded into the shape desired by the potter.

However, if one reverts to the classic, albeit largely discredited, theory of the Rule of Law as propounded by the Victorian Oxford Professor A V Dicey one finds a formal legal analysis which is at least capable of being used to measure the actions of government, and which even today is invoked from time to time to criticise abuses of power. It might well still be a political concept dressed up as law, but it is not as vague as the Declaration of Delhi or other modern variants.

Dicey contended that the Rule of Law has three essential elements:

a) that no one should be punished or lawfully made to suffer in body or goods except for a distinct breach of the law established in the ordinary legal manner before the ordinary courts of the land;

b) that no one should be above the law: that every person, whatever his rank or con should be subject to the ordinary law and answerable to the ordinary courts; and

c) that the general principles of the constitution, such as the right to personal liberty and right of public meeting, are the result of judicial decisions and that so we have a judg made constitution.

Dicey summed up the objective of those three elements as being 'the absolute supremacy or predominance of regular law as opposed to the influence of arbitrary power, and the exclusion of arbitrariness, of prerogative or even of wide discretionary authority on the part of government': from *Introduction to the Study of the Law of the Constitution* (1885).

Dicey's views proved immensely influential on thinking throughout the twentieth century in the British constitution. Element (a) lay behind Parliament's caution in setting up tribunals and in granting delegated law-making powers to ministers and others. Committees such as Donoughmore (1932) and Franks (1957) recommended safeguards against the risks of abuse of power by ministers, tribunals and inquiries, which, of necessity, had to operate in a fashion far removed from the due process of law administered by the ordinary courts of the land. Supervisory bodies such as Parliament's Committees on Statutory Instruments and the independent Council on Tribunals, as well as the relatively modern British phenomenon of ombudsmen (imported from Sweden), show how the British constitution has adapted to the social welfare needs of the twentieth century without losing sight of Diceyan concepts.

Element (b) of Dicey's theory, concerning equality under the law, was said to have been gravely weakened by certain power groups in society which were able to operate at times seemingly with utter contempt for the law, eg the mineworkers' union in the period of 1972–4 which flouted statutory income restraint legislation; trades unions generally in the period 1974–9; and the state security services where control and accountability seemed so minimal as to be virtually nonexistent until very recently. However the 'Thatcher Years' of 1979–90 witnessed a reassertion of the rule of law over trades unions (it took a year-long miners' strike to end in failure to achieve it, in 1984) and steps were even taken to establish a statutory framework and system of parliamentary control for the security services, first with the home service, MI5, under the Security Service Act 1989 and then, during John Major's government, with the foreign service, MI6, under the Intelligence Services Act 1994. Even the long established common law immunities of the Crown, which sometimes seemed to put ministers above the law, suffered a blow with the recent historic decision that ministers, in their public capacity as Crown servants, could be made subject to the law of contempt of court, a decision which Sir William Wade QC hailed as a tremendous victory for the Rule of Law: *M* v *Home Office* (1993).

Dicey's third element, which some have regarded as descriptive rather than normative in character, has also proven a useful weapon in the armoury of those who believe in vigorous judicial review of administrative action and perhaps the creation eventually of a domestic human rights court to enforce a Bill of Rights against an over-mighty executive (ironically Dicey was against a Bill of Rights because he thought it would undermine parliamentary sovereignty; but in his day Parliament was not the executive-dominated institution which it is today; if he had lived to see the power of the Whips and executive patronage Dicey may well have changed his view). The rapid growth of principles of judicial review in the last 30 years is regarded by many senior judges as their most significant contribution to establishing constitutional restraints against abuse of power and, indeed, Wade & Bradley call judicial review a modern constitutional fundamental.

…eing vague and transitory, has proven of solid and lasting value …nt of controls over decision makers and in bringing government

…s does the British constitution conform to, or contradict, the doctrine of …powers?

University of London LLB Examination
(for External Students) Constitutional Law June 1996 Q1

…eneral Comment

The question involves an understanding of the basic structure and workings of the British constitution. The candidate should be familiar with what is meant by the doctrine of separation of powers and how this idea is put into practice in the context of the unwritten constitution of the United Kingdom. This will also involve an appreciation of the workings of conventions and the role of important 'actors' in the constitution.

Skeleton Solution

- Definition of the doctrine.
- Its strict application in other constitutional jurisdictions, eg the US.
- Relevance to the UK; the Westminster model – the comments of Bagehot – the role and functions of the Attorney-General, Lord Chancellor, the Law Lords.
- In contradistinction, the independence of the judiciary, Act of Settlement, House of Commons Disqualification Act 1975 and the judiciary.
- The status of the Crown.
- Conclusion.

Suggested Solution

The doctrine of separation of powers divides the workings of a constitution into three distinct branches. These are the legislature, the executive and the judiciary. The legislature passes the laws, the executive puts them into practice and the judiciary interprets them. The 'highpoint' of this doctrine is to be found in the works of the eighteenth century philosopher Montesquieu. In this book *The Spirit of the Laws*, published in 1748, the author advances the view that the best foundation for individual liberty and good governance is to separate the three branches of government. The three branches of government will have distinct functions and none will be powerful enough to dominate the others. Montesquieu wrongly believed that this formula applied to the England of his time, but the theory served to influence the founding fathers of the American constitution, which does apply the doctrine in practice. A member of the United States Congress is forbidden, for example, to be a member of the United States government: art 1, s6.

How, then, is this doctrine relevant to the UK? First, the United Kingdom constitution is characterised by the blending of the executive and the legislature. It is unusual, as a result of constitutional conventional practice, for a member of the executive *not* to be a member of the legislature. If the government of the day wishes to bring in an outsider – a non-professional politician – into government then that individual must be found a seat in the legislature,

either in the House of Commons through election or in the House of Lords t
ennoblement. Walter Bagehot in his classical work *The English Constitution* (1867) des
the constitution as displaying 'the close union, the nearly complete fusion of the exec
and legislative powers'.

He then went on to argue that the fusion takes place in the Cabinet, a body which h
graphically described as: 'a combining committee – a hyphen which joins a buckle which fastens the legislative part of the state to the executive part of the state. In its origin it belongs to the one, in its functions it belongs to another.'

The Cabinet and government only come into existence because the majority of the legislature wish it so, but, as Bagehot points out, the Cabinet (and now the Prime Minister) may request a dissolution of Parliament and 'annihilate the legislature'. In contrast, the United States' President cannot dissolve the Congress, nor is his existence dependent upon a majority in the legislature. The amalgamation of the executive and the legislature and the answerability of the executive to the legislature, demonstrated in Question Time, is one of the fundamental characteristics of the Westminster model of government.

The role and functions of particular offices in government display this amalgamation of the branches of government. The Attorney-General has a function as a quasi-judicial officer of the Crown. In this role he decides in a limited number of offences and cases whether or not to initiate a prosecution. In this he is answerable to Parliament – usually the House of Commons – and may in theory be removed by them in a vote of no confidence. The Attorney-General is a member of the government, although not a member of the Cabinet, a convention which resulted from the alleged pressure which was placed upon the then Attorney-General, Sir Patrick Hastings, who withdrew a prosecuting against J R Campbell, acting editor of a Communist paper, for 'incitement to mutiny'. The Attorney-General does take into account the views of the Cabinet when performing his functions, but he is not bound by the views of the Cabinet or Prime Minister. When Lord Denning, in an inventive phase, tried to make the Attorney-General answerable to the courts, this was firmly repudiated by the House of Lords in *Gouriet* v *Union of Post Office Workers* (1977). Similarly, the Divisional Court in *R* v *Solicitor-General, ex parte Taylor* (1995) reiterated that the Attorney-General, or the Solicitor-General acting on his behalf, is not amenable to judicial review of his official decisions.

It is with the office of Lord Chancellor that the absence of separation of powers is most marked. The Lord Chancellor is a member not only of the government but also of the Cabinet. He is chosen by the Prime Minister, and previous Lord Chancellors, such as Lord Hailsham, have had an active political career before ascending to the office. Indeed, Lord Hailsham once ran for the leadership of the Conservative Party. The Lord Chancellor has important administrative functions to perform in connection with the judiciary and is responsible for law reform, some of which may be politically controversial, as with Lord Mackay's proposed reform of the divorce laws. The Lord Chancellor is also a judge and may preside over the Judicial Committee of the House of Lords. This office also entitles the holder to sit in the legislature (in the House of Lords), and the Lord Chancellor acts as Speaker of the upper chamber, performing a Janus-type role of acting as an umpire – although less active than the House of Commons Speaker – and participant. The Lord Chancellor is also instrumental in the appointment of members of the judiciary in practice and theory. Justices of the Peace (JPs) are appointed by the Lord Chancellor on the advice of local advisory committees. Without the benefit of an advisory committee he appoints, for instance, High Court judges, circuit judges and recorders. He also has the power to remove members of the judiciary below the status of superior court judges.

the doctrine of separation of powers would imply the disconnection of e legislature this is *not* found with regard to the role of the Lords of . The Law Lords can and do play a part in the proceedings of the upper e it used to be correct to say that they avoided politically controversial issues, trictly the case. The response of Lord Taylor, the then Lord Chief Justice, ome Secretary's proposed reform of sentencing casts doubt over the previously

g the above discussion then how may Lord Diplock accurately state that 'the British tion is firmly based upon the separation of powers' (see *Duport Steel* v *Sirs* (1980))? umably what is meant by this statement is the adherence to the concept of the dependence of the judiciary. The Act of Settlement 1700 provided that the superior court judges should hold office upon 'good behaviour' rather than the 'King's pleasure' as had been the case. The independence of the judiciary and the inability of the executive to remove them is one of the hallmarks of the separation of powers. Since 1700 superior court judges can only be removed by the Crown on an address presented to it by both Houses of Parliament. It has to be said, however, that circuit judges and recorders may be removed from office by the Lord Chancellor for 'inability or misbehaviour'.

Also, in accordance with the separation of the judiciary from the legislature and the executive is the statutory prohibition of full time members of the judiciary from the House of Commons: House of Commons Disqualification Act 1975.

All of the above, of course, is based upon the conventional (in the technical sense) role of the monarchy. While the Queen is forbidden to enter the House of Commons this is of little or no practical significance as her ministers dominate the chamber. One may conclude that although under the Westminster model the theory of separation of powers is more honoured in the breach than the observance, nevertheless the adherence to the practice of the independence of the judiciary has meant that the courts may maintain an independent and separate existence from the law-makers.

3 Constitutional Principles: The Sovereignty of Parliament

3.1 Introduction

It is important to understand in outline the means by which Parliament's legislative supremacy came to be established, and to understand the ways in which the British constitution differs markedly from countries with a written constitution. The British constitution has evolved out of the long struggle between the Crown and Parliament that culminated, in 1689, with Parliament conclusively asserting its predominance over many of the powers previously exercised the Crown acting alone.

In countries with written constitutions there are normally express limits on the powers of the legislature. In addition, their courts may be able to rule on whether an act of the legislature is 'unconstitutional'. Notwithstanding the absence of any higher law in the United Kingdom that limits the power of the legislature there are clearly political limitations in terms of legislation that would be regarded as acceptable by the population at large. One must be careful not to equate sovereignty – the power to make any law – with effectiveness – the observance of the law by the people and indeed the judges.

The political integration of European countries has been a post-war objective within Europe. In 1957 Belgium, France, West Germany, Italy, Luxembourg and The Netherlands signed the Treaty of Rome establishing the European Economic Community. In 1973 Denmark, Ireland and the United Kingdom became members.

The United Kingdom became a member by virtue of the Treaty of Accession 1972. It was necessary for Parliament to pass legislation incorporating the provisions into domestic law. This was achieved by the European Communities Act 1972. Political and legal integration has proceeded since then. The political and legal issues are:

a) The extent to which the United Kingdom Parliament is obliged to pass legislation which is consistent with Community provisions – is this a negation of sovereignty?

b) The position of the United Kingdom courts where Community law and domestic law conflict.

3.2 Key points

The phrase 'the sovereignty of Parliament' is generally used to mean the absence of any legal restraint on the legislative powers of the United Kingdom Parliament. This absence of legal restraint has three aspects:

a) Parliament is legally competent to legislate on any subject matter – as evidenced by the Act of Settlement 1700; His Majesty's Declaration of Abdication Act 1936; *Burmah Oil Co* v *Lord Advocate* [1965] AC 75 and the War Damage Act 1965; *Mortensen* v *Peters* 1906 14 SLT 227; Parliament Acts 1911 and 1949; Ireland Act 1949, s1(2); Scotland Act 1998; Human Rights Act 1998.

b) No Parliament can bind its successors or be bound by its predecessors. There is one and only one limit to Parliament's legal power: it cannot detract from its own continuing sovereignty (Dicey, *Law of the Constitution*). A later Parliament can expressly repeal an earlier statute. A later Parliament can impliedly repeal an earlier statute: *Vauxhall Estates* v *Liverpool Corporation* [1932] 1 KB 733; *Ellen Street Estates Ltd* v *Minister of Health* [1934] 1 KB 590.

c) In theory once Parliament has legislated no court or other person can pass judgment upon the validity of the legislation. All the courts may do when faced with an Act of Parliament is apply it, subject to their limited powers of statutory interpretation. What the courts would do when confronted by a primary Act of Parliament that confounded all basic notions of fairness any civilised society remains a matter of academic speculation. It should not be assumed that the courts would not 'discover' a common law doctrine whereby they were not required to give effect to such an Act. At common law a Bill becomes an Act of Parliament when it has been approved by the House of Commons and the House of Lords (unless passed under the provisions of the Parliament Acts), and has received the Royal Assent. The enforcement of these procedural rules is entirely a matter for the House concerned and the courts refuse to consider the question as to whether there have been any procedural defects in the passage of a Bill through Parliament: *Pickin* v *British Railways Board* [1974] AC 765.

d) Only Parliament can limit its own sovereignty and such limitations must have been enacted in the form of a statute. However, no Parliament can bind its successors. Therefore, whatever limitations are imposed upon the sovereignty of Parliament by one statute may be repealed by a subsequent Act. However, in practice there are limitations upon the sovereignty of Parliament.

   i) Limitation as to the scope and subject matter of parliamentary legislation: Statute of Westminster 1931, s4.

   ii) Limitation as to the manner and form which legislation must take: *Attorney-General for New South Wales* v *Trethowan* [1932] AC 526 – but note that this applied to a colonial legislature.

   iii) Other practical limitations on the exercise of sovereignty

   - The doctrine of the mandate
   - Public opinion
   - Political and economic constraints

e) Membership of the European Community has inevitably lead to a reassessment of the doctrine of parliamentary sovereignty, given that the Community acquires its sovereignty as a result of member states each giving up sovereignty to some extent in order to be bound by Community law. The Community organs have law-making, executive and judicial powers.

i) The Council of Ministers – the final policy and law-making body of the Community. It has representatives from each member state with a president holding office for six months. Note the decision-making process of the council.

ii) The European Commission – members are chosen by national governments. The Commission can propose law, make law itself and enforce Community law against member states.

iii) The European Parliament – members of the European Parliament are directly elected by member states. They are independent of national party policies. The Parliament has no law-making powers but is consulted by the council. Both the Council and the Commission are accountable to the Parliament.

iv) The European Court of Justice – the European Court of Justice consists of 15 judges appointed by member states. Its function is to enforce Community law and treaty provisions. The role of the Court is crucial to Community law being applied uniformly through all member states.

f) *The sources of Community law*

i) The treaties

Proceedings can be brought in the European Court if a member state fails to fulfil its obligations.

ii) Acts of the Community institutions

- Regulations – made by Council of Ministers or the Commission, these are directly applicable in member states.
- Directives – these establish Community objectives but leave the responsibility of implementation to member states: see *Van Duyn* v *Home Office* [1974] 3 All ER 178.

iii) Decisions of the Court of Justice

- Actions against member states
- Rulings on the interpretation of Community law referred by national courts: art 234 (previously art 177); see *Bulmer (HP)* v *J Bollinger SA* [1974] Ch 401 and *Finnegan* v *Clowney YTP* [1990] 2 AC 407.

Note s3(1) European Communities Act 1972: 'For the purpose of all legal proceedings any question as to the meaning or effect of any of the Treaties, or as to the validity, meaning or effect of any Community instrument, shall be … for determination as such in accordance with the principles laid down by … the European Court.'

g) *Direct applicability*

Section 2(1) of the European Communities Act 1972 provides:

'All such rights, powers, liabilities, obligations and restrictions from time to time created or arising by or under the Treaties, and all such remedies and procedures from time to time provided for by or under the Treaties, as in accordance with the Treaties are without further enactment to be given legal effect or used in the United Kingdom shall be recognised and available in law, and be enforced, allowed and followed accordingly; and the expression "enforceable Community right" and similar expressions shall be read as referring to one to which this subsection applies.'

The effect of this subsection is that all the provisions of Community law which are, in accordance with Community law, intended to take direct effect in the United Kingdom are given the force of law. This applies to Community law made both before and after the coming into force of the Act.

h) *Direct effect*

The term 'direct effect' refers to the enforceability of Community law. 'Vertical' direct effect is the term applied to those measures that can be invoked by a private individual against a member state. 'Horizontal' direct effect applies to those provisions that can be invoked by an individual against another private party. Essentially, the criteria to be satisfied before a provision can be regarded as having direct effect are that it is sufficiently precise in its terms to be said to be creating individual rights, and does not require any further implementation in order to become effective in law. Treaty provisions and regulations are normally regarded as having both vertical and horizontal direct effect provided the above criteria are met: see *Van Gend en Loos* v *Nederlandse Administratie der Belastingen* [1963] ECR 1; *Politi* v *Ministry of Finance* [1971] ECR 1039; *Walrave and Koch* v *Union Cycliste Internationale* [1974] ECR 1405; and *Defrenne* v *SABENA* [1976] ECR 455. Directives can also have vertical direct effect, see *Van Duyn* v *Home Office* Case 41/74 [1974] ECR 1337, but not horizontal direct effect: see *Marleasing SA* v *La Comercial Internacional de Alimentacion SA* [1992] 1 CMLR 305 and *Faccini Dori* v *Recreb Srl* Case C–91/92 [1994] ECR 1–3325. In *Marleasing SA*, however, the European Court of Justice ruled that, whilst directives were not of themselves capable of having direct effect between individuals, the national courts of member states were obliged to interpret domestic law so as to ensure conformity with EC directives, whether the domestic law originated before or after the incorporation of the directive.

i) *The supremacy of Community law over national rules*

Section 2(4) of the European Communities Act provides:

'The provision that may be made under subsection (2) above includes, subject to Schedule 2 of this Act, any such provision (of any such extent) as may be made by Act of Parliament, and any enactment passed or to be passed, other than one contained in this part of this Act, shall be construed and have effect subject to the foregoing provisions of this section.'

The 'foregoing provisions' include s2(1), which states that directly applicable Community law shall have effect in the United Kingdom. Therefore s2(4) seems to amount to a statement that United Kingdom Acts of Parliament 'shall be construed and have effect subject to' directly applicable Community law. The primacy of Community law over national law can be seen in decisions of the European Court of Justice: *Costa* v *ENEL* [1964] ECR 585; *Amminstrazione delle Finanze dello Stato* v *Simmenthal SpA* [1978] 3 CMLR 263; [1978] ECR 629.

j) *Community law and the United Kingdom*

European law will be followed in preference to inconsistent pre-1972 statutes: *Conegate* v *HM Customs and Excise* [1987] 2 WLR 39. It is suggested that there is a new canon of statutory interpretation so that relevant provisions of United Kingdom law can bear a meaning that is consistent with Community law: *Garland* v *British Rail Engineering Ltd* [1983] 2 AC 751; *Macarthys Ltd* v *Smith* [1979] 3 All ER 325; *Pickstone* v *Freemans plc* [1988] 2 All ER 803. More radical approaches are being adopted which suggest that the duty of the national court is to give effect to Community law and frustrate the provisions of an Act of Parliament where there is a conflict. In *R* v *Secretary of State for Transport, ex parte Factortame Ltd and Others (No 2)* [1990] 3 WLR 818 the court granted interim relief suspending those parts of the Merchant Shipping Act 1988 which conflicted with Community law.

k) *Conclusion*

The doctrine of direct applicability and the supremacy of Community law over national rules has led to a surrender of sovereignty on the part of the Westminster Parliament. But while there can be no implied repeal of Community law by national legislation, the position regarding the express repeal of Community law by Act of Parliament is a matter of controversy. While the European Court of Justice maintains that a national court should give effect to Community law even when subsequent national legislation is inconsistent with it, some lawyers argue that the express wish of Parliament must prevail. Two points are however clear:

i) It is only a partial surrender of sovereignty in that it only affects those matters within the competence of the European Community treaties.

ii) It is only a temporary surrender of sovereignty in that it only applies so long as the European Communities Act 1972 is in force.

3.3 Recent cases and developments

In *Mighell* v *Reading and Another; Evans* v *Motor Insurers Bureau; White* v *White and Another* (1998) The Times 12 October the Court of Appeal ruled that the Second Council Directive (84/5/EEC) (OJ 1984 L8/17), which dealt with the approximation of the laws of EC member states regarding civil liability arising from the use of motor vehicles, was not of direct effect and could thus not be relied upon to provide a right to compensation in respect of damage caused by uninsured drivers.

The Human Rights Act 1998, which gives effect to certain provisions of the European Convention on Human Rights in domestic law, does not directly affect the doctrine of parliamentary sovereignty as such, but raises a number of interesting issues. The courts will not be empowered to strike down primary legislation found to be in conflict with the Convention, but higher courts will be empowered to declarations of incompatibility, thus clearly flagging that domestic law is not consistent with the operation of the Convention as incorporated. It will then be for ministers to take remedial action. The Act also places ministers under a duty when presenting new Bills to the House of Commons to make a statement on the extent to which the Bill complies with the 1998 Act.

The Scotland Act 1998 provides for the devolution of power to a Scottish Parliament. The Scottish Parliament will be sovereign in respect of devolved issues, but the United Kingdom Parliament at Westminster retains power over certain reserved areas such as constitutional reform, foreign affairs and social security. The 1998 expressly provides that the United Kingdom Parliament at Westminster can legislate in respect of any matter, including devolved matters, if it so chooses, but it may be the case that a convention develops to the effect that it will not do so without the consent of the Scottish Parliament.

3.4 Analysis of questions

Questions can be either essay or problem style. Problem questions tend to focus on the issue as to whether or not Acts of Parliament can be entrenched against future repeal. Essay questions are more wide ranging and may examine the student's knowledge of the relationship between parliamentary sovereignty and conventions of the constitution. The extent to which the United Kingdom Parliament remains sovereign becomes an ever more important political question. The legal issue raised in exam questions focuses on the relationship between Community law and United Kingdom law where there is a conflict and the approach of the judiciary to such a conflict.

3.5 Questions

QUESTION ONE

In July 1993 Parliament passed the Puffins Act: s1 provides that it shall be a criminal offence to kill a puffin; s2 provides that no Bill to repeal the Puffins Act shall be laid before Parliament unless the consent of the Birds Council has previously been obtained.

In 1994 a Bill repealing the Puffins Act is laid before Parliament, without the consent of the Birds Council having been previously obtained, and this is subsequently enacted as the Puffins Repeal Act 1994.

Advise the Birds Council whether they can challenge the 1994 Act and still bring a prosecution against Mr Toad who killed a puffin in 1995.

How, if at all, would your advice differ if the European Commission had made a Regulation in October 1993 providing that puffins were vermin and that a cash premium would be paid in respect of each puffin killed?

Adapted from University of London LLB Examination
(for External Students) Constitutional Law June 1986 Q3

General Comment

A relatively simple question on the sovereignty of Parliament and the effects of membership of the European Union. As regards the first part of the question, after stating the content of the doctrine of parliamentary supremacy, students should argue as best they can the likely effect of the Puffins Repeal Act. There is no answer; just state the likely alternatives. The second part of the question is more straightforward as the supremacy of Community law over national rules is now firmly established in situations such as the one in the problem.

Skeleton Solution

- Introduction: the content of the doctrine of parliamentary sovereignty.
- The Puffins Repeal Act 1994: the application of the doctrine of parliamentary sovereignty to the Act; the effects of s2 of the Act on the traditional doctrine.
- The European Communities Act 1972 s2(4); the supremacy of Community law over national laws.

Suggested Solution

Under the doctrine of the sovereignty of Parliament there exists no legal limitation upon the legislative competence of the United Kingdom Parliament. This absence of legal restraint has three aspects: Parliament is legally competent to legislate upon any subject matter, no Parliament can bind its successors or be bound by its predecessors, and, once Parliament has legislated, no court or other person can pass judgment upon the validity of the legislation.

This rule that Parliament may not bind its successors (and that no Parliament is bound by Acts of its predecessors) is often cited both as a limitation upon legislative supremacy and as an example of it. As Dicey wrote: 'The logical reason why Parliament has failed in its endeavours to enact unchangeable enactments is that a sovereign power cannot, while retaining its sovereign character, restrict its own powers by any parliamentary enactment' (*The Law of the Constitution*, 10th edition, 1959, p68). It is inherent in the nature of a legislature that it should continue to be free to make new laws and, within the United Kingdom legal system therefore, all statutes that have been enacted by the Queen in Parliament remain in force until they are repealed or amended. An Act can be repealed either expressly or impliedly (see *Ellen Street Estates Ltd* v *Minister of Health* (1934)). In the latter case if Parliament passes an Act which is contrary to a previous statute (or certain provisions of the earlier statute) the earlier statute (or those particular provisions) are held to have been repealed.

The doctrine therefore consists, in essence, of a rule that governs the legal relationship between the courts and the legislature, namely that the courts are under a duty to apply the legislation made by Parliament and may not hold an Act of Parliament to be invalid or unconstitutional.

In order for the Birds Council to challenge the Puffins Repeal Act 1994 and prosecute Mr Toad, the Council will have to satisfy the courts that the Act is invalid due to the failure to comply with the consultation provisions of the 1993 Act. Normally of course, under the doctrine of parliamentary supremacy, there will be no problem. The courts will consider the 1994 Act to have expressly repealed the 1993 Act. But in the present case, what is the effect of s2? The principle that the Parliament which passed the 1993 Act cannot bind the Parliament which purports to enact the 1994 Repeal Act may mean simply that, notwithstanding s2, the repeal is valid and the courts will be bound to give effect to the express wishes of the legislature. However, it can also be argued that s2 creates a provision as to the manner by which repeal of the 1993 Act must be achieved and that this will be binding upon future Parliaments until s2 itself is expressly repealed. Therefore any attempt to repeal the whole Act without first removing s2 will be invalid. Of course it may also be argued that by expressly repealing the whole of the 1993 Act Parliament is in any case impliedly repealing the consultation provisions of s2.

The situation concerning the effect of the purported repeal is therefore somewhat uncertain. No uncertainty would exist, however, had the European Commission made a regulation in October 1993 providing that puffins were vermin and that a cash premium would be paid in respect of each puffin killed. Section 2(4) of the European Communities Act 1972 provides in effect that United Kingdom Acts of Parliament shall be construed and have effect subject to directly applicable Community law. Under art 249 (previously art 189) of the Treaty of Rome, regulations have direct applicability and are binding in all member states without requiring implementation or adoption by national law. Therefore any regulation made by the European Commission in October 1993 would have supremacy over national laws and take effect notwithstanding the conflict with the then already existing Puffins Act 1993. In this respect it is both clear from the Treaty and from statements made by the European Court of Justice (see *Costa* v *ENEL* (1964)) that Community law should prevail over national law in all circumstances and therefore any United Kingdom constitutional law doctrine of the legislative supremacy of Parliament is irrelevant.

Of course, the approach taken by the European Court of Justice indicated above runs completely contrary to the traditional doctrine of the sovereignty of Parliament. This has resulted in controversy, with some arguing that, while the doctrine of implied repeal has been abandoned so far as Community law is concerned, the doctrine of express repeal of earlier law, including Community law, is nevertheless retained. However it is yet to be seen how the United Kingdom courts would act if faced by a United Kingdom Act of Parliament expressing an intention of Parliament to legislature contrary to Community law. It is worth noting, however, that in *R* v *Secretary of State for Transport, ex parte Factortame (No 2)* (1990) the House of Lords did, following a reference to the European Court, grant an injunction effectively suspending the operation of a United Kingdom statute to the extent that it was inconsistent with European law. Such a situation is, perhaps, unlikely to arise since it would amount to a blatant repudiation by the United Kingdom of its international obligations under the European Community treaties. But, in the absence of such express repeal of Community law by our Parliament, it is clear that as in *Macarthys Ltd* v *Smith* (1979), where a conflict does exist between United Kingdom legislation and Community law, the latter will prevail and accordingly, not withstanding the Puffins Act 1993 and its provisions, the Community Regulation of October 1993 will bind our courts.

QUESTION TWO

'Attempts to entrench legislation by legal means will inevitably be futile unless the basic rule of the United Kingdom's constitution is abandoned.'

Discuss.

University of London LLB Examination
(for External Students) Constitutional Law June 1991 Q1

General Comment

A question requiring an explanation of the terms used, particularly entrenchment, and the basic rule of the constitution. It is important to explain how parliamentary sovereignty manifests itself thus indicating the difficulties with entrenchment. Obviously the impact of European Union membership upon parliamentary sovereignty also needs to be considered.

Skeleton Solution

- Explain nature of sovereignty.
- Express and implied repeal – examples.
- Nature of European Communities Act decisions thereunder.
- *Factortame* cases – conclusion.

Suggested Solution

Entrenchment of legislation involves the enactment of clauses that prevent the Act concerned from being repealed by simple majority vote by the legislative body. A typical example is provided by art V of the United States constitution under which two-thirds of the members of Congress have to approve an amendment to the constitution, which in turn has to receive the support of three-quarters of the state legislatures. The purpose of entrenchment is clearly to protect those constitutional measures that are seen as being particularly fundamental. A constitution that could not be altered at all would soon become obsolete and disregarded in practice. One that could be changed by a simple majority vote would be at the mercy of passing political trends, especially where a small party held power because an election had produced a 'hung' Parliament. The question under consideration refers to attempts at entrenchment within the British constitution being futile because of the constitution's basic rule. By this it is assumed that the question is referring to the doctrine of parliamentary sovereignty, under which Parliament has the ultimate power to pass or repeal any legislation it sees fit. In short it is being suggested that it will not avail Parliament to include entrenchment provisions in a piece of legislation in an effort to protect it, as a natural consequence of parliamentary sovereignty is that no parliament can bind its successor parliaments. To what extent does the operation of the British constitution support this view?

Traditionally constitutional lawyers have pointed to the operation of two doctrines as evidence of the inability of any parliament to bind its successors; express repeal and implied repeal. Under the former, any parliament could enact legislation expressly repealing existing legislation. The effect of the doctrine was that the courts would always apply the most recent legislation. Where two pieces of legislation appeared irreconcilable, but the later Act did not expressly state that its effect was to repeal the terms of the earlier Act, the latter doctrine of implied repeal would be brought into play by means of which the courts would assume that it was implicit in the passage of the later legislation that Parliament had intended to repeal the earlier legislation since they could not stand together. Attempts by Parliament to circumvent the doctrine of implied repeal in the earlier part of the 20th century met with little success.

This is illustrated by the cases of *Vauxhall Estates* v *Liverpool Corporation* (1932) and *Ellen Street Estates Ltd* v *Minister of Health* (1934). In the first of these cases, the Corporation of Liverpool proposed a scheme for the improvement of a certain area of the city. The Minister of Health confirmed the scheme in an order that incorporated the provisions of the Acquisition of Land (Assessment of Compensation) Act 1919 and the Housing Act 1925. These two Acts each provided a different scheme of compensation for compulsorily acquired land. The 1919 Act provided in s7(1):

'The provisions of the ... order by which the land is authorised to be acquired, or of any Act incorporated therewith, shall in relation to the matters dealt with in this Act, have effect subject to this Act, and so far as inconsistent with this Act those provisions shall ... not have effect.'

The question arose as to whether the compensation due to the appellants should be calculated in accordance with the 1919 Act or in accordance with the 1925 Act. The appellants argued that, because of s7(1) of the 1919 Act, it must be calculated in accordance with that Act. It was held that the compensation should be assessed in accordance with the later Act. Parliament had exercised its power of overriding the provisions of s7(1) of the 1919 Act by enacting in the later Act of 1925 a set of provisions totally inconsistent with those of the 1919 Act. Similarly, in the *Ellen Street* case it was held that the provisions of an earlier Act could always be repealed, by implication, by provisions in a later Act which were inconsistent with those in the earlier Act. Maugham LJ stated the effect of the doctrine as follows:

'The legislature cannot, according to our constitution, bind itself as to the form of subsequent legislation, and it is impossible for Parliament to enact that in a subsequent statute dealing with the same subject matter there can be no implied repeal.'

It should be clear from the above that the doctrine of parliamentary sovereignty depends in large measure on the adherence by the judiciary to the practice of applying the later Act in preference to an earlier one.

Since the entry into the European Community (EC) by the United Kingdom, however, the assumptions implicit in the question need to be reassessed, however. Section 2(1) of the European Communities Act 1972 provides that all EC law became part of United Kingdom law with effect from 1 January 1973. Section 2(4) further provides that 'any such provision (of any such extent) as might be made by Act of Parliament, and any enactment passed or to be passed, other than one contained in this Part of this Act, shall be construed and have effect subject to the foregoing provisions of this section'. In other words any subsequent Act passed by the United Kingdom Parliament was to take effect only to the extent that it did not conflict with the provisions of EC law. This was clearly another attempt to bypass the doctrine of implied repeal, but it was one that was necessary if the United Kingdom was going to be able to abide by its obligations under the terms of the Treaty of Rome, which requires each member state to give primacy to EC law: see *Costa* v *ENEL* (1964). The result has been that the domestic courts have modified the doctrine of implied repeal as regards domestic law and EC legislation, by holding that domestic law should always be interpreted in a manner that produces a result consistent with the United Kingdom's obligations under the Treaty: see *Macarthys Ltd* v *Smith* (1981), and *Garland* v *British Rail Engineering Ltd* (1983), wherein Lord Diplock stated that, in a case of clear conflict, domestic courts would still have to produce an interpretation of domestic law that ensured conformity with EC law, no matter how wide a departure from the prima facie meaning may be need to achieve consistency.

Following *R* v *Secretary of State for Transport, ex parte Factortame (No 2)* (1990), it is now clear that the domestic courts have to be prepared to go as far as effectively suspending the operation of an Act of Parliament if it is impugned on the ground that it conflicts with EC law whilst that issue is being considered by the European Court of Justice. It is submitted that short of the United Kingdom reneging upon its obligations under the Treaty of Rome, unilaterally withdrawing from the EC, and expressly repealing the European Communities Act 1972, the Act effectively entrenches EC law, by making it impossible for any later Act to be applied in preference to EC law by means of implied repeal.

Note that this result is achieved because of the existence of bodies outside the United Kingdom (such as the European Commission and Court of Justice) given jurisdiction by the United Kingdom Parliament over matters formerly within its control, and further given power to invoke sanctions against the United Kingdom if it attempts to reassert that sovereignty by indirect means.

QUESTION THREE

'It is often said that it would be unconstitutional for the United Kingdom Parliament to do certain things, meaning that the moral, political and other reasons against doing them are so strong that most people would regard it as highly improper if Parliament did these things. But this does not mean that it is beyond the power of Parliament to do such things. If Parliament chose to do any of them the courts could not hold the Act of Parliament invalid.' (*Madzimbamuto* v *Lardner-Burke* (1969), per Lord Reid).

Discuss.

University of London LLB Examination
(for External Students) Constitutional Law June 1995 Q1

General Comment

This question is a general theoretical problem that requires some discussion of basic constitutional theory. The candidate must take care with this problem and not merely launch into it because it appears to be straightforward. Obtaining a strong mark in very generally based questions can be difficult unless the candidate is scrupulous to ensure that the answer is well structured. Beyond that, it is a question asking for a discussion of the interaction between Parliament and the courts, which might be useful to settle in the student, or as a general final question.

Skeleton Solution

- Comparison with the USA.
- Discussion of the scope of judicial review in English law to review executive action.
- Discussion of the Criminal Justice and Public Order Act 1994 as an example of courts' ability to control Parliament.
- Use of statutory interpretation to control legislation partially.
- Overall sovereignty of Parliament explained.

Suggested Solution

There is a tension between the theoretical constitutional powers of Parliament and those acts that Parliament can perform without attracting political censure. The basic rule of constitutional law is that Parliament is the sovereign body and that any Act of Parliament passed by the Queen in Parliament supersedes any other rule or decree. Therefore, at least in theory, there is a possibility that Parliament can act in any way that it sees fit.

In the United States of America, the seminal decision of the Supreme Court in *Marbury* v *Madison* (1803) found that the Supreme Court has the power to review any legislative act of the executive or the legislature. Therefore, the principle of sovereignty under United States constitutional arrangements is that the Supreme Court has a residuary power to find that any particular act is unconstitutional. There is no such power in the United Kingdom legal jurisdiction. The English law doctrine of judicial review has led to a power in the High Court to review certain acts of public bodies or the acts of ministers in the exercise of the prerogative powers of the Crown. There is, therefore, a development of the ability of the courts to look at the powers of the executive and their exercise. However, these powers derive directly from the Supreme Court Act 1981 and therefore can be said to be constitutional 'long-stop' functions created by the powers of Parliament itself, rather than judicial powers to curtail the exercise of those of Parliament. Judicial powers are restricted to the categories of *Wednesbury* unreasonableness (see *Associated Provincial Picture Houses Ltd* v *Wednesbury Corporation* (1948)) or breaches of natural justice.

It is important to note that judicial review cannot curtail the power of the legislature or executive by retaining a power to overturn legislation, nor can it affect the power of the legislature, Parliament, to pass legislation by exercising judicial review principles. There is no ability to say that an Act of Parliament offends some principle of natural justice or that it is *Wednesbury* unreasonable in some way. Therefore, there is no judicial control over Parliament.

As a result of a lack of judicial competence, and in the absence of a written constitution making plain any other control over the powers of Parliament, judicial review principles have grown to fill the gap. Indeed, it would be undesirable if it were possible for some agency other than Parliament itself to overturn its powers. That would lead to a political conflict outside the scope of the British constitutional arrangement of parliamentary elections and the sovereignty of the Queen in Parliament.

The question arises: to what extent does Parliament act against the interests of the constitutional order by doing things that are, per se, unconstitutional? The answer to that question is that Parliament does not tend to do things that are unconstitutional on such a regular basis that the constitutional order would be threatened. The system of democratic elections ensures that the House of Commons has a vested interest in not exercising powers which it would be unable to justify to the British electorate.

Therefore, legislation like the Criminal Justice and Public Order Act 1994 can be passed by Parliament, despite the fact that it seems to interfere with the rights of citizens to freedom of movement and action in prescribed circumstances. On the United States model, it would be possible for the Supreme Court to consider whether or not this exercise of power was unconstitutional. If it were found to be unconstitutional, then it would be possible to refer the legislation back to Parliament as constitutionally invalid.

The Westminster model, however, invests no such power in the courts. The Criminal Justice and Public Order Act 1994 cannot be declared invalid. The courts, however, are able to interpret it in such a way that the sense it appeared to have when passed through Parliament is tempered somewhat to ensure that it complies with a level of fairness on the facts of any case. In September 1995 (in an unreported decision), s70 of the 1994 Act was invoked against an individual claiming to be King Arthur. He sought to gain access to Stonehenge at the time of the Solstice. However, the police arrested him for criminal trespass on the basis that there were more than 20 people gathered together seeking to trespass on land. The court held that of the 20 or more people in attendance, most were not known to the defendant, being either television crews or simply bystanders. Therefore, s70 was held not to apply on these facts. This is an example of the way in which a court can interpret the wording of an Act to suit the court's view of what is appropriate in the circumstances. However, the statute still remains effective.

The fact that this legislation can be passed without any power to prevent it is perhaps more a testament to shortcomings in the democratic system than to the constitutional rules per se. It might be possible to vote for a different political party committed to the repeal of this legislation; however, there is no political party currently committed in this way. Therefore, there is a gap between constitutional theory, which might hold that there has been a technical breach of some standard of natural justice, and the political realities of democratic power.

QUESTION FOUR

Parliament wishes to promote affirmative action and decides to allow women to be paid more than men for the same work. It passes the Turning the Tables Act 1995, s1 of which states:

'This Act is to be given effect notwithstanding any decision of the European Court of Justice or any provisions of Community law or any provisions of the European Communities Act 1972.'

Would a British judge still give primacy to Community law if this new Act came into conflict with it?

Adapted from University of London LLB Examination
(for External Students) Constitutional Law June 1987 Q3

General Comment

A relatively simple question concerning the effect of membership of the European Communities on the sovereignty of the Westminster Parliament.

Skeleton Solution

- Introduction. The European Communities Act 1972.
- The principles of direct applicability and the supremacy of Community law over national rules. Section 2(1) and s2(4) of the European Communities Act 1972.
- The sovereignty of Parliament. Express repeal and the doctrine of implied repeal. Effect of Community law.
- Effect of parliamentary legislation expressly contrary to Community law: *Macarthys Ltd* v *Smith* (1979); *R* v *Secretary of State for Transport, ex parte Factortame (No 2)* (1990).
- The position with regard to the Turning the Tables Act 1995.

Suggested Solution

The United Kingdom became a member of the European Communities with effect from 1 January 1973, by virtue of the Treaty of Accession 1972. For the Treaty of Accession and the Community treaties and law to have legal effect in the United Kingdom it was necessary for Parliament to pass legislation incorporating them into domestic law. This was achieved by the European Communities Act 1972.

The legal regime of the European Community is founded upon the principle of direct applicability. Certain rules of Community law contained both in the treaties and in regulations made by the Council or the Commission are directly applicable in that, of their own force, they create legal rights and duties enforceable in municipal courts. Community law also forms part of the national law of every member state. The European Court of Justice has held that Community law prevails over national law to the extent that they are inconsistent with one another. These two principles are given effect in the law of the United Kingdom by virtue of s2(1) and s2(4) of the European Communities Act 1972.

By virtue of s2(4) of the European Communities Act 1972 therefore all United Kingdom legislation shall only take effect to the extent that it is consistent with Community law however clearly it may appear from the United Kingdom legislation that it is intended to have effect notwithstanding any Community law to the contrary: *Costa* v *ENEL* (1964); *Amministrazione delle Finanze dello Stato* v *Simmenthal SpA* (1978). It is clear both from the Treaty and from statements made by the European Court of Justice that community law should prevail over national law in all circumstances. Any United Kingdom constitutional law doctrine of the legislative sovereignty of Parliament is irrelevant. This approach taken by the European Court of Justice runs completely contrary to the traditional doctrine of the sovereignty of Parliament as enunciated in *Vauxhall Estates* v *Liverpool Corporation* (1932) and *Ellen Street Estates Ltd* v *Minister of Health* (1934). Certainly the doctrine of implied repeal as set out in *Ellen Street Estates* v *Minister of Health*, that later United Kingdom legislation always, by implication, repeals earlier legislative provisions with which it is inconsistent, would not survive.

But what about the situation such as that under the Turning the Tables Act 1995, where Parliament legislates expressly contrary to Community law? In such a case it may be possible to treat s2(4) as amounting to a rule of interpretation that there shall be a presumption that the United Kingdom Parliament, in passing legislation, intends to legislate consistently with Community law. This approach allows that if the United Kingdom Parliament were to make it clear in a piece of legislation that it intended to legislate contrary to Community law or that it intended the legislation to take effect notwithstanding any provision of Community law to the contrary, then the United Kingdom legislation would prevail over the inconsistent Community law. This is the approach that was favoured by the Court of Appeal in *Macarthys Ltd* v *Smith*

(1979). A man had been employed as a stockroom keeper at £60 per week. Subsequently a woman was employed in this position at £50 per week. She took the matter to an industrial tribunal on the grounds that this was contrary to law. Two questions arose. Firstly, was this contrary to art 119 (now art 141) of the Treaty of Rome which provides that each member state shall ensure and maintain the application of the principle that men and women should receive equal pay for equal work? Secondly, in the event of a conflict between the United Kingdom legislation and art 119 of the Treaty, which should prevail in English courts?

In the Court of Appeal Lord Denning MR felt that if there were a conflict between the United Kingdom legislation and art 119 (now art 141) of the Treaty, art 119 should prevail since this is required by s2(1) and s2(4) of the European Communities Act 1972. Lord Denning here assumed that Parliament, when it passes legislation, intends to fulfil its obligations under the Treaty. But he felt that if the time should come when Parliament deliberately passes an Act with the intention of repudiating the Treaty or any provision in it or intentionally of acting inconsistently with it and says so in express terms, then it would be the duty of the United Kingdom courts to follow the Act of Parliament. But unless there is such an intentional and express repudiation of the Treaty, it is the duty of the United Kingdom courts to give priority to the Treaty.

Thus Lord Denning put forward the view that if Parliament in an Act stated an express intention to legislate contrary to Community law or notwithstanding Community law, then in that one situation the United Kingdom court would give preference to the United Kingdom legislation over the Community law. This interpretation was also favoured by Lord Diplock in *Garland* v *British Rail Engineering Ltd* (1983) when he too stated that statutes must be construed in a way consistent with Treaty obligations if they are capable of bearing such a meaning.

This amounts to a retention of the doctrine of express repeal of earlier law by later legislation, but involves the abandonment of the doctrine of implied repeal as far as Community law is concerned. In the case of *R* v *Secretary of State for Transport, ex parte Factortame (No 2)* (1990) the court granted temporary injunctive relief suspending those parts of the Merchant Shipping Act 1988 which were in conflict with Community law. A reference to the European Court of Justice ruled that domestic courts were required to give effect to directly enforceable provisions of Community law. The approach is not consistent with the traditional United Kingdom doctrine of the sovereignty of Parliament. However, it is yet to be seen how the United Kingdom courts would act if faced with a United Kingdom Act of Parliament expressing a clear intention of Parliament to legislate contrary to Community law. Regarding the Turning the Tables Act 1995 therefore the position is far from clear. The court may be inclined to uphold the express wish of Parliament and give effect to the Act notwithstanding art 119 of the Treaty of Rome. However the European Court of Justice would almost certainly declare this to be invalid and hold that s1 of the 1995 Act amounts to a blatant repudiation by the United Kingdom of its international obligations under the European Community Treaties.

QUESTION FIVE

'The United Kingdom Parliament is said to have forfeited its sovereignty by the European Communities Act 1972. However this forfeiture of sovereignty is better described as a limited and partial surrender of sovereignty.'

Discuss.

The University of Wolverhampton
Constitutional Law September 1991 Q1

General Comment

A topical question which continues to arouse political controversy. The United Kingdom's membership of the European Union has far reaching political and constitutional implications.

Skeleton Solution

- An outline of the idea of parliamentary sovereignty.
- The European Communities Act 1972 ss2(1), (4) and 3(1).
- Sources of Community law and its integration into the United Kingdom.
- The response of the United Kingdom courts.
- Conclusion.

Suggested Solution

The doctrine of parliamentary sovereignty according to Dicey means that Parliament has the right to make or unmake any law whatever, that no person or body is recognised by the law of England as having a right to override or challenge the legislation of Parliament and that Parliament cannot bind its successors. Thus Parliament has passed legislation which has retrospective effect (see *Burmah Oil Co* v *Lord Advocate* (1965)), legislation which conflicts with international treaties (see *Mortensen* v *Peters* (1906)), and the cases of *Vauxhall Estates* v *Liverpool Corporation* (1932) and *Ellen Street Estates Ltd* v *Minister of Health* (1934) illustrate the principle that Parliament cannot detract from its own continuing sovereignty – that is to say it cannot bind a future Parliament.

There are of course certain ultimate limitations on what Parliament can do which derive from the influence of public opinion and the political realities any government faces: see Lord Sankey in *British Coal Corporation* v *R* (1935). By and large such issues tend to be academic. However, the United Kingdom's membership of the European Union has posed a constitutional dilemma in that the United Kingdom is obliged to legislate in a way that is consistent with treaty obligations and European law has direct effect in the United Kingdom.

The United Kingdom became a member of the European Communities with effect from 1 January 1973. The Community treaties and Community law were given legal effect by the European Communities Act 1972. The objective of the Community is to create a 'partnership' of member states. To achieve this a degree of harmonisation of individual states' laws is necessary. The objectives of the Community are contained in art 2 of the Treaty of Rome and whilst specifically aimed at commercial and agricultural activity they permeate many other areas of United Kingdom law, for example sex discrimination and environmental control.

Community law originates from the Community Treaties, Acts of the Community institutions and decisions of the European Court of Justice. Whilst the United Kingdom is not bound by international treaties the particular feature of the Community is that laws made by the Community organs are transferred into United Kingdom law by virtue of the European Communities Act and furthermore the United Kingdom must legislate in a way consistent with Community law and Community treaties: see *Bulmer* v *Bollinger* (1974). Community law has become a source of law in the United Kingdom. Where then does this leave the doctrine of parliamentary supremacy as defined by Dicey?

Section 2(1) of the European Communities Act 1972 provides that 'rights, powers, liabilities, obligations and restrictions ... and all such remedies and procedures from time to time provided for under the Treaties ... are without further enactment to be given legal effect ... in the United Kingdom'. Section 2(4) provides that United Kingdom Acts of Parliament shall be construed and have effect subject to directly applicable Community law.

The approach of the European Court of Justice, which under s3 of the Act is the ultimate authority on the interpretation of Community law, is to assert the primacy of that law: see *Costa* v *ENEL* (1964) and the *Simmenthal* case (1978). The approach of the United Kingdom courts has been to interpret both treaty provisions and directives (see *Van Duyn* v *Home Office* (1974)) in a way consistent with treaty obligations. This was the case in *Macarthys Ltd* v *Smith* (1979), which concerned the equal pay provisions under art 119 (now art 141) of the Treaty of Rome. In that particular case there was a degree of interpretative latitude under the Equal Pay Act 1970 as amended by the Sex Discrimination Act 1975, and Denning MR argued that the court could look to the treaty provisions as an aid to construction, the assumption being that the United Kingdom Parliament would not intend to legislate in a way inconsistent with European law.

The case of *R* v *Secretary of State for Transport, ex parte Factortame (No 2)* (1990) further underlines the conflict. The Merchant Shipping Act 1988 contained provisions at variance with Community law. On a reference to the European Court of Justice the Court predictably ruled that measures of EC law rendered any conflicting national law inapplicable. The House of Lords granted an injunction effectively suspending the provisions of the Act that were in conflict thus frustrating, albeit temporarily, the objectives of the statute. The developing jurisprudence of the European Court can be seen in two cases: *Marleasing SA* v *La Comercial Internacionale de Alimentacion SA* (1992) and *Francovich* v *Italy* (1992). In *Marleasing* the Court held that national courts should interpret their existing national law taking account of a clearly worded directive, notwithstanding it had not been implemented. In *Francovich* v *Italian Republic* (1992) an individual was given the right to sue the state for damages for the non-implementation of a directive that would, if implemented, have conferred a remedy.

It can therefore be seen that, in the context of our membership of the European Union, the purist view of parliamentary sovereignty is no longer tenable. Forfeiture of sovereignty is limited and partial in the sense that in the United Kingdom constitution it is not possible to entrench legislation and the European Communities Act could be repealed. However, a 'European constitutional order' is emerging despite some political resistance and the present integration of the United Kingdom into the Community does mean a limited sovereignty in practical terms.

QUESTION SIX

'The traditional doctrine of parliamentary sovereignty requires revision in light of the United Kingdom's membership of the European Communities.'

Do you agree?

University of London LLB Examination
(for External Students) Constitutional Law June 1993 Q2

General Comment

Despite its mild, almost understated appearance, this is probably the most difficult of all questions which a constitutional student is likely to face. The effect of EC membership on national sovereignty involves very sophisticated and intricate analysis; there will be no time to give elementary explanation of concepts at any length, and so the examiner will be prepared to assume a large degree of knowledge, eg on the character of EC articles, regulations and directives, the differences between horizontal and direct effect, etc. It is essential to concentrate on rulings of the European Court of Justice in recent cases that have spelled out the enormity of the constitutional changes.

Skeleton Solution

- Brief definition of concept of sovereignty.
- Brief outline of changes made by European Communities Acts 1972 and 1993.
- Detailed consideration of 1972 Act, ss2 and 3.
- Rulings of European Court of Justice on harmonisation of national laws and supremacy of EC law.
- Ruling of European Court of Justice on methods of interpreting national laws so as to comply with EC directives.
- Ruling of European Court of Justice on remedies for failure to implement directives.
- Brief reference to likely effect of ratification of Treaty of Maastricht.
- Conclusion.

Suggested Solution

The traditional doctrine of parliamentary sovereignty contends that Parliament can make or unmake any law whatsoever; that no Parliament can bind future Parliaments as to the manner or form of legislating or as to the policy of legislation; and that no court is competent to question the validity of an authentic Act of Parliament. The doctrine evolved in the context of the United Kingdom's unwritten constitution as a result of Parliament's struggle for power against the monarchy and judges in the seventeenth century. However, the enactment of the European Communities Act (ECA) 1972 and the incorporation of the Maastricht Treaty on European Union (now referred to as TEU 1992) by the European Communities (Amendment) Act 1993, and the ratification of the Treaty of Amsterdam (now referred to as TEU 1997) changed all that. It would, indeed, be something of an understatement to say that the traditional doctrine requires mere revision; it must be questionable whether it even exists any more, since the ECA 1972 gave the United Kingdom an external written constitution superior (in cases of conflict) to the internal unwritten one. EC law today affects so much of English law that, so far as fundamentals are concerned, it would be fantasy to assert that United Kingdom judges could continue to recognise a claim to sovereignty which had effectively been surrendered to (or 'pooled' with) a different kind of sovereignty, that of the EC.

The combined effect of the 1972 Act, s2(1) and s2(4) is that conflicts between English law and EC law must be resolved in favour of EC law, whether the English law existed before or after the coming into force of the 1972 Act. The effect of the 1972 Act s3 is to make the European Court of Justice at Luxembourg the supreme judicial authority for deciding issues of EC law, including conflicts of law. Long before the United Kingdom joined the EC, the European Court of Justice had made rulings for other member states emphasising the primacy of EC law in order to facilitate harmonisation of laws, regarded as essential to lay the foundations for a Single Market and eventual economic and political union: *Van Gend en Loos* (1963) and *Costa* v *ENEL* (1964). National courts were instructed by the European Court of Justice to suspend conflicting national law by granting injunctions to applicants without waiting for their national legislatures to bring in amending legislation: the *Simmenthal* case (1978). It was only a matter of time before the European Court of Justice was given an opportunity to rule that the same obligation applied to United Kingdom judges and that any national doctrine (such as parliamentary sovereignty) which appeared to stand in the way was 'irrelevant' and could and should be ignored: the *Factortame (No 2)* case (1991).

The acceptance of that ruling by the House of Lords and the consequent disapplication of the Merchant Shipping Act 1988 (found to have been in conflict with art 52 (now art 43) of the Treaty of Rome) illustrated what Bingham LJ (as he then was, in the Court of Appeal) described as the 'constitutional enormity' of the change to the British constitution made by the United Kingdom's membership of the EC. One academic commented in the following terms: 'The House of Lords has given the clearest indication yet that the British courts accept the full implication of the constitutional foundations of the Community legal order; and that the British constitutional doctrine of parliamentary sovereignty can no longer be relied on in the British courts to frustrate the application of Community Law': Gravells ([1991] PL 180 at 181).

There appears to be no escape from the logical consequences of belonging to a system in which the objective is the harmonisation of laws. Thus, even attempts by United Kingdom judges to preserve a degree of national sovereignty by giving a literal interpretation to laws passed prior to EC membership have been rejected by the European Court of Justice's adoption of a 'broad' approach under which national judges are obliged to construe such law so as to comply as far as possible with EC law (especially directives), even if this means considerable judicial rewriting of the statutory text and ignoring the intentions of the Parliament which passed the pre-ECA 1972 law in question: see *Duke* v *GEC Reliance* (1988), which cannot now stand with the ruling of the European Court of Justice in the *Marleasing* case (1992).

The impact of *Marleasing* will be considerable because although directives strictly have only vertical effect (imposing duties on national state authorities only), the broad approach to construction will permit directives to be 'interposed' in purely private disputes between Community citizens and therefore give them a kind of horizontal effect, thereby immensely extending the scope of existing directives. This is precisely what the European Court of Justice hoped to achieve, because the European Court of Justice had been faced with the problem that the efficacy of EC law was being undermined by the difficulty of enforcing EC harmonisation rules contained in nonimplemented Directives because of the absence of horizontal effect.

The recognition in *Francovich* v *Italian Republic* (1992) that a member state could be liable in damages for failure to implement a directive, has given rise to a developing jurisprudence, notably evidenced by decisions such as *Brasserie du Pêcheur SA* v *Federal Republic of Germany* Case C–46/93; *R* v *Secretary of State for Transport ex parte Factortame Ltd and Others (No 4)* Case C–48/93 (1996). It is now clear that damages will be available if a member state fails to comply with, or implement Community law, and an individual suffers loss as a result, provided three conditions are met: (i) the rule of law infringed must be intended to confer rights on individuals; (ii) the breach must be sufficiently serious; and (iii) there must be a direct causal link between the breach of the obligation resting on the state and the damage sustained by the injured party.

There is considerable support for the view that, as the process of integration with the rest of Europe through EC membership continues, the concept of sovereignty as we have known it may no longer have a place in the dictionary of the British constitutional lawyer.

QUESTION SEVEN

Discuss, by reference to decided cases, the legal status of European Community law within the United Kingdom and its priority in relation to provisions in domestic Acts of Parliament.

University of London LLB Examination
(for External Students) Constitutional Law June 1996 Q4

General Comment

This is a relatively straightforward question involving the case law relating to the United Kingdom's membership of the European Community. The candidate should highlight the leading cases in this area and avoid getting enmeshed in a descriptive analysis of the plethora of cases in this area. A detailed knowledge, inter alia, of the course and implications of the *Factortame* litigation is required.

Skeleton Solution

- United Kingdom's membership of the EC and the method by which treaties are signed.
- Implications for domestic law of the signing of treaties.
- Sections 2(1), 2(4) and 3 European Communities Act 1972.
- Question of express and implied repeal.
- *Macarthys* v *Smith*.
- *Factortame* cases – art 177 (now art 234).
- How the EC sees itself and conclusion.

Suggested Solution

The United Kingdom as an international legal personality joined the European Economic Community (as it then was) by the act of signing and ratifying the Treaty of Rome under the power vested in the Royal Prerogative. This was not as such a departure from previous practice dealing with treaties. The power so to do cannot be impugned or questioned in the courts (*Blackburn* v *Attorney-General* (1971)). The Royal Prerogative is not, however, capable of enacting new laws and, as the *Case of Proclamations* (1611) established, the Crown is unable to make new prerogative powers or laws imposing rights or obligations upon the Crown's subjects. Therefore, in order to give domestic effect to the Treaty of Rome it was necessary to incorporate the Treaty into United Kingdom municipal law. This was done by the enactment of the European Communities Act 1972. The terms of the statute are far-reaching. By s2(1) both primary – the Treaty – and secondary Community law is to be given legal effect in the United Kingdom.

This applies to Community law past, present and future. Moreover, under s3 of the statute the interpretation of Community treaties and legislation is regarded as a question of law to be interpreted either by the European Court of Justice at Luxembourg or, if it is decided by the courts of the United Kingdom, the matter is to be decided in accordance with European Court of Justice decisions. The wording of s2(4) presents the United Kingdom courts with the dilemma of how to interpret Community law and subsequent Acts of Parliament, stating that: 'any existing or future enactments are to be construed and have effect subject to the foregoing provisions of this section'.

This would appear to be constitutional nonsense. According to the traditional doctrine of parliamentary sovereignty one Parliament cannot bind future Parliaments. Sovereignty is continuing and one Parliament cannot see itself up as being superior to any future Parliament or Parliaments. A subsequent Act of Parliament may expressly or impliedly repeal any previous legislation. English case law contains a plethora of decisions substantiating the above proposition. In the case of *Ellen Street Estates Ltd* v *Minister of Health* (1934) Maugham LJ held, inter alia:

'If in a subsequent Act, Parliament chooses to make it plain that the earlier statute is being to some extent repealed, effect must be given to that intention just because it is the will of the legislature.'

Such is, or was, the theory. In the case of *Blackburn* v *Attorney-General* Lord Denning chose to cast doubt on the orthodox theory and its relation to reality. Speaking obiter he said:

'We have all been brought up to believe that in legal theory one Parliament cannot bind another and that no Act is irreversible. But legal theory does not always march alongside political reality.'

He then went on to discuss the unlikely instance of Parliament reversing an Act of independence to a former colony, arguing 'Freedom once given cannot be taken away. Legal theory must give way to practical politics.'

What then is the position with relation to European Union law and any conflicting Acts of Parliament? In the case of *Macarthys Ltd* v *Smith* (1979) Lord Denning again turned his attention to this problem. Speaking obiter he hypothesised:

'Thus far I have assumed that our Parliament whenever it passes legislation intends to fulfil its obligations under the Treaty. If the time should come when our Parliament *deliberately passes an Act* – with the intention of repudiating the Treaty or any provision in it – or intentionally acting inconsistently with it – and says so in express terms – then I should have thought that it would be the duty of our courts to follow the statute of our Parliament. I do not, however, envisage any such situation.'

Thus Lord Denning is acknowledging that if Parliament intends to repudiate Community law (as it then was), then the United Kingdom courts will give effect to it. However, one should be aware and pay attention to the phrase used: 'express terms'. It is submitted that this is less than express repeal and an implied repeal may be in express terms. In his judgment Lord Denning also provides for an escape clause from any possible conflict by talking about 'some oversight of our draftsmen' when a conflict with Community law is apparent. So what is 'express terms' or what is 'an oversight of our draftsmen' is conveniently left to the United Kingdom courts to interpret.

Another aspect of the potential conflict between the two jurisdictions, which the courts have had to tackle, arises when there is a *perceived* conflict between the United Kingdom law and EC law. This is discussed in the series of *Factortame* cases. The Common Market Fishing Policy devised a system to conserve fish by fixing quotas for national fishing fleets. The British government established a licensing system in 1985, which was expanded upon in the Merchant Shipping Act 1988 and which empowered the Secretary for Transport to make regulations and introduce a new register of British fishing vessels designed to prevent so-called 'quota hopping', whereby non-British Community nationals, Spanish fishermen, established companies in the United Kingdom in order to avail themselves of the British fishing quota. The question that arose before the United Kingdom courts was if a United Kingdom Act of Parliament supposedly infringed a party's Community rights – in this case as a result of discrimination based on the grounds of nationality – could that Act could be suspended pending a final outcome? The House of Lords (*R* v *Secretary of State for Transport, ex parte Factortame* (1989)) initially answered 'no' but referred the case to the European Court of Justice, under art 177 (now art 234), for a preliminary ruling. The United Kingdom courts will avail themselves of art 177 when, inter alia, a question of interpretation of Community law needs to be answered (*Bulmer Ltd* v *Bollinger* (1974); see also *Customs and Exercise Commissioners* v *APS Samex* (1983)).

The European Court of Justice in its preliminary ruling argued that the full effectiveness of Community law would be impaired if the United Kingdom argument that they could not suspend an Act of Parliament in such circumstances were to prevail. The European Court of Justice (*R* v *Secretary of State for Transport, ex parte Factortame* (1990)) argued that, pending a final outcome, interim relief should be granted and the House of Lords (*R* v *Secretary of State for Transport, ex parte Factortame (No 2)* (1991)) granted the said relief. A temporary injunction was issued against the Secretary of State preventing him from enforcing the offending provisions of the statute. Injunctive relief was therefore granted against the Crown and an Act of Parliament was suspended. In *Factortame (No 3)* (1991) the ruling of the European Court of Justice upheld the complaints of the Spanish fishermen. Therefore, for the first time in United Kingdom constitutional history an Act of Parliament was suspended upon the basis of a violation of alleged rights, never mind established rights, and injunctive relief was given against the Crown.

The legal revolution as a result of joining the European Community has also been commented upon in other areas of litigation. Hoffmann J (as he then was) put it succinctly:

'The EC Treaty is the supreme law of this country, taking precedent over Acts of Parliament. Our entry into the EC meant that Parliament surrendered its sovereign right to legislate contrary to the provisions of the Treaty on matters of social and economic policy which it regulated' (*Stoke-on-Trent City Council* v *B & Q plc* (1991)).

Whether or not the courts of the United Kingdom would disallow an Act of Parliament if it were to say 'notwithstanding EC law to the contrary' such and such is to apply is an open question. As it is the United Kingdom courts have clearly absorbed the philosophy of the European Court of Justice in *Costa* v *ENEL* (1964), when it argued in effect that a new legal order had been created. The United Kingdom courts will now not only suspend the workings of a statute but will also entertain an application for judicial review from, for example, the Equal Opportunities Commission (*R* v *Secretary of State for Employment, ex parte Equal Opportunities Commission* (1994)) for a declaration that United Kingdom law is incompatible with Community law. It is indeed true to say, as Lord Denning stated in *Bulmer* v *Bollinger*, that 'the Treaty [ie the Treaty of Rome] is like an incoming tide. It flows into the estuaries and up the rivers. It cannot be held back.'

4 The Electoral System

4.1 Introduction

The membership of the House of Commons is elected on the basis of adult suffrage. A general election must be held at least every five years: Parliament Act 1911.

4.2 Key points

a) *The franchise*

In order to vote in a parliamentary election a person must be included on the electoral register for a parliamentary constituency: Representation of the People Act 1983. To qualify for inclusion a person must:

i) be 18 years of age (or be due to attain his eighteenth birthday within twelve months of the publication of the register);

ii) be a British subject or a citizen of the Republic of Ireland;

iii) not be subject to any legal incapacity;

iv) be resident in the constituency on the qualifying date for compiling the register: *Fox* v *Stirk* [1970] 2 QB 463; *Hipperson* v *Electoral Registration Officer for Newbury* [1985] QB 1060.

b) *Disqualification*

The following persons are not entitled to vote, even if their names appear on the register.

i) Aliens (excluding citizens of the Republic of Ireland).

ii) Minors (persons under 18 years of age).

iii) Peers and peeresses in their own right (Irish peers may vote).

iv) Convicted persons serving sentences of imprisonment.

v) Persons convicted of corrupt practices at elections are disqualified from voting for five years. Persons convicted of illegal practices at elections are disqualified from voting for five years in the constituency in question.

vi) Those who for reasons such as mental illness, subnormality or other infirmity lack the capacity at the moment of voting of understanding what they are about to do.

c) *Parliamentary constituencies*

The United Kingdom is divided into constituencies each of which is represented by a member in the House of Commons.

i) Constituency boundaries are delimited by the Boundary Commissioners.

ii) The basic principle that each constituency should have the same number of electors is to ensure that all votes have equal value.

Quota = number of electors divided by number of constituencies

iii) Boundary Commissioners have discretion to depart from strict application of the rules if there are special geographical or other considerations that render departure desirable: House of Commons Redistribution of Seats Acts 1949–79; see, too, Schedule II.

iv) The re-drawing of the constituency map can result in challenges: *R* v *Boundary Commission for England, ex parte Foot* [1983] 1 All ER 1099; *Harper* v *Home Secretary* [1955] Ch 238; *R* v *Home Secretary, ex parte McWhirter* [1969] CLY 2636.

d) *Electoral campaign*

i) It is an offence to incur expenditure 'with a view to promoting or procuring the election of a candidate at an election' without authorisation of the candidate or his agent for public meetings and displays and advertisements or 'otherwise presenting to the electorate the candidate or his views or the extent or nature of his backing or disparaging another candidate': s75 Representation of the People Act 1983.

ii) There are limits placed on the amount a candidate can spend: s76 Representation of the People Act 1983; *R* v *Hailwood* [1928] 2 KB 277; *R* v *Tronoh Mines* [1952] 1 All ER 697; *Grieve* v *Douglas-Home* 1965 SC 315; *Director of Public Prosecutions* v *Luft* [1976] 2 All ER 569.

e) *Broadcasts*

i) Other broadcasts: *Marshall* v *BBC* [1979] 3 All ER 80. See s93 Representation of the People Act 1983.

ii) Broadcasting Act 1990: see s6 requiring impartiality in relation to 'major matters'.

f) *The election of Members of Parliament*

At present Members of Parliament are elected under the simple majority voting system. Each parliamentary constituency returns a single member. Each elector can vote for one candidate only and the candidate who polls the most votes within a given constituency wins the seat.

i) Disadvantages of the simple majority voting systems

- There are many wasted votes.
- It is a very crude system.
- There is no relationship between the number of votes cast nationally for a particular party and the number of seats allocated to that party in the House of Commons.
- The system produces exaggerated majorities for the two major parties and discriminates against the minority parties.

ii) Advantages of the simple majority voting system

- The voting procedure is simple and the results may be quickly calculated.
- There is a link between the member and his constituency.
- One party usually obtains an absolute majority of seats in the House of Commons thus leading to strong government.

g) *Electoral reform*

The three main alternatives to our present system are:

i) The Alternative Vote. Voters list the candidates in order of preference. If no candidate gains an absolute majority of first preference votes then the lowest candidate is eliminated and his second preference votes are distributed among the other candidates. The process may be repeated until a candidate emerges who has an absolute majority.

ii) The Party List System. One constituency comprising the whole country. The parties present lists of candidates and electors vote not for individual candidates but for the whole party list. Seats are then allocated to the parties in proportion to the votes received by each party list.

iii) The Single Transferable Vote. Requires multi-member constituencies of between five and seven members. Voters list the candidates in order of preference. The candidate needs a quota of votes to be elected. Any votes he receives beyond this figure are surplus and so they are redistributed among the other candidates according to second preference. The quota is usually established by the following formula:

$$\frac{\text{number of votes cast} + 1}{\text{number of seats} + 1}$$

4.3 Recent cases and developments

R v *British Broadcasting Corporation and Another, ex parte Referendum Party* (1997) The Times 29 April – allocation of party political broadcasts – policy of regarding the fielding of at least 50 candidates by a political party as a threshold requirement for the granting of one party political broadcast held not to be irrational.

Bowman v *United Kingdom* (1998) The Times 23 February European Court of Human Rights – UK electoral expenditure restrictions held to be a violation of art 10 of the ECHR – s75 of the Representation of the People Act 1983 regarded as effectively imposing a complete ban on the applicant disseminating her views effectively in the pre-election period, as the spending limit was so low and she had no access to other forms of broadcasting.

Reform of party funding proposed – the Committee on Standards in Public Life (Neill Committee), which reported in 1998, proposed that donations to the funds of political parties from one source of more than £5,000 or more in one year must be publicly disclosed. It further recommended the establishment of a Policy Development Fund 'to enable the political parties to engage more fully in policy development'. The report also recommended an increase in the funding available to opposition parties in the House of Commons. The Committee felt that the limits on expenditure by candidates should be reviewed with a view to their being increased. In terms of the overall election campaign, however, the Committee felt that there ought to be an upper limit on the campaign spending of political parties. The report also contained a number of proposals aimed at ensuring that referendums are conducted on a 'level playing field'. To this end it recommended that each 'side' should be given equal access to an amount of core funding sufficient to enable it to mount at least a minimal campaign and to make its views widely known.

The Registration of Political Parties Act 1998 has been enacted primarily to allow political parties to register their names and emblems so as to eliminate the use of potentially confusing party names by rival candidates at elections. Parties will have to be registered if they are to submit lists for the additional member aspect of elections to the Scottish Parliament, Welsh National Assembly, the Assembly for London and the elections to the European Parliament.

The report of the Jenkins Commission – the Labour government appointed Lord Jenkins of Hillhead to head the commission of inquiry into the voting system and it produced its report at the end of October 1998. It recommended that the current first-past-the-post system should be replaced by an enhanced alternative vote system.

4.4 Analysis of questions

Questions on this area seem to be set when the subject is topical ie just before or just after an election. Examiners favour essay type questions on the voting system in the UK – its advantages and disadvantages – a question that requires students to have some knowledge of alternative systems.

Students need to be aware of the role of the Boundary Commissioners and the problems that can arise when they report.

Problem questions could be set on the rules governing elections.

4.5 Questions

QUESTION ONE

a) What is the function of the Boundary Commission and what problems can occur when it reports?

b) Rupert is a newspaper proprietor. He stood as candidate for the Freedom Party at a general election. His newspapers carried advertisements extolling the virtues of the Freedom Party and urging people to vote for it. Rupert was elected.

   Blake, a constituent, seeks to challenge Rupert's election as MP on the grounds that he incurred unauthorised expenditure.

   Discuss.

Written by the Editors

General Comment

An easy question if students know the cases and statutes below.

Skeleton Solution

a) • The function of the Boundary Commission – House of Commons Redistribution of Seats Acts 1949–79.
   • An explanation of the effect on political parties when constituencies are redefined.
   • *R* v *Boundary Commission for England, ex parte Foot* (1983).

b) • The provisions of s75 Representation of the People Act 1983.
   • An analysis of cases on unauthorised expenditure: *R* v *Tronoh Mines* (1952); *Grieve* v *Douglas-Home* (1965); *Director of Public Prosecutions* v *Luft* (1976).

Suggested Solution

a) The function of the Boundary Commission as laid down by the House of Commons Redistribution of Seats Acts 1949–1979 is to regulate the size of parliamentary constituencies in the United Kingdom. The purpose is to achieve, as far as is practicable, constituencies which are approximately equal in terms of voters. A figure is arrived at by dividing the number of voters by the number of constituencies which produces a current figure of approximately 65,000.

   The commissioners do have, however, discretionary powers to vary the size of constituencies taking into account county boundaries and special geographical considerations including the size, shape and accessibility of a constituency. In the exercise of their discretion the commissioners should observe a balance between the countries of the UK, ie Great Britain should not have substantially more or less seats than 613, Scotland should not have less than 71, Wales 35 and Northern Ireland between 16 and 18.

   Under their powers the commissioners present their recommendations to the Home Secretary whose duty it is to lay these before Parliament for approval. The objective is to remove the decision from the political process because changes are perceived by one party or another as disadvantaging them and political agreement is therefore unlikely. The only circumstances in which a review of their decision is likely is if 100 or more affected voters petition or if a county council petitions. The only other way is to challenge through judicial review the exercise of the commissioners' discretion.

   The Labour Party has traditionally been disadvantaged by changes largely because of migration from urban areas, traditionally labour strongholds, to the country. In the late 1960s the Labour Party sought to delay the implementation of proposals: see *R* v *Home Secretary, ex parte McWhirter* (1969). More recently Michael Foot, then leader of the Labour Party, sought to challenge the proposals on the grounds that the commissioners had exercised their powers wrongly and that the decision was ultra vires: *R* v *Boundary Commission for England, ex parte Foot* (1983). The court held that the discretion of the commissioners was very wide and that they had not acted unreasonably. The challenge failed.

b) Section 75 of the Representation of the People Act 1983 makes it an offence to incur expenditure with a view to promoting or procuring the election of a candidate at an election without the authority of the candidate or his agent and s76 goes on to place limits on the candidate's expenditure. The amount is varied from time to time by means of statutory instrument. The objective here is to ensure that one candidate does not gain advantage by virtue of the fact that he may have substantial personal wealth to wage a campaign and can be contrasted with other countries notably America where there are no limits.

   There are however no limits in this country on the amount that a national party can spend on a campaign. It can be argued that this is a disadvantage to some political parties, more particularly the smaller parties whose ability to wage a national campaign is limited by a lack of money. It is a tradition in this country that political parties grow out of grass roots support. The issue in the question therefore would seem to be simply whether the newspaper advertisement can be seen as essentially part of a national campaign or whether the intention and effect is to ensure the election of the local candidate Rupert.

In support of the principle that expenditure incurred cannot exceed the permitted maximum it has been held that a local campaign urging the electorate not to vote for a particular candidate falls foul of s75 because by implication it is of advantage to the other: see *Director of Public Prosecutions* v *Luft* (1976). However, on the question of national newspaper campaigns it has been held that an advertisement advocating the defeat of a Labour government was not an election expense within the meaning of s75: see *R* v *Tronoh Mines* (1952). Furthermore, in *Grieve* v *Douglas-Home* (1965), an unsuccessful Communist candidate who argued that Douglas Home the then Prime Minister gained an unfair advantage in respect of his local campaign when he appeared on national television did not convince the courts. Such a broadcast was not held to be expenditure with a view to procuring his election.

By analogy then it would seem unlikely that Blake would be successful in his challenge unless the advertisement referred to in the problem specifically relates to Rupert's own campaign. Whilst he may gain some advantage from such an advertisement, on the facts the advertisement is aimed at furthering the interests of the party nationally.

QUESTION TWO

What difference, if any, would reforming the electoral system make to the British constitution?

Written by the Editors

General Comment

This is a very straightforward question involving discussion of the present electoral system and the effect reform would have on the British constitution.

Skeleton Solution

- Introduction. The operation of the relative majority system (the first-past-the-post system).
- The problems with the present system. Parliamentary seats not allocated on a proportional basis; discrimination against small parties; wastage of votes; problems with constituency size.
- The advantages of the present system. Simplicity; results in strong government; constituency link with MP.
- Effect of reform. Loss of the advantages of the present system; election of a Parliament but not a government.

Suggested Solution

Under the present parliamentary electoral system the United Kingdom is divided into 659 parliamentary constituencies, each of which returns a single member to the House of Commons. Each elector may vote for one candidate only and the successful candidate is the one who receives the highest number of valid votes in the constituency. This system of 'first past the post' is known as the relative majority system as wherever there are more than two candidates in a constituency, the successful candidate need not have received an absolute majority of votes, but simply a majority over the runner-up. This system has the advantage of being very simple, but as a means of providing representation of the electorate in Parliament it is very crude. It is a system which, according to its critics, is not truly democratic and one which has several inherent disadvantages which, it is argued, can only be overcome by reform.

Certainly any reform of the present electoral system will seek to remedy the major problem that at present the system does not ensure that the distribution of seats in the House of Commons is in any way proportionate to the national distribution of votes. There is no consistent relationship between the number of votes cast nationally for a political party and the seats which they obtain. This is illustrated by the May 1997 general election result. The Labour Party polled 45 per cent of the votes cast and won 419 seats. The Conservative Party polled 31 per cent of the votes cast and won 165 seats. The Liberal Democrats polled 17 per cent of the votes cast and won only 46 seats. The Liberal Democrats were therefore was under-represented in relation to their national vote. By dividing the number of votes cast for each party by the number of seats won it can be seen that, in the 1997 general election, it took: 58,124 votes to elect each Conservative MP; 32,342 votes to elect each Labour MP; 113,985 votes to elect each Liberal Democrat MP; 108,049 votes to elect each 'minor party' MP.

The result of the 1997 general election is commonly referred to as a landslide victory for the Labour Party, but the statistics reveal that it polled only 1.9 million votes more than it had in 1992. The problem for the Conservative Party appeared to be defections to the Liberal Democrats and abstentions by those who would normally have supported the party. The curious variable geometry of the electoral system ensures that any party thus squeezed suffers disproportionately.

This tendency of the system to exaggerate the representation of the large parties and reduce that of the smaller parties leads to the allegation that the present electoral system makes no provision for the representation of minority interests. It discriminates against the smaller parties whose support is evenly spread throughout the country rather than being concentrated in particular constituencies. Votes for the smaller parties are, in effect, wasted votes. It doesn't matter whether the person elected has one more or twenty thousand more votes than his nearest rival. So where there are more than two candidates a person may be elected by less than 50 per cent of the total votes cast in that constituency. The votes for the losing candidate have no parliamentary importance, they are in a sense wasted. This system, it is argued, perpetuates the two party system and helps destroy any possibility of consensus politics in the United Kingdom.

A further problem arises from the constituency basis of the present system. If votes are to carry equal weight throughout the country each constituency must be of equal size. The size of every constituency is determined by the Boundary Commissioners who keep the situation under constant review and try to ensure that each constituency has the same number of voters in it. However, disparity does exist between constituency populations and, as a result, the weight of your vote may vary according to where you live.

Reforming the electoral system would therefore help remove these problems and help achieve fairer representation for all political parties in the House of Commons. But it must always be remembered that the present electoral system has considerable advantages and that these advantages may be lost as a result of any reform. For example the voting procedure itself is very simple and easy to understand, ensuring quick results. The outcome of the election is known within a matter of hours of the close of poll. The system also ensures a close link between the Member of Parliament and his constituency. The constituents know who their parliamentary representative is and can approach him with their problems. He in turn will serve their interests, in the knowledge that their continued support is necessary if he is to be re-elected.

But the major advantage claimed for the present system is its tendency to produce an absolute majority of seats in the House of Commons for one party. The function of a general election is to elect a government as well as a parliament and the present system does precisely that, producing strong government. The United Kingdom system avoids the problems, often found in European countries, which use different electoral systems, of coalition or minority governments which can find it difficult to govern effectively because of their unstable electoral position.

Despite these advantages there is a case for reforming the electoral system so as to secure better representation of minority parties and a distribution of seats which bears some relation to the votes cast. The most favoured alternative systems are the alternative vote system, the party list system and the single transferable vote system. The adoption of any one of these systems would bring about changes to the British constitution which, while welcomed by some, would be abhorrent to others.

The Jenkins Commission's key proposal is that the current first-past-the-post system should be replaced by an enhanced alternative vote system. Approximately 80 per cent of MPs would be elected on a constituency basis – the number of constituencies being reduced to around 525. The remaining MPs would be drawn from party lists and would represent other geographical areas such as cities and counties. Electors would cast two votes in order to elect a constituency MP, numbering the candidates in their order of preference. If a candidate secured a 50 per cent share of the votes on the first count he or she would be elected as the MP for that constituency. If no candidate secured 50 per cent of the votes on the first count, the candidate with the lowest number of first preference votes would be eliminated and his or her second preference votes redistributed amongst the remaining candidates. The process of eliminating lowest scoring candidates would continue until a candidate achieved 50 per cent of the first preference and redistributed second preference votes. Voters would also cast a party list, or 'top-up' vote for MPs who would represent cities or counties. The proposal is that this vote could simply be for a party, or for a specific candidate appearing on the party list. If the two most recent general elections had been conducted using the enhanced alternative vote system proposed by the Jenkins Commission the allocation of seats would have been as follows:

1997: Conservatives – 167 seats; Labour – 367 seats; Lib Dem – 92 seats; Nationalists – 14 seats.

1992: Conservative – 316 seats; Labour – 240 seats; Lib Dem – 74 seats; Nationalists – 11 seats.

The major result of adopting these systems is that they will help achieve legislative representation which accords with the relative electoral strengths of the political parties. Minority parties and independent candidates will therefore stand a better chance of election and the number of wasted votes will be reduced. But while these systems may to an extent maintain a local basis for representation, they may weaken the link between Members of Parliament and constituents. These systems of election are also complex. Most important, however, is the likely result that the traditional two party system may be destroyed. To some of course this may be no bad thing but, if the European experience is repeated and one party is less likely to secure an absolute majority of seats in the House of Commons, this will lead to minority or coalition governments giving smaller parties political importance out of all proportion to their popular support. Such a system of government is totally alien to the British tradition.

QUESTION THREE

'In a really equal democracy, every or any section would be represented, not disproportionately, but proportionately.' (J S Mill)

Discuss this statement with respect to the British system of general elections.

University of London LLB Examination
(for External Students) Constitutional Law June 1995 Q3

General Comment

This is a beguilingly straightforward question about differing forms of electoral systems. The statement is brief and therefore gives a lot of scope to the candidate to use all the knowledge that can be amassed. The statement itself focuses on 'sections' of society rather than the individual voter. This aspect should be discussed to focus on the right aim for an electoral system, before considering the variety of possible electoral systems.

Skeleton Solution

- Discuss the detail of the statement in the question.
- Discuss the pros and cons of the first-past-the-post system.
- Discuss the pros and cons of the party-list system.
- Discuss the pros and cons of the single transferable vote.
- Discuss the pros and cons of the alternative member system.
- Conclusion.

Suggested Solution

The question of the desirability of equality in systems of democracy is one that is easy to answer in rhetorical terms, but difficult to deal with in systemic terms. In general, it is possible to say that an ideal system of elections would aim to provide each citizen of majority age with one vote which would be of equal value to the vote of every other citizen. However, Mill's formulation of this proposition looks at society not in terms of individual citizens but rather in terms of 'sections'.

The difficulty with this formulation is that it requires it to be possible for every section to be identified in a two-dimensional format. To identify the opinions of the electorate as sectional interests casting their votes in the same manner is to ignore the broad range of issues which are active in the minds of the voters, and which may cause people of ostensibly similar backgrounds and with seemingly similar views to vote or act in very different ways. One may choose not to vote, whereas the other might decide that one should vote for the least worst option. Both are valid choices, but it is difficult to identify exactly which 'section' best represents each voter. Therefore, the individual citizen model, it is suggested, offers the better model for assessing whether or not a given democratic system is 'equal' or not.

Mill's conception of the issue is more useful when looking at the issue of proportional representation. While it is still focused on the notion of 'sections', it does identify the need to create a Parliament which does, to some extent, reflect the political composition and views of society. The result of an election is the creation of a Parliament which enacts the political programme of the majority party or a coalition of parties.

The first-past-the-post system fails to admit the views of the minority interests in society. Where there is insufficient support for a particular interest or shade of opinion in a given geographic region, there will not be enough support to elect a Member of Parliament in any constituency. Therefore, special interest groups are unrepresented. The growing cynicism of the population with the political system can potentially be traced to the failure of the current electoral system to reflect adequately the opinions of the population in more than a two-party, two-dimensional format. The weight of a vote for Party A will be weaker in a constituency where Party A either stands no prospect of victory or where Party A is sure to win. A vote for Party A will be more important in a constituency where Party A might win or lose by a very few votes.

The advantages of this system appear in ways other than straightforward 'equality' or parity of votes. The constituency system does provide representation for a particular region through a given individual politician. Therefore, there is a mechanism for ensuring responsiveness from the political system to the local needs of a particular constituency. The conduct of representational and democratic politics can therefore be made more accountable to specific units of the population. Voting patterns mirror more closely the views of general geographic areas measured in trends large enough to affect those overall local majorities. The simple majority system also aids ease of comprehension, which makes it easier for politicians to analyse the views of the population and also, more importantly, for the population to understand the outcomes of elections.

The proportional representation models are many and varied. The simplest system is that used in Israel where people vote on a party-list, non-constituency basis. The proportion of the total national vote obtained by each party is then attributed to that party. The percentage of the total that represents is then allotted to each party as a corresponding percentage of seats in the parliamentary assembly. The advantage of this system is that every vote has exactly the same weight. Similarly, each section in society is represented precisely. The disadvantages with this system are, firstly, that there is no link between local people and any individual politician: therefore local democratic ties are very weak. Secondly, the system places enormous powers in the hands of the parties to select who the politicians are.

The single transferable vote method is a more complicated system of proportional representation. This system retains the use of large constituencies from which a number of candidates are elected at the same time. Voters mark their ballot papers with their candidates placed in order of preference. A threshold level of votes is calculated above which a candidate is elected. This threshold is itself calculated by reference to the mean number of votes required for the prescribed number of candidates to be selected out of the votes cast. This enables a broader range of preferences to be tested because, once a candidate crosses the threshold, the remaining votes for that candidate as first choice are reallocated to the second choice on the ballot paper. The drawbacks are the complication of the system and the loose ties which are established on a local democratic basis. There is also an element of mathematical chance involved with the reallocation of votes.

The alternative member system is practised in a variety of countries, and it enables the voter to vote for a constituency MP and then to have that vote counted a second time as a vote for a party-list candidate selected by the party. Therefore, there are two cadres of MP, one who represents the constituency and another who is selected by the political party. There is a drawback to having two streams of politicians in that it raises questions as to which of the two has a better mandate from the electorate. The electoral process is also slightly complicated by the use of this system.

It is clear that there are a number of means of carrying out elections. However, it is difficult to measure which is the best electoral system to use. Mill's conception points towards a simple party list system which may, in fact, diminish the service and representation which many constituents are able to obtain from the first-past-the-post system.

It is interesting in this regard to note that the Jenkins Commission, which published its report on alternatives to the first-past-the-post system in October 1998, proposed is that it should be replaced by an enhanced alternative vote system. The proposal would seek to equalise the value of votes. Pending the introduction of such major changes moves have been made that would go some way towards satisfying Mill's views in so much as the party list system is to be used for the first time to elect MEPs in Great Britain from June 1999, and will also be used to select some candidates for the Scottish Parliament and Welsh Assembly.

QUESTION FOUR

'In practice, the legal rules providing for the delineation of electoral constituencies and the rules regulating the conduct of election campaigns reveal many defects.'

Critically assess this statement.

University of London LLB Examination
(for External Students) Constitutional and Administrative Law June 1992 Q7

General Comment

This is a difficult question. It requires a detailed knowledge of a fairly restricted subject and many students would find it hard to provide sufficient information.

Skeleton Solution

- Introduction.
- The Parliamentary Constituencies Act 1986.
- Inconsistencies in size of constituency.
- Political objections.
- Finance in elections.
- Broadcasting.
- Conclusion.

Suggested Solution

There are very precise rules both for the delineation of constituencies and for the conduct of campaigns. However, no rules can cover all of the variables and the political impossibility of drawing lines in a way that pleases all parties or of regulating conduct during a contest to general approbation make it possible to find defects. However, what may seem a defect from one partisan view is seen as a strength from another.

Dealing firstly with the rules for the delineation of electoral constituencies: the Parliamentary Constituencies Act 1986 retains four permanent Boundary Commissions – for England, Wales, Scotland and Northern Ireland. Their purpose is continuously to review the distribution of seats and recommend, in a report to the Home Secretary at intervals of between ten and 15 years, such redistribution as they consider necessary.

The Home Secretary cannot ignore or reject these recommendations but he can, when he lays them before Parliament, add modifications. If they are approved by resolutions of each House the recommendations take effect as Orders in Council and operate from the next election.

What, if any, defects are there in the system? Firstly, the Act determines the minimum number of seats per Commission area. The electorate of a constituency is to be as near as practicable to the quota, which is found by dividing the total electorate of the area by the number of constituencies. Scotland and Wales have fewer electors per constituency than England and there is a wide variation nationally in size of constituency, both numerically and geographically. This is inevitable but it means that your vote can carry more weight depending upon where you live.

Secondly, each set of recommendations always proves controversial and might not be implemented. For example, the 1969 recommendations proposed major changes to 271 constituencies. The Labour Party feared losing some ten seats as a result, so the Labour government decided to implement then only in part but could not get the Bill past the Lords. The Orders in Council containing the complete recommendations were not passed until after the next election, by a Conservative Government.

In 1983, the Labour Party again objected to the effects of recommendations and took the case to the Court of Appeal (*R* v *Boundary Commission for England, ex parte Foot* (1983)), which held that the Commission had acted reasonably. This ability to challenge the Commission through the courts is clearly a safeguard and a strength in the system.

Turning to the rules for regulating the conduct of election campaigns, these are contained in the Representation of the People Act 1983 (and to a lesser extent subsequent Representation of the People Acts).

Firstly, election expenditure is strictly controlled at a constituency level, but the national expenditure of the parties is not, which might seem anomalous in terms of advertising in the national press. The Conservative Party in recent elections has had greater resources for this, therefore the attempt to avoid unfair advantage to the wealthier party at local level may be seen to have been avoided at national level.

Secondly, broadcasting at election times is also controlled and the major parties are allowed to make party political broadcasts on television. This does not favour small, minority parties. Thirdly, there is no limit on opinion polls, although after the 1987 election the Speaker's Conference on electoral law recommended they should be banned for the 72 hours before an election. The inefficiency of opinion polls in the 1992 election and their influence on news programmes with the consequent influence on voters would strengthen this recommendation.

However, if these are defects, there are many positive features of the rules on election campaigns. There are clear rules in the event of dispute, with an Election Court investigating any misconduct. Corrupt practices are vigorously opposed and it is significant how few complaints are made.

Overall, one might conclude that no single system will provide better solutions. On the one hand, there is a shifting population, unevenly distributed and locally diverse. On the other hand, there is a short period of intense campaigning involving massive expenditure, saturation coverage and mass participation. It is submitted that the system, in general terms, is a successful one.

QUESTION FIVE

Consider the view that 'our method of election to the House of Commons is in the highest degree unjust, unsatisfactory and dangerous'.

University of London LLB Examination
(for External Students) Constitutional Law June 1996 Q3

General Comment

This question invites a discussion of the workings of the present electoral system. Candidates should discuss not only the present electoral system but also its consequences in the representation of the parties in Parliament. The advantages and disadvantages of the system should be set out and the student must be willing to agree or disagree with the polemical statement. A brief summary of some of the alternative electoral systems needs to be included to complete the essay.

Skeleton Solution

- Introduction – the franchise in the UK.
- Constituency basis of the MP.
- First past the post.
- The reflection of first past the post in the Commons.
- Advantages of the present system.
- Disadvantages of the present system.
- Alternative electoral systems.
- Conclusion.

Suggested Solution

The membership of the House of Commons is elected on the basis of universal adult suffrage. In order to vote in a parliamentary election the individual must be listed in the electoral register for a parliamentary constituency. To be placed on the register the individual must be a British subject, a Commonwealth citizen or a citizen of the Irish Republic (such citizens are not classified as aliens for electoral purposes), be eighteen years of age or be due to attain his/her eighteenth birthday within twelve months of the publication of the register, not suffer any legal incapacity and be resident in the constituency on the qualifying date for compiling the register.

The above is without controversy and has raised little or no political discussion. It is the electoral system, rather than issue of who is eligible to vote, which is the cause of political disquiet. Following the 1997 general election the Labour government evidenced its qualified enthusiasm for electoral reform by setting up a Commission under Lord Jenkins of Hillhead to investigate possible reforms to the current system.

How then is the electoral system to the House of Commons based? The United Kingdom is divided into 659 parliamentary constituencies, each of which is represented by one member in the House of Commons. The constituency boundaries are determined by the Boundary Commission, which works on the theory that each constituency should have the same number of votes within it to ensure that all votes in the country are of equal value. This is summed up by the maxim: 'one man, one vote, one value'. The Boundary Commission reviews the electoral population of the parliamentary constituencies and may recommend that extra constituencies be formed in an area under-represented owing to an increase in population, or an abolition of constituencies owing to a decrease in population. These changes largely reflect the change in the balance of the population away from urban areas and into the shires. The Boundary Commission is not, however, obliged to reflect the voting population exclusively, as its terms of reference (Parliamentary Constituencies Act 1986) include the proviso that the number of constituencies in Scotland shall not be less than 71, a directive which results in the relative over-representation of Scotland at Westminster.

This division of the UK by the Boundary Commission is normally accepted by the political parties but its findings are still capable of judicial review, as the Court of Appeal accepted in their judgment in *R* v *Boundary Commission for England, ex parte Foot* (1983).

Of much more controversy though is the electoral system. The UK system is categorised as first past the post. Each elector is eligible to vote for one candidate only and the candidate who obtains the most votes within a constituency wins. It is possible, therefore, for a candidate to win even though the majority of the electorate in a constituency vote against him. If, for instance, J Bloggs obtains 10,000 votes, J Smith obtains 7,000 votes and J Jones obtains 6,000 votes, J Bloggs wins despite the fact the majority of the electorate voted against him. All the votes given to J Bloggs over 7,001 are 'wasted'. The number of wasted votes may be significant in a safe Labour seat, for example in South Wales, or in a safe Conservative seat, for instance in Surrey. There is no way in the existing system that the votes, or more accurately the surplus votes, may be distributed elsewhere in the country.

This system is reflected in the final outcome of the votes as there is little relationship between the number of votes cast nationally for a party and the number of seats that party may obtain in the House of Commons. Thus, in 1992 general election the Conservatives obtained 41.9 per cent of the votes but achieved 51.6 per cent of the seats. Minority parties do particularly badly in this system, as illustrated by the Liberal Democrats who obtained 17.8 per cent of the votes in 1992 but only 3.1 per cent of the seats. As with racing, or even more so, there is little merit in coming second. Parties that come second in a significant number of constituencies, as with the Social Democratic Party in 1983 may as well have come third or fourth. The only minority parties likely to survive in such a system are those with a strong regional base, such as the Scottish Nationalists, or to some extent the Liberals in the 'Celtic fringe'. They are able to target particular constituencies rather than have their votes spread out throughout the country.

It should be pointed out, however, that the first-past-the-post system has a number of advantages. It is simple and the electorate has a clear understanding of how it works. The results are easily arrived at and it avoids delays in establishing the winner on both a national and local level. It also establishes a link between the MP and his/her constituency; the other systems (see below) often fail to achieve this. The link between an MP and his/her constituency enables other institutions such as the Parliamentary Commissioner for Administration (PCA) to function effectively as the MP puts forward the complaints and grievances of the constituent. An MP may also pursue a particular matter that is of concern to his or her constituents. For example, MPs who have a large proportion of immigrants amongst their constituents are more likely to be involved in immigration issues. In taking up an issue raised by a constituent the MP is obliged to help the constituent to his or her best ability no matter whether the constituent is likely to vote for the MP or not.

A further advantage of the present system is that it usually creates an absolute (overall) majority of seats in the House of Commons. At the end of the day the electorate can understand the result of the election, while in other electoral systems (see below) this is not necessarily the case. The majority of British elections do not result in inter- and intra-party manoeuvres as a government is trying to be formed. A proportional representation system, with its possible result of a 'hung' Parliament, would also have the effect of politicising the role of the monarch as she would have to exercise her discretion as to which candidate would be the most suitable Prime Minister.

While it may be seen as unjust in the manner in which it penalises minority parties, the present electoral system does have the beneficial effect of preventing extremist minority parties obtaining a presence in the House of Commons. In the 1930s the British Fascist Party led by Oswald Mosley failed to obtain a seat in the House of Commons because its followers were spread throughout the country and the party failed to gain enough following to achieve a majority in a single constituency. Indeed, countries with a system of proportional representation, such as Germany, have a threshold requirement of about 5 per cent before a party can enter Parliament, the purpose being to prevent extremist minority parties gaining a platform.

What then are the alternatives to the British electoral system? The main options are these systems:

a) alternative vote;

b) party list; and

c) single transferable vote.

The alternative vote system operates by the voter listing the candidates in their constituency in order of preference. If no candidate gains an absolute majority of the first preference then the lowest candidate is eliminated and his/her second preference votes are distributed amongst the other candidates. This process can be repeated until one candidate emerges with an absolute majority. The principal inadequacy of the system is that the overall result does not reflect the actual proportions of the votes. The voter has the potential to be confused with the procedure and the winner might not have a clear mandate from the voters. Significantly the Jenkins Commission, which published its report on alternatives to the first-past-the-post system in October 1998, proposed that the current system should be replaced by an enhanced alternative vote system.

The party list system is perhaps the method which best reflects the real proportion of the votes. The country is classified as one constituency and the parties present lists of candidates and the electors vote for the whole party list. Seats in Parliament are allocated to the parties in proportion to the votes received by each party list. Such a system strengthens the party bureaucracy as potential candidates compete to be placed as near the top of the list as possible. The link between the MP and the constituency is destroyed and minority parties will be given greater potential power as they offer their conditional support to any putative government. This effect is increased as an outright winner in such a system is unusual. The party list system will be used for the first time in Great Britain in May 1999 to elect a proportion of members of the Scottish Parliament and the Welsh Assembly and in June 1999 to elect MEPs representing constituencies in Great Britain.

The single transferable vote (STV) is the system that is looked upon with most approval by the advocates of electoral reform. This system would see a diminution in the number of constituencies in Parliament, as it requires multi-member constituencies with between five and seven members. Voters list the candidates in order of preference. The candidate needs a quota of votes to be elected. The 'surplus' votes of the winning candidate are then redistributed among the other candidates in accordance with the voter's second preference. While this system would weaken the link between the MP and his constituents it is not unknown in the UK. In the nineteenth century multi-member constituencies (usually two MPs) were present in the UK Parliament.

The call for reform of the electoral system in the UK is heard especially from those parties such as the Liberal Democrats who are penalised by being minority parties. There is no manner in which their votes may be distributed. Unfortunately, the debate is often centred on the economic and social success of a particular country. The advocates of electoral reform point to the German voting system while the detractors point to Israel or Ireland. The message elsewhere is unclear; while New Zealand has introduced a system of proportional representation, Italy has moved away from it. One might conclude that our method of election is unjust and unsatisfactory, but so are all the others.

5 Legislature I – The House of Commons

5.1 Introduction

The Monarch is one of the three constituent parts of the legislature but the role of the monarchy is now largely ceremonial and formal. The United Kingdom has a bicameral legislature – there are two Houses of Parliament – the House of Commons and the House of Lords. The House of Commons dominates.

One of the central issues relating to the legislature is the accountability of government to Parliament. The House of Commons is dominated by the government particularly if following a general election the government has a large majority. The House of Lords challenges the government at a political level on unpopular policies. However, ultimately the Commons can successfully achieve its political will in the unlikely event of a confrontation.

Textbook analysis of the topic describes the rules and procedures of the House of Commons. Students must be able to place this knowledge in the context of executive power and understand the nature of the relationship between government and the Commons – see Chapter 8.

5.2 Key points

The main functions of Parliament include the passing of legislation and the scrutiny of the administration through debate, the committee system and the control of national finance.

a) *The legislative process*

i) A distinction must be drawn between Public and Private Bills:

- Public Bills seek to alter the general law and affect the whole community.
- Private Bills affect only a section of the community and relate to matters of individual, corporate or local interest.
- Hybrid Bills are Public Bills that are classified by the Speaker as having a particular effect on one section of the community.

ii) Public Bill procedure

Most Public Bills are government Bills, but some may be Private Members Bills introduced by backbench Members of Parliament. Bills may be introduced into either House, but legislation which is politically controversial, financial or electoral begins in the House of Commons.

- First reading: The Bill is presented to Parliament.
- Second reading: The House considers the principles and merits of the Bill.
- Committee stage: The Bill is normally referred to a standing committee for detailed clause by clause consideration.
- Report stage: The Bill as amended is reported to the whole House.
- Third reading: The Bill is debated in general terms with only oral amendments allowed.
- House of Lords stages and amendments: After its third reading, the Bill is sent to the House of Lords where it goes through stages similar to those in the Commons. But note the effects of the Parliament Acts 1911–1949.
- Royal Assent: Now a formality. After the Royal Assent has been given the Bill becomes an Act.

iii) Private member's Bill procedure

There are a number of procedures under which private members may initiate Bills.

- The Ballot: The Ballot establishes an order of priority enabling those members successful in it to use the limited private members' time for debate of their Bills which, given the governments' control of the parliamentary timetable, might otherwise not make progress.
- The Ten Minute Rule: Not, in general, serious attempts at legislation. The member may speak briefly in support of the Bill and an opponent may reply. The House may then decide on whether the Bill should be introduced.
- Standing Order No 39: Allows every member the right to introduce a Bill of his choosing after due notice.

iv) Private Bill procedure

Private Bills are initiated by petition from persons or bodies outside Parliament. Full notice must be given to those whose legal rights may be affected by the proposed legislation so that they may oppose it. In the House of Commons the Bill is introduced by being presented at the Table by the Clerk of the Private Bill Office. It is then deemed to have been read for the first time. At the Second Reading Debate, the House determines whether the Bill is unobjectionable from the point of view of national policy. If read a second time, the Bill is committed to a committee of four members in the Commons (or five members in the Lords). The committee stage has some of the features of a quasi-judicial proceeding.

v) Hybrid Bill procedure

The Standing Orders for private business apply to a hybrid Bill so that if opposed after its second reading it goes before a select committee, where those whose legal rights are affected by the Bill may raise their objections and petition against it. After the petitioners have been heard by the select committee, the Bill then passes through its committee stage and later stages as if it were an ordinary Bill.

b) *Opportunities for debate in the House of Commons*

Apart from the opportunities for debate during the legislative process, there are various other opportunities for debate in the House of Commons.

i) Adjournment debates

At the end of every day's business, when the adjournment of the House is formally moved, half an hour is made available for a private Member to raise a topic in debate and for a ministerial reply to be given.

ii) Standing Order No 10 – Motion to Adjourn

This allows members to suggest that a specific and important matter should have urgent consideration and that an emergency debate be held upon it.

iii) Other opportunities

The final day before each of the four parliamentary recesses is also devoted to a series of private members' debates and ten Fridays per session are also set aside for private members' Motions. Other opportunities for debate occur in the debate on the address in reply to the Queen's Speech, the debate on the Budget, debates on motions of censure, the twenty Opposition Days, the three Estimate Days and on the second reading of Consolidated Fund Bills.

iv) Devices for curtailing debate

Delay of Bills in the House of Commons is a threat to the government's legislative programme. To overcome this threat, various methods of curtailing debate have been adopted by the House.

- Standing Order 22: The Speaker or Chairman may require a member to discontinue his speech if he persists in irrelevance or tedious repetition.
- The Closure: Any member may move 'that the question now be put'. If not less than 100 members vote for the motion the debate ceases and the motion under discussion must be voted upon.
- The Kangaroo: This is the power of the Speaker at the Report Stage to select from amongst the various proposed amendments those which are to be discussed.
- The Guillotine Motion: Such a motion provides that one or more stages of a Bill be disposed of either by a fixed date, or by a fixed number of sittings.

c) *Parliamentary questions*

There are three categories of question:

i) Question for oral answer which is intended to be given an oral answer in the House during Question Time.

ii) Private notice question which can be asked if the Speaker judges its subject matter to be urgent and important. These are taken orally in the House at the end of Question Time.

iii) Question for written answer, which is not taken orally in the House but is printed in the official report (Hansard).

d) *Parliamentary committees*

The committees of the House of Commons fall into two main categories:

i) Standing committees

These are responsible for the committee stage in the passing of a Bill.

ii) Select committees

- Ad-hoc select committees: These are set up for a specific purpose when the need arises.
- Sessional select committees: These are set up at the beginning of the session and remain throughout the session.
- Departmental select committees: These are appointed to examine the expenditure, administration and policy of the principal government departments and associated public bodies.

e) *Parliamentary control of national finance*

Parliamentary control of national finance has two aspects:

i) Parliamentary control of government expenditure

- Estimate Days: There are now three annual days devoted to consideration of the main and Supplementary Estimates.
- The Public Accounts Committee: This is a select committee concerned with public money already spent, to see that it has been spent economically, and not wastefully.
- National Audit Act 1983: This Act provides for the appointment of the Comptroller and Auditor General, establishing a Public Accounts Commission and a National Audit Office and making new provisions for promoting economy, efficiency and effectiveness in the use of public money by government departments and other authorities and bodies.

ii) Control over taxation

Budget Resolutions and the Finance Bill: These provide an opportunity for Members to debate government proposals for taxation and duties etc.

5.3 Recent cases and developments

R v *Parliamentary Commissioner for Standards, ex parte Al Fayed* [1998] 1 All ER 93 – remarks made in debate, discussions in committee, parliamentary questions and answers, and votes are clearly within the concept of proceedings in Parliament.

The process by which Public Bills make the transition from statements of government policy to Acts of Parliament was considered by the House of Commons Modernisation Committee in its report published in July 1997. The Committee highlighted several areas where it felt that changes could and should be made: pre-legislative consultation; scrutiny by First Reading committees; making the standing committees more effective; and improving the Report stage.

In July 1997 Sir Patrick Downey was appointed as the first Parliamentary Commissioner for Standards, responsible for maintaining the Register of Members Interests, advising MPs on a confidential basis regarding possible conflicts of interest, and investigating complaints from MPs and members of the public regarding the Register of MPs' Interests and the propriety of MPs' conduct. The operation of this new regime is scrutinised by the Select Committee on Standards and Privileges (replacing the Privileges and Members' Interests Committee).

One of first changes introduced by Prime Minister Blair on taking office in May 1997 was to introduce the longer weekly Wednesday session of Prime Minister's questions, in place of the twice-weekly sessions. His aim is to provide a more informative and less adversarial exchange with MPs.

5.4 Analysis of questions

Questions are essay type. They tend to examine the student's understanding of the relationship between government and the legislature and so require a broadly based knowledge which includes the separation of powers, conventions of the constitution and Cabinet government.

5.5 Questions

QUESTION ONE

The parliamentary function of legislation has effectively passed to the Cabinet.

Discuss.

University of London LLB Examination
(for External Students) Constitutional Law June 1986 Q5

General Comment

This question revolves around the old argument as to whether Parliament legislates or merely legitimates executive policy. As well as examining the role of the backbench MP and the House of Lords in the legislative process, students should also consider whether in fact today legislation is not so much decided by the Cabinet as the Prime Minister.

Skeleton Solution

- Introduction: the enactment of legislation by the Queen in Parliament.
- The House of Commons: does it legislate or merely legitimate; the control of the Commons by the executive.
- The role of the House of Lords: the ability of the Lords to check the executive.
- The role of the backbench MP: private members' Bills.
- Conclusion: Cabinet legislation or Prime Ministerial legislation.

Suggested Solution

For purposes of constitutional analysis, the functions of government have often been divided into three broad classes – legislative, executive and judicial. The legislative function involves the enactment of general rules determining the structure and powers of public authorities and regulating the conduct of citizens and private organisations. In the United Kingdom, legislative authority is vested in the Queen in Parliament: new law being enacted when it has been approved by Commons and Lords and has received the Royal Assent.

The passing of legislation therefore is one of the primary functions of Parliament. Bills, which may be either public or private, cannot become law until they have been passed by Parliament and received the Royal Assent. However many consider that Parliament no longer legislates but rather that it merely legitimates proposed legislation already decided upon by the executive. Certainly, the great majority of Public Bills are prepared for Parliament by the government, which is also responsible for supervising their passage through each House. The executive therefore participates actively in the process of legislation. Party domination of the House of

Commons and the use of the whip system ensures that, generally speaking, when the government has a working majority in the Commons, no new legislation can be enacted by Parliament which is not approved also by the government and that those Bills which are approved are passed.

There are however occasions when in spite of the government's control of the Commons its members may exert their independence and refuse to act as a mere rubber stamp for executive policy. For example the Commons effectively blocked attempts by the Labour government to reform the House of Lords in 1968 and attempts by Mrs Thatcher to reform the law on Sunday trading were defeated following a backbench Conservative revolt in the Commons. One must also remember that Parliament also includes the House of Lords and that although the legislative powers of the Lords have been severely curtailed under the Parliament Acts 1911 and 1949 the chamber, retaining as it does a large degree of political independence, may still act as an effective check on government Bills.

Although the House of Lords no longer has power over money matters, under the Parliament Acts their Lordships do retain the power to amend non-money Bills and although the House cannot impose its will on the Commons in legislation, it can effectively delay government Bills for one year. In practice therefore where the government has a heavy legislative programme amendment or delay in the Lords can seriously threaten the legislative timetable for that particular session and the government will be forced to take notice and attempt a compromise with the Lords. If compromise fails and the government implements the procedure under the Parliament Acts, even a one year delay may prove fatal to the government's plans. Recent events have illustrated how the House of Lords can exert its independence and challenge government legislation. The Local Government Finance Act 1988 and the Education Reform Act 1988 both were amended by the House of Lords. It must however be conceded that a determined government will successfully achieve its purpose in the face of the House of Lords. Mrs Thatcher's first administration sustained 45 defeats in their Lordships' Chamber.

It must also be remembered that not all Public Bills are initiated by the executive. Although the bulk of the legislative programme of Parliament is taken up by government Bills, a small but significant part of the programme consists of Bills introduced by backbench MPs. Although the scope for legislative initiative by individual MPs is severely limited, both because of restricted parliamentary time and of the tight hold which the government maintains over departmental responsibilities, standing orders, while generally giving precedence to government business, nevertheless set aside ten Fridays in each session on which private members' Bills have priority. The fact that not many of these Bills reach the statute book does not detract from their value as expressions of the independent legislative function of Parliament.

However, in spite of the opportunities for private members to introduce their Bills, the independence of the House of Lords and the occasional rebellion amongst backbench members of the government party in the House of Commons, it is probably true to say that in the main the parliamentary function of legislation has effectively passed to the Cabinet, at least in the sense that the Cabinet is the core of collective responsibility.

Traditionally it is in the Cabinet where government policy is thrashed out before being put to Parliament for what has largely become the formality of approval. However, this may not necessarily be the case today. In the 1980s, under Margaret Thatcher, we experienced a period of prime ministerial government where policy decisions were made by the Prime Minister and her small inner-Cabinet based largely upon the advice of Cabinet committees and the

Prime Minister's own policy unit. The full Cabinet, if consulted at all, merely approved whatever was put before it. It did therefore mean that the parliamentary function of legislation had effectively passed to the Prime Minister. More recently, under John Major and Tony Blair ministers have been more involved in the decision-making process. Much depends on the personality of the Prime Minister.

QUESTION TWO

Evaluate the following statement:

'A serious weakness of the House of Commons is the ineffectual role of so many backbenchers.' (de Smith)

University of London LLB Examination
(for External Students) Constitutional Law June 1984 Q3

General Comment

In this question de Smith is commenting upon the fact that backbench MPs have opportunities available to scrutinise government policy but that because of the procedure of the Commons and the stranglehold of the government over the legislative system, these opportunities are mostly ineffectual. However, following this quote in his *Constitutional and Administrative Law* de Smith goes on to describe the success of the select committees in increasing the effectiveness of backbench MPs. Students, in evaluating the statement, should therefore weigh against the traditional factors limiting the effectiveness of the backbench MP in the Chamber, the success and achievements of the specialist select committees. Mention should also be made of the benefits to the backbenchers' role following the passing of the National Audit Act 1983.

Skeleton Solution

- Introduction – an outline of the opportunities available to backbenchers to participate in the business of the House of Commons.
- Examination of the system of select committees including their function.
- Limitations of select committees and the role of backbenchers.
- Conclusion – evaluation of the backbenchers' role.

Suggested Solution

The role of any backbenchers in the scrutiny of government policy and administration is largely ineffectual. Backbenchers have their opportunities to call the government to account on the occasions set aside for private members' motions, on the motions for the adjournment each day and before a recess, at question time and, if any succeed in catching the Speaker's eye, in the course of general debate.

However, many Members of Parliament soon discover that their opportunities to contribute significantly to debate are few. All such debates are limited by the political framework in which they are held and individual members have no means of probing behind the statements of ministers seeking to justify departmental decisions. The influence of the member on government policy from the backbenches or in opposition is also negligible, and it often seems that the conduct of public administration cannot be effectively scrutinised by the House of Commons. It has been said that any effective participation of backbench Members of

Parliament in decision-making will continue to present very great difficulties as long as governments maintain majorities in the House with the aid of an electoral system under which the winner can expect to take almost all, and as long as constitutional rules leave the spending power entirely in the hands of the executive.

It is these limitations that have given rise to demands for other procedures by which the House may inform and concern itself more directly with the work of government. In this respect experience has shown that it is possible within the existing British parliamentary system for members to influence the conduct of administration and to modify aspects of policy by their scrutiny of administrative activity as members of select committees. Indeed many people have seen in the increased use of select committees the key to a more effective role for Parliament vis-à-vis government. Between 1967 and 1978 these committees did offer some detailed and imaginative suggestions for administrative reorganisation, and made themselves, the House in general and interested members of the public better informed about central administration and the views of the administration.

However, it was not until 1979 that a bold experiment to extend the opportunity for members to scrutinise the executive through specialised select committees was started. Twelve select committees were established to monitor the activities of particular government departments or groups of departments. Their terms of reference were to examine the expenditure, administration and policy of the principal government departments, with the power to send for papers and witnesses and to appoint sub-committees. The committees also have the power to appoint technical advisors to supply information which is not readily available or to elucidate matters of complexity.

But while their investigation and reports show that they are effective in putting pressure on the government, there are limitations. No sanctions exist in respect of ministers who refuse to appear. There is still no guaranteed time for debating their reports. Also the party whips effectively choose the members of their party who are to serve on a particular committee. This enables the party frontbench to exclude from a committee any member who is likely to oppose frontbench policy. Thus the government will attempt to exclude from a committee members of its own party who are likely to join with the opposition to produce a report critical of the government.

Nevertheless, reports critical of the government are produced, but this 'packing' of committees by the party whips clearly reduces the potential effectiveness of select committees as a device for exercising control over the government. A further step towards increasing the effectiveness of members over government policy, this time in the field of national expenditure, has been the enactment of the National Audit Act 1983. The Act provides for the Comptroller and Auditor General to become an officer of Parliament and to head a National Audit Office. A Public Accounts Commission is also established consisting of the Chairman of the Public Accounts Committee, the Leader of the House and seven other MPs who are not ministers of state. This has vastly increased parliamentary control over national expenditure.

Therefore the ineffectual role of so many backbenchers may be a serious weakness of the House of Commons. But while the role of the backbencher in the chamber itself may be ineffectual, opportunities do exist through the select committee system for his full participation in serious and effective scrutiny of government policy and administration.

QUESTION THREE

Critically assess the statement that Parliament legitimates but does not legislate.

University of London LLB Examination
(for External Students) Constitutional Law June 1983 Q4

General Comment

This question requires discussion of the idea of a separation of powers in the British parliamentary system. You need to write an introduction explaining the basic principles of separation of power and then decide if, as between the executive and legislature, it exists in this country. Does the executive control the legislature or vice versa? Remember the statement does not mention the independence of the judiciary – so you in answering should also not really discuss it. We are concerned only with executive/legislature relations.

Skeleton Solution

- The doctrine of the separation of powers with the example of the USA which is based on the theory.
- The evolution of Cabinet government in the UK with particular reference to government dominance in the Commons.
- The nature of the relationship between Parliament and the government with reference to parliamentary controls on government.

Suggested Solution

The doctrine of the separation of powers has taken several forms at different periods and in different contexts. Aristotle is probably its first exponent, followed much later by John Locke in his second treatise of Civil Government in 1690, and then given a more popular treatment by Montesquieu in the eighteenth century. John Locke simply reasoned that as power corrupts men 'The three organs of state must not get into one hand'. Montesquieu developed the theory basing his analysis on a idealised picture of the British constitution in 1700s. He decided that there are three main classes of government function: the legislative, the executive and the judicial and that these should be exercised by three main organs of government – the legislature, the executive and the judiciary. He felt that to concentrate more than one class of function in any one person or organ of government is a threat to individual liberty. For example, the executive should not be allowed to make laws, or adjudicate on alleged breaches of the law and it should be concerned only with the making and applying of policy and general administration.

The best modern model of the doctrine is in the United States. The President and his 'Cabinet', the executive, cannot be members of Congress, the legislature. The judiciary can declare legislation void, however this has in reality produced judges who are political appointments. The doctrine is embodied in the constitution. In contrast no one would claim that the separation of powers is a central feature of the modern British constitution.

Since the evolution of the Cabinet system with the ministers of the Crown exercising executive power, and also sitting in Parliament the legislative body, there has been a direct link between executive and legislature power. In a sense the statement in question is true, but to see how true it is, a closer examination of the system is needed.

By convention ministers of the Crown who form the Cabinet should be members of one or other House of Parliament. However since the House of Commons Disqualification Act 1975 the maximum number of ministers in the Commons is 95. Except for these ministers, under the same statute, the vast majority of persons who hold positions within the executive are disqualified from membership of the Commons, namely all members of the civil service, armed forces, police and holders of many other public offices. It is only really the ministers who form part of the legislature and the executive.

The statement in essence is suggesting that the executive controls the legislature. Ultimately this is untrue as Parliament can oust a government it does not like by withdrawing support. However the system of electoral representation together with the use of Whips makes such a reversal highly unlikely. A government usually is returned with an overall majority in the House of Commons and has virtual control over Parliament. The government will have a majority on all House of Commons committees. The whips ensure that the party line is not broken and also that a majority can be summoned at short notice to vote in the Commons. Devices such as the guillotine are used to curtail parliamentary debate of legislation. A government such as the one returned in 1987 under Mrs Margaret Thatcher with a large majority had little trouble in pushing through legislation designed to implement Tory policies. Similarly the Blair government elected in May 1997. In substance the government does seem to make law.

It is possible to argue that the legislature is not merely a 'rubber stamp' and that it controls the government through ministers' Question Time, Adjournment Debates, select committees, Opposition Days and just general opposition to the executive policy. It is true to say that probing questions can disturb the path of government policy. An example may be the Local Government Finance Act 1988. Matters of great public concern can usually be at the very least delayed by the legislature.

The executive also produces a great number of statutory instruments which are a form of delegated legislation and not questioned in the Commons. This usually is to deal with details within the minister's domain (eg planning for the Secretary of State for the Environment) but it is in theory a powerful example of the executive exercising the functions of the legislature. In conclusion it is true to say that on most occasions Parliament merely legitimates the actions of the executive but this blending of executive and legislature is a fundamental characteristic of the British system of government. It existed to a lesser extent in Montesquieu's day and with the growth of Cabinet and Prime Ministerial government it has grown too – any attempt to change it would produce startling results for our unwritten constitution.

QUESTION FOUR

'Parliamentary procedures provide adequate opportunities for backbenchers to scrutinise government policy.'

Do you agree?

University of London LLB Examination
(for External Students) Constitutional Law June 1991 Q2

General Comment

A straightforward question requiring a brief account of procedural matters such as debates, question time and committee work, with a brief comment on their effectiveness.

Skeleton Solution

- Set out three main devices – debate – questions – committee work.
- Comment on the effectiveness of each.
- Conclusion.

Suggested Solution

There are three principal means by which backbenchers can scrutinise government policy: first, in general or specific debates in the House of Commons; secondly, through questions asked of ministers at Question Time; thirdly, through cross examination of ministers appearing before select committees.

a) *Debates*

The main opportunities for debate in the House of Commons are provided by adjournment debates, debates on motions to adjourn, and debates that occur as part of the legislative process.

The adjournment debate normally occurs at the end of the day's business, when the adjournment of the House is formally moved. Half an hour is made available for a private member to raise a topic in debate and for a ministerial reply to be given. Topics are selected by ballot. The topic under discussion is usually one of local interest, so the debates tend to be constituency orientated. Often, if a member is dissatisfied with an answer he has received in correspondence with a minister and/or in answer to a parliamentary question he may raise the matter 'on the adjournment'. A serious drawback in terms of publicity generation is that these debates usually take place in an almost empty House and at an inconvenient time for press coverage.

Debates on motions to adjourn, held under Standing Order No 10, allow members to suggest that a specific and important matter should have urgent consideration and that an emergency debate be held upon it. It is for the Speaker to decide whether the matter is sufficiently important and urgent to warrant giving it precedence; the Chair in general very seldom gives leave. If leave is granted, and if the motion is approved by the House or supported by 40 members, the motion will be debated either that evening or the following day. Again, the length of time available for debate dictates that such devices can only be of limited use in bringing ministers to account.

As part of the legislative process members can question government policy during the debate on the Second Reading of a Bill. The general principles and policy behind the Bill are debated and a defeat at this stage will be fatal for the legislation in question.

The effectiveness of backbench scrutiny depends to a large extent on the role of the Speaker in ensuring that all members who wish to do so have the opportunity to speak. The Speaker acts as chairperson during debates and generally presides over the House, except when it is in committee. It is the Speaker who calls members to speak and decides how many supplementary questions shall be allowed at Question Time.

The effectiveness of backbench scrutiny can be limited by the government's resorting to the various devices that exist for curtailing debate. Under the Closure Motion (Standing Order 30), debate will cease where at least 100 members vote for the motion. Under the 'Guillotine Motion' (allocation of time motion), one or more stages of a Bill are disposed of either by a fixed date, or by a fixed number of sittings (either of the House, or a

Committee, or both). The effect is clearly to leave some issues undiscussed in the House of Commons. On the whole, these devices are unpopular with parliamentarians because they can restrict valuable criticism and amendment of legislation. If used extensively (and they are being used increasingly), it can be argued that they deny the legislative role of Parliament.

b) *Parliamentary questions*

These can be questions for an oral answer in the House during Question Time; or Private Notice Questions, which can be asked if the Speaker judges their subject matter to be urgent and important (these are taken orally in the House at the end of Question Time); and questions for a written answer, the reply to which is printed in the Official Report (*Hansard*).

The effectiveness of Question Time as a means of scrutiny of ministers by backbenchers is limited by a number of factors. Generally, the backbencher is no match for the minister with his Civil Service brief. When a parliamentary question is submitted it is passed immediately to the relevant government department, and the officials in that department will give priority to preparing a brief for the minister enabling him to answer not only that question, but also any supplementary questions that the officials anticipate. The department knows by whom the question is asked and in preparing the brief will bear in mind the interest and concerns of the questioner and other MPs who are similarly interested and likely to put supplementary questions. Ministers rarely gain or lose in reputation at Question Time. Most of them can cope quite satisfactorily with it, having risen through the House themselves. Often a minister will deal with a question simply by a party gibe, stonewalling or evasion.

c) *Select committees*

The most powerful select committees are those shadowing the work of government departments. The present system of committees was instituted in 1979, with the aim of strengthening the accountability of ministers to the House for the discharge of their responsibilities. The committees can send for persons, papers and records, and from time to time report to the House. The committees have proved to be a very effective way of allowing backbenchers to question ministers, and their reports frequently engender publicity embarrassing to the government of the day, but a number of limitations still exist.

There is still no effective sanction available against a minister who refuses to appear, or refuses to allow civil servants to appear, before a select committee to give evidence. In the past, ministers have sometimes refused to appear or to answer certain questions.

In the past, select committees, partly because of inadequate funding, have enlisted the assistance of too few support staff, viz secretarial staff, researchers and technical experts, and thus their inquiries and reports have not been as penetrating as they could have been. MPs themselves also have limited time available for committee work. There is still no guaranteed time set aside for debating committee reports (other than those of the Public Accounts Committee).

In conclusion it is submitted that whilst the formal methods of control, outlined above are important, government backbenchers can have their greatest effect on government policy when they threaten to rebel and withdraw their support from government sponsored legislation in the House of Commons. Such a threat is likely to result in 'horsetrading' between backbenchers and the government whips, to produce the required modifications in policy.

QUESTION FIVE

In the British Parliament today, are a government's backbenchers its most effective opposition?

University of London LLB Examination
(for External Students) Constitutional and Administrative Law June 1992 Q4

General Comment

This is not the usual question on the power of backbenchers, therefore it is not a general essay on the methods open to the backbencher to check the executive. It requires a discussion of the role of the government's own backbenchers, who will often exercise their influence in less overt ways. As a result it is quite a difficult question to answer fully.

Skeleton Solution

- Introduction.
- The whips.
- Backbench groups.
- Procedural opportunities.
- Debates.
- Restrictions on the backbencher.
- Conclusion.

Suggested Solution

A party which wins an election with an outright majority of seats in the House of Commons is virtually unassailable. Even if the opposition gathers together all the minority parties, the government cannot be defeated. In such a position, only a backbench revolt will threaten the government. Where the majority is thinner, the need for party discipline increases. Whatever the case, it is true that the government's backbenchers can be a most effective check on the government.

Immediately following the general election in 1992 John Major's government had an outright majority of 21 seats – 81 seats fewer than that of the previous Conservative government. In due course he lost his overall Commons majority, and faced the prospect of backbench revolts over monetary union, the ban on handguns, and the culling of livestock affected by BSE. It is during such times that a small number of dissident backbenchers can exercise an inordinate amount of power, effectively blackmailing the front bench with treats to defeat the government on key votes. The only weapon the Prime Minister has is to threaten an election at a time when the same backbenchers might lose their seats because of the government's unpopularity.

What can the backbencher do? He is under the control of the party whips, to the extent that they will try to ensure that MPs will turn up and vote when needed and will perform such parliamentary duties as are required. Most of the time, most MPs obey the whips. Ambitions of joining the front benches will soon be thwarted if an MP takes too independent a line, but, that apart, most of the time MPs willingly follow the party line.

The whips also convey to the party leaders the feeling amongst the backbenchers. These feelings are more directly conveyed by backbench groups. For example, the Conservative 1922 Committee is quite capable of taking ministers, even the Prime Minister, to task over their policies. During the last Conservative administration the Chairman of the 1922 Sir Marcus Fox, a former whip, was effectively the spokesman for the Conservative backbenchers and any Conservative Prime Minister faced with contentious legislation must first ensure he has the 1922 on his side. Faced as he will be with unanimous opposition from the other parties, he needs to rely on his own members and these unofficial channels will tell him whether this support will be provided.

There are, of course, plenty of opportunities within House of Commons' proceedings, short of voting against the government, by which a backbencher can make his voice heard. Parliamentary questions – both oral and written – are one such opportunity. Another would be through participation in parliamentary committees. To some extent, the selection process will ensure that maverick MPs are kept away. However, the select committees have shown themselves quite capable of confronting government policies and criticism may well come from the government's backbench members as, for example, in the Select Committee on Defence during the 'Westland Affair' (1986). In other words, their loyalty to the government does not prevent them from taking a critical stance. The government is not directly threatened by that stance and yet its source probably makes the criticism more effective.

A further opportunity for the backbencher will be during debates. During Mrs Thatcher's premiership the most significant backbench speeches came from those she had just removed from the front bench. Sir Geoffrey Howe's speech shortly after his departure is a good example. If such a speech voices opposition and if others share that view then it is obviously of greater significance than the inevitable opposition from the other side of the House.

In conclusion it should be said that most politicians are ambitious; none would want to see their own government defeated. These two factors limit the extent of backbench opposition. Further, MPs are answerable to their constituents who might take a dim view of opposition. A government may not wish to call the backbencher's bluff, but the backbencher certainly does not hold all the cards.

6 Legislature II – The House of Lords

6.1 Introduction

The House of Lords is currently a non-elected chamber. It plays a part in the legislative process but ultimately its powers are very limited. Nevertheless many argue that the quality of debate in the House of Lords is high and the House can sometimes effectively challenge the Commons.

The reform/abolition of the House of Lords has been on the political agenda for many years but other than the Life Peerages Act 1958 which has very much re-vitalised the House no significant attempts at reform have been successful. Following the election of a Labour government committed to reform, changes are likely during 1999.

6.2 Key points

a) *The composition of the House of Lords*

i) The Lords Spiritual: Archbishops of Canterbury and York, the Bishops of London, Durham and Winchester, and the next 21 diocesan bishops of the Church of England in seniority of appointment.

ii) The Lords Temporal:

- Hereditary peers and peeresses in their own right of England, Scotland, Great Britain and the United Kingdom.
- Life peers created under the Life Peerages Act 1958.
- Lords of Appeal in Ordinary.

b) *The functions and work of the House of Lords*

The 1968 Government White Paper *House of Lords Reform* referred to seven functions of the House of Lords.

i) Its appellate role as the supreme court of appeal.

ii) The provision of a forum for free debate and matters of public interest.

iii) The revision of Public Bills brought from the House of Commons.

iv) The initiation of Public Bills.

v) The consideration of subordinate legislation.

vi) The scrutiny of the activities of the executive.

vii) The scrutiny of private legislation.

c) *House of Lords' reform*

i) The Parliament Act 1911

- A Bill certified by the Speaker as a Money Bill should receive the Royal Assent and become an Act of Parliament without the consent of the House of Lords if, having been sent up from the House of Commons at least one month before the end of the session, it had not been passed by the Lords without amendment within one month of its being sent up.
- Any other Public Bill, except one for extending the life of Parliament, could become an Act of Parliament without the consent of the House of Lords if it had been passed by the House of Commons in three successive sessions, two years having elapsed between its Second Reading and its final passing in the House of Commons, and if it had been sent up to the House of Lords at least one month before the end of each of the three sessions.
- The maximum duration of a Parliament was reduced from seven years to five.

ii) The Parliament Act 1949

Amends the Parliament Act 1911 by reducing the number of sessions in which a Bill must be passed by the House of Commons from three to two, and reducing the period between the Second Reading and final passing in the House of Commons from two years to one.

iii) Life Peerages Act 1958

This Act empowers the Crown to create life peers who vote in the House of Lords. The on-going result of the Act is that the House of Lords has become rejuvenated and appointments are made from people with wide ranging experience in different walks of life. The role of the House of Lords as a debating chamber is consequently significant.

iv) The Peerage Act 1963

This Act enables hereditary peers, other than those of first creation, to renounce their titles for life by disclaimer. The peerage remains dormant and devolves upon the heir in the normal manner on the renouncer's death. A person who has disclaimed a peerage is entitled to vote in Parliamentary elections and is eligible for election to the House of Commons.

v) The Parliament (No 2) Bill 1969

In November 1968 the Labour government published a White Paper, *House of Lords Reform*, which was later embodied in the Parliament (No 2) Bill 1968–69. Its main proposals were as follows:

- The reformed House of Lords was to be a two-tier structure comprising voting peers and non-voting peers.
- Succession to a hereditary peerage was no longer to carry the right to a seat in the House of Lords, but existing peers by succession would have the right to sit as non-

voting members during their life time, or might be created life peers to enable them to continue in active participation as voting members.

- Voting peers were expected to play a full part in the work of the House and be required to attend at least one-third of the sittings. They would be subject to an age of retirement. Non-voting peers would be able to play a full part in debates and in committees, but would not be entitled to vote.
- The voting House would initially consist of about 230 peers, distributed between the parties in such a way as to give the government a small majority over the Opposition parties, but not a majority of the House as a whole when those without party allegiance were included.
- The reformed House would be able to impose a delay of six months from the date of disagreement between the two Houses on the passage of non-financial public legislation. After this delay a Bill could be submitted for Royal Assent by resolution of the House of Commons.
- The Lords would be able to require the House of Commons to reconsider subordinate legislation, but would not be able to reject it outright.
- A review would be made of the functions and procedures of the two Houses once the main reform had come into effect.

The Bill was abandoned on 17 April 1969.

vi) The Labour government elected in May 1997 is committed to reform of the House of Lords and to this end intends to introduce a House of Lords Bill early in 1999. Given the large majority the Labour government currently enjoys in the House of Commons it would appear that the Bill will become law even if the Parliament Acts 1911–49 have to be invoked in order to ensure that it reaches the statute book.

6.3 Recent developments

As indicated above the key development in this area has been the announcement by the Labour government of its proposals to reform the House of Lords. It seems likely that the Bill to be presented to the House of Commons in early 1999 will seek to end membership of the House of Lords by virtue of a hereditary peerage. The Bill will also provide for the removal of voting and sitting rights of current hereditary peers. As a quid pro quo hereditary peers will be eligible to stand for election as members of the House of Commons.

It seems likely that a Royal Commission or Speaker's Conference will be established to examine the logistics of replacing the hereditary peers with other elected or appointed members to deflect the criticisms of the Lords on the grounds of it being an unrepresentative and undemocratic body. The question nevertheless arises as to what extent the *life* peers can claim that they have any stronger claim to vote. Critics have pointed out that this change would convert the House of Lords into a powerful quango. If the Labour government's argument is taken to its logical conclusion *all* current peers should be deprived of the right to vote. There will be a transitional period between the time when the current hereditary peers lose the right to sit and vote and the point at which the new method of appointing members of the House of Lords comes into effect. During that transitional phase a new, more independent system for nominating peers will be introduced as an interim measure. Details as to how this will work are not yet available.

The European Parliamentary Elections Act 1999 was enacted utilising the procedures under the

Parliament Acts 1911–49. As a result of objections in the House of Lords to the closed party list system adopted by the government for the election of MEPs in Great Britain, the Bill was lost at the end of the 1997–98 session. The government immediately reintroduced it at the commencement of the 1998 –99 session to ensure its enactment in time for the June 1999 Euro-elections.

6.4 Analysis of questions

The House of Lords has, in the past, been a popular topic for examiners. Questions generally have demanded a knowledge of the role and functions of the House and have required the student to consider the relationship between the House of Commons and the House of Lords. Given recent events the emphasis is likely to shift much more to the issue of reform. It is not clear at present how examiners are going to respond to the uncertainty surrounding this issue. The questions set out below will help you prepare some basic answers but caution is advised – in the light of impending changes the type of question set in the future regarding the House of Lords may be markedly different when compared to the past questions examined below. You will have to keep up with the progress of the reform proposals in order to be able to tackle questions on the subject.

For present purposes the answers set out below reflect the position as at 31 December 1998.

6.5 Questions

QUESTION ONE

'While a second chamber is needed to serve a number of legislative purposes the present House of Lords is restricted by its composition from exercising its powers effectively.' (Wade and Bradley).

Discuss.

University of London LLB Examination
(for External Students) Constitutional Law June 1986 Q4

General Comment

The usual House of Lords question. As always don't write everything you know about the House of Lords and don't be tempted to simply turn out the traditional (and now largely discredited) criticisms of the Lords. Remember that while the undemocratic nature of its composition is a major criticism of the House, it is also one of its greatest assets.

Skeleton Solution

- Introduction; the need for a second chamber.
- The criticisms of the hereditary and life peerage systems.
- The advantages which flow from the undemocratic nature of the composition of the House of Lords.
- The factors limiting the effective exercise of the powers of the House.

Suggested Solution

For many years there has been opposition to the continued existence of the House of Lords as the second chamber in our present bicameral parliamentary system. Nevertheless the fact remains that a second chamber is needed to assist in the legislative process and the House of Lords performs the functions of a second chamber extremely well.

However, despite the success of the House of Lords in performing its functions it can be argued that the House is nevertheless restricted by its aristocratic and unrepresentative composition from exercising its powers effectively. In a democracy, it may be argued all legislators should be directly accountable to the people at elections or at least accountable indirectly, for example, by election by the House of Commons. Their Lordships, however, take their seats in the legislature either because they are hereditary peers or because they have been created life peers under the Life Peerages Act 1958. The former are criticised on the grounds that high office should be awarded to those who earn it on merit and not by accident of birth, and as most hereditary peers are Conservative this leads to a permanent Conservative majority in the House. The life peers are criticised because of the considerable powers of patronage left in the hands of the Prime Minister to reward party loyalists and retiring ministers with seats in the Upper Chamber. It is also thought by some that since the members of the House of Lords do not represent any body of constituents they speak for a small privileged section of the community.

But criticism of the composition of the House of Lords is often ill-founded and uninformed. It can be argued that the composition of the House does not directly affect the effectiveness of the chamber – quite the opposite. The quality of members and speeches is often very high. Debates are well informed. Those upon whom peerages are conferred are usually persons with considerable experience of politics, public service or industry, or who have otherwise made their mark in public or intellectual life. They bring to the House a wide range of expertise. The hereditary element also provides many young peers and because the Lords do not have any constituencies to consider they can devote more time to their parliamentary duties and do not have to worry about re-selection or re-election. In many respects therefore the membership of the House of Lords is far superior to that of the House of Commons. The only difficulty is the undemocratic nature of their appointment.

It is the consciousness of their undemocratic nature of appointment which is the major impediment to the effectiveness of the House. While the Parliament Acts 1911 and 1949 did have a direct effect on the effectiveness of the House of Lords – for example, the House no longer has power over money matters and governments no longer depend on the favour of the Lords for their continuation in office – nevertheless under the Parliament Acts their Lordships do retain the power to amend non-money Bills. Although the House of Lords cannot impose its will on the Commons in legislation, it can effectively delay government Bills for one year. But the Lords are reluctant to exercise their suspensory powers over legislation which they still retain. If they interfere with government business they may lay themselves open to allegations of seeking to frustrate the wishes of the people as expressed through their democratically elected government.

This makes the House of Lords extremely vulnerable. How can they act as a check on the House of Commons in such circumstances? The government can brush aside opposition in the House of Lords 'because they don't represent the people', and the threat of abolition or reform is always present. Their Lordships are well aware of this. This is perhaps one reason why in spite of their inbuilt Conservative majority they have always shown restraint when dealing with Labour government legislation. Recent events have shown however that the reports of the impotence of the House of Lords have been exaggerated and that, given the right circumstances, its effectiveness and efficiency is not altogether impaired by these legislative and political constraints.

In the past, when the threat of abolition has been absent, as was the case under the previous Conservative government, their Lordships were effective in carrying out their constitutional functions. The Lords retain a high degree of political independence inherent in their undemocratic character. They do not have to rely upon the continued support of a political party for their seats in the legislature and while the majority of hereditary peers may be Conservative, a Conservative government is not guaranteed a majority in the House. They vote according to their conscience, not the demands of the Whips. Where the government has a heavy legislative programme, amendment or delay in the Lords can seriously threaten the legislative timetable for that particular session and the government will be forced to take notice and attempt a compromise with the Lords. If compromise fails and the government implements the procedure under the Parliament Acts, even a one year delay may prove fatal to the government's plans.

But such opposition is possible only where the House of Lords retains popular support for its action, where, for example, the government is acting unconstitutionally or outside the terms of its mandate. In other situations their Lordships may be reluctant to seriously oppose the government's wishes. The fear of abolition or public censure would be decisive.

Therefore while the effectiveness of the House of Lords in respect of its legislative functions and powers is relatively unimpeded and in many respects enhanced by the anachronistic and undemocratic nature of its composition, its effectiveness as a check upon the House of Commons, and thus in reality upon the government of the day, is limited.

QUESTION TWO

Outline the constitutional problems and benefits, if any, that would arise if the House of Lords were abolished.

University of London LLB Examination
(for External Students) Constitutional Law June 1985 Q3

General Comment

This question involves discussion of the role of the House of Lords as the second chamber in our bicameral parliamentary system and the constitutional problems and benefits which would arise if the Lords were abolished in favour of an unicameral parliamentary system. Don't write everything you know about the House of Lords and don't be tempted to simply turn out the traditional (and now largely discredited) criticisms of Lords as justification for their abolition. Remember, the House of Lords plays a vital function as a revision chamber and helps relieve the pressure of work on the already overburdened House of Commons. Events in recent years have also shown that the House of Lords is the only effective check on a Government which dominates the House of Commons. It is doubtful whether any real benefits would arise from the abolition of the House of Lords. Reform yes, abolition no.

Skeleton Solution

- Introduction: arguments for reform/abolition of the House of Lords.
- The problems caused by adopting a unicameral parliamentary system. The position of the Judicial Committee; role of the House as a revision chamber for Public Bills; inability of Commons to deal adequately with all Bills passed; need for fundamental change in House of Commons procedure; role of Lords as a check on the executive; need for written Constitution/Bill of Rights.

- Benefits of abolition: saving of costs; space; forcing of change and reform of House of Commons procedures.

Suggested Solution

For many years there has been opposition of some sort or another to the continued existence of the House of Lords as the second chamber in our present bicameral parliamentary system. The argument is that as presently constituted the House of Lords is undemocratic, outdated and unsuitable in a modern society. Some therefore favour reform, so that, for example, its composition becomes more democratic and its powers perhaps increased so that it can act as a more effective check on the House of Commons, (and thus, in reality, on the government of the day), than it does at present. Others, however, wish to go further still and see the abolition of the second chamber in favour of a unicameral parliamentary system.

If the House of Lords were abolished certain constitutional problems would undoubtedly result. Whether these problems would be insuperable is a matter of opinion. What cannot be denied, however, is that despite the problems regarding its composition, the fact remains that the House of Lords does perform a valuable service within the present parliamentary system and if abolished many of its functions would still have to be performed by some other body, presumably the House of Commons. In 1968, the government White Paper *House of Lords Reform* referred to seven functions of the House of Lords. An examination of each of these functions serves to illustrate some of the problems that might result from abolition.

Firstly, the House of Lords acts as the final court of appeal for the whole of the United Kingdom in civil cases and for England, Wales and Northern Ireland in criminal cases. If the House were abolished therefore a new 'supreme' court would have to be established to take its place, unless of course the Court of Appeal were to become the final appeal court for England and Wales. However, as the judicial work of the House is separate from its other functions and only involves the Judicial Committee – drawn from the Lord High Chancellor, the Lords of Appeal in Ordinary and Lords who hold or have held high judicial office – the separation of the Judicial Committee from the rest of the House of Lords or its replacement by some new body would not perhaps cause too great a constitutional problem.

Secondly, the House provides a forum for free debate on matters of public interest, Wednesday in particular being traditionally set aside for special debate on a wide range of subjects. Apart from the fact that these debates are usually of a very high standard; a standard that would perhaps never be reached in the Commons, even if the time were available, this loss would not pose any great constitutional problem.

Thirdly, and perhaps most importantly, the House acts as a revising chamber for Public Bills brought from the House of Commons. About one half of the time of the House of Lords is devoted to the consideration of Public Bills. The majority of this time is spent on revising Bills which have already passed the Commons, where the great majority of government legislation is introduced. The House of Commons does not have the time to fully debate all the legislation it has to pass each session and the use of procedures for the curtailment of debate, such as the guillotine, often means that Bills are passed by the Commons without really being considered at all. A second chamber is therefore required to examine and revise such Bills. If the second chamber is abolished then the procedures of the House of Commons for enacting legislation will have to be changed if the present standard and volume of legislation is to be maintained. This could be achieved by membership of the House of Commons becoming full-time and by making even more use of committees. However, even then the volume of legislation may still prove to be too great, necessitating either a shortening of the procedure by which a Bill is enacted or making more use of subordinate legislation, which some would argue is already over used as it is. Certainly some fundamental changes would have to be made to the proceedings of the House of Commons and these may prove unacceptable to many of the present MPs.

Also it must be remembered that the House of Commons, because of the distortion produced by our electoral system, is largely controlled by a government which does not represent even 50 per cent of the electorate. A second chamber is thus required to at least delay substantially controversial legislation which may be unpopular with the majority of the people of the country. If the second chamber is abolished then the only way to control a government with an absolute majority in the House of Commons may be to have either a written Constitution or a Bill of Rights containing entrenched clauses, perhaps requiring a referendum for amendment.

The House of Lords also initiates Public Bills. While the more important and controversial Bills almost invariably begin in the House of Commons, Bills which are relatively uncontroversial in party political terms are regularly introduced in the House of Lords. If abolished, these Bills will have to be wholly dealt with by the Commons thus adding to its already overburdened workload. Similarly, the subordinate legislation and the private legislation at present dealt with by the House of Lords would also fall to be wholly dealt with by the Commons if the second chamber were abolished.

The arguments in favour of a unicameral Parliament are mainly political and it is doubtful whether any real practical benefit would result from the abolition of the House of Lords. Certainly it is doubtful that the loss of the Lords could ever be compensated. However, there are benefits of sorts which would flow from abolition, such as the saving of money and the making available of more space in the Palace of Westminster. Abolition would also have to result in the widespread reform of the House of Commons if any semblance of a parliamentary democracy is to be maintained. Such reform may be viewed as a substantial benefit. However, the main fear, and indeed the most likely consequence of the abolition of the House of Lords, is that it will simply serve to strengthen the executive control of the legislature.

QUESTION THREE

'Paradoxically, the House of Lords is an essential and valuable second chamber.'

Critically assess this statement.

University of London LLB Examination
(for External Students) Constitutional Law June 1991 Q3

General Comment

A question inviting one to consider the shortcomings and advantages of the second chamber. It is advisable to deal with the two issues separately, citing specific examples.

Skeleton Solution

- Examine common criticisms of the House of Lords; membership, unelected, powers.
- Consider its contribution to scrutiny of the executive, and the legislative process.

Suggested Solution

The quotation under discussion assumes that, in the normal course of events, a body such as the House of Lords would not normally be able to function properly as the second legislative chamber, but that, despite its theoretical shortcomings, it performs that task very well. This answer will first address itself to those aspects of the House of Lords that one might suppose render it unable to play such an important constitutional role.

Firstly its membership. None of the members of the House of Lords is elected. All members are there either through appointment, birth, or by virtue of the office they hold. The institution is, therefore, an affront to democracy. Peers in theory represent no-one but themselves, or the interests of those exercising the power of appointment, and as such are not accountable to the people despite the influence they might have over the law making process. It is added that peers are paid a daily attendance fee and this is an unnecessary extra burden on the taxpayer. The Commons is short of space and could make use of the room currently used by the Lords.

Secondly, there is the argument that one elected chamber is enough. To have a second (particularly in a unitary system) is simply a confusion. If there are faults in the way the House of Commons operates at present that should be dealt with by reform of the House of Commons. For example, the introduction of a system of proportional representation and/or the adoption of a really effective system of select committees to scrutinise the government's activities and with the powers necessary to exercise a great deal more influence than at present over the government. Rather than being 'controlled' by a Second Chamber, the government could be controlled by a written constitution containing some entrenched clauses, perhaps requiring a referendum for amendment.

Thirdly, the House of Lords has a majority of Conservative Party supporters who, although they may seldom attend, can always be relied upon to turn up and vote in favour of that party's legislation (or opposition to legislation). These are the so-called 'backwoodsmen'.

Despite all of the foregoing, the House of Lords continues to be a respected and valuable part of the British constitution. Why should this be? There are a number of reasons.

The House provides a forum for free debate on matters of public interest. Wednesday is traditionally set aside for special debates on a wide range of subjects. Debates may be initiated either by the government, opposition, backbench or independent members. Once a month, from the beginning of the Session until the Spring Bank Holiday recess, there are two 'Short Debates', limited to two and a half hours each. The right to initiate such debates is confined to backbenchers and crossbenchers and the subjects for debate are chosen by ballot.

The House of Lords serves a valuable purpose in scrutinising Bills passed by the House of Commons, with about one half of the time of the House of Lords devoted to the consideration of Public Bills. This process is especially important because, unlike the Commons, the Lords have nothing corresponding to the guillotine and there is therefore no effective machinery for curtailing debate. Also the Lords have no provision for the selection of amendments for debate and therefore all amendments tabled may be debated. To some extent the House of Lords can compensate for inadequate scrutiny of legislation by the House of Commons. The powers of the House of Lords to thwart the wishes of the House of Commons are, of course, limited by the provisions of the Parliament Acts 1911 and 1949, under which certain Public Bills may be presented for the Royal Assent without the consent of the Lords: see the War Crimes Act 1991.

The House of Lords does not stand idle at the start of a parliamentary session waiting for legislation to work its way up from the House of Commons. Bills which are relatively uncontroversial in party political terms have been introduced in the House of Lords with a fair degree of regularity. These include the Wildlife and Countryside Bill (1980–81 Session), the National Heritage Bill, Data Protection Bill and the Health and Social Services and Social Security Adjudications Bill (1982–83 Session). By convention all Consolidation Bills (Bills which do not alter the law but replace a number of Acts dealing with a particular subject by a single Act) and most Bills to give effect to changes in the law proposed by the Law Commissions, are introduced in the Lords.

Unlike members of the House of Commons, members of the Lords are free to introduce Private Members' Bills into the House and there is usually sufficient time for them to be debated. However if they are passed there is no guarantee that time will be found for them in the House of Commons. The fact that the Lords have no constituents makes it easier for them to discuss measures proposing controversial changes in the law in this way. The Lords thus played a significant part in reforming the law relating to homosexuality and abortion.

Their Lordships also contribute to the scrutiny of delegated legislation. The powers of the House of Lords over delegated legislation were not curtailed by the Parliament Acts and are therefore the same as those enjoyed by the House of Commons. When a resolution of each House approving the instrument is required, the House of Lords always has an opportunity to debate the instrument. In the case of negative instruments, any member may move a motion to annul the instrument and while in the Commons time often cannot be found to debate such motions, in the Lords there is no such difficulty.

The government departments will have representatives in the House of Lords who can be questioned about policy by peers in the same way that ministers can be questioned in the House of Commons. Each day up to four oral or 'starred questions' may be asked of the government and are taken as first business. No Lord may ask more than two questions on any day nor may he have more than three questions on the order paper at any time. Supplementary questions may be asked by any Member, but there may not be a debate. 'Unstarred questions' are taken at the end of business. The Lord asking the question makes a speech, and a debate may take place before the minister makes his reply, which concludes the proceedings. Private notice questions may be asked on matters of urgency. It is for the Leader of the House or as a last resort for the House itself, to decide what constitutes a matter of urgency. The process of question time in the House of Lords therefore provides a valuable adjunct to the procedure in the House of Commons.

In conclusion, it is submitted that there is one further argument in favour of the retention of the House of Lords, namely that the House of Commons, because of the distortion produced by our electoral system, is largely controlled by a government which does not represent even 50 per cent of the electorate. A Second Chamber (and one with greater powers than the present House of Lords) is thus required to at least substantially delay controversial legislation which may be unpopular with the majority of the people of the country. During the 1980s, with its succession of Conservative governments with large majorities, it was the House of Lords that inflicted over 100 defeats upon the government in votes on various controversial pieces of legislation. The Labour Party in opposition was virtually powerless, given the nature of the parliamentary process.

QUESTION FOUR

'The increasing willingness of the House of Lords over the past 15 years to amend and delay government Bills may be viewed either as an affront to democracy or a legitimate constitutional safeguard for the citizen.'

Discuss.

University of London LLB Examination
(for External Students) Constitutional Law June 1994 Q4

General Comment

Careful reading of this question is required: it is not a question on the House of Lords in isolation, but rather deals primarily with the relationship between the Lords and the Commons. As such, it admits of quite a general treatment and allows the candidate to discuss not merely the composition, functions and powers of the Lords, but also issues such as the electoral system, the 'elective dictatorship' and the inadequacy of scrutiny of government by the Commons. All these must, of course, be integrated into discussion of the specific quote. While it would be possible to argue that recent activism in the Lords is an affront to democracy, or that it is a legitimate constitutional safeguard, the approach taken here is that it is a bit of both.

Skeleton Solution

- Composition of Lords: hereditary and life peers.
- Electoral system: effect on composition of Commons.
- House of Lords' functions: scrutiny.
- Reform?

Suggested Solution

Figures suggest that the House of Lords has indeed been increasingly willing to amend government Bills: thus, while in the mid-1960s the average number of amendments per session was in the region of 500, by the mid-1980s there were well over 1,000, and between 1987 and 1993, this figure had risen to some 2,300 (see, generally, J A G Griffith and M Ryle, *Parliament: Functions, Practice and Procedures* (1989); D N Clarke & D Shell 'Revision and Amendment of Legislation by the House of Lords – A Case Study' [1994] PL 409). While it is important to realise that many of these amendments will be minor, technical, or moved by the government, there has been a consistent increase, during the period since 1979, in policy amendments, those dealing with the substance of the proposed legislation, and, moreover, in government defeats on policy issues. The effect of any increase in amendments will obviously have a delaying effect on the passage of legislation, but it is worth noting that the Lords attempted recently not merely to delay but to reject, on second reading, the War Crimes Bill. Only the eventual use of the Parliament Acts 1911–1949 – the first use of the 1949 Act and the first use of the procedures by a Conservative administration – ensured passage of the legislation.

If, then, we accept the statement in the quote for discussion, it is necessary to consider whether this recent tendency in the Lords to delay or amend Bills is either 'an affront to democracy' or a 'legitimate constitutional safeguard for the citizen'. Of course, the quote assumes that it is either one or the other. The approach taken here, however, will be to argue that it is more likely to be a bit of both.

Arguments that the role of the House of Lords in the legislative process is an 'affront to democracy' focus primarily on the composition of the Lords. As an unelected body, comprised largely of both hereditary peers, whose status as members of the legislature is derived from blood rather than the ballot box, and of life peers (Life Peerages Act 1958), who are political appointees, the House is fundamentally unrepresentative. As Lord Birkenhead once memorably said in debate to a member who annoyed him: 'The noble Lord represents no-one but himself – and I don't think much of his constituency!'

It is arguable, however, that the composition of the Commons, albeit that the members are directly elected by the people, is itself somewhat lacking in democratic foundations. The effect of the electoral system, when combined with the modern development of the party system, is to ensure 'strong government' – or, as Lord Hailsham has suggested, an 'elective dictatorship' – at the expense of representation of the electorate. The experience of the Alliance and, subsequently, the Social and Liberal Democratic parties since 1979, when a popular vote of roughly 25 per cent is regularly translated into a percentage of seats in the Commons in the region of 5 per cent, bears eloquent testimony to the inadequacies of the current electoral system in ensuring truly democratic representation in the House of Commons.

It follows that, while there is force in the assertion that the role of the Lords does constitute an affront to democracy, it does not tell the whole story. Concern, moreover, has been expressed of late that the powers of government are no longer subject to adequate scrutiny by the Commons; with the advent of the party system and party discipline, it is rare in modern times for a government not to enjoy a majority in the Commons. While rebellion by supporters of the government is less rare of late, it remains true that in the vast majority of cases scrutiny of the government is the function of the opposition; as, almost by definition, a minority, it is clear that such scrutiny can scarcely claim to be effective. Further, pressure on the parliamentary timetable has increased – as evidenced by the dramatic increase in the use of the guillotine in recent years – to such an extent that the adequate scrutiny of legislative proposals is often lacking.

It is in this context that it is possible to argue that the recent activism in the House of Lords can be seen as a 'legitimate constitutional safeguard for the citizen'. It is generally accepted that, particularly since the advent of life peers in 1958, the level of expertise and ability in the Lords has been significantly enhanced. This factor, when taken together with the lack of time in the Commons and the possibility of a 'strong' government inclining too much towards elective dictatorship, suggests that there is both merit in and justification for this increasing willingness to amend and delay government bills. It is also worth noting that while the Conservatives generally enjoy a majority in the Lords (albeit not over opposition and cross-benchers combined), it is paradoxically easier for the Lords to amend, delay and even defeat Bills proposed by a Conservative government than a Labour administration – for the simple reason that the latter is more likely to honour the promise in the preamble to the Parliament Act 1911 'to substitute for the House of Lords ... a Second Chamber constituted on a popular instead of hereditary basis'.

In conclusion, while it is undeniable that as an unelected and unrepresentative body it is certainly anomalous that the House of Lords should exercise so much influence, if not power, in the legislative process, it is going too far to describe its willingness to amend and delay government bills as an affront to democracy; ultimately, as the enactment of the War Crimes

Act 1991 suggests, a government sufficiently determined will ensure it has its way. Equally, and for much the same reasons, it is hard to see how the House of Lords could be an effective constitutional safeguard for the citizen. Ultimately, the House will almost always respect the convention of deference to the will of the elected chamber; at best, the House can make the government think again. Rather, the true situation is that the House of Lords, undemocratic as it is, still has a useful role to play in the constitution in enhancing scrutiny of an increasingly powerful executive. Advocates of abolition or reform might better consider how an alternative electoral system, coupled with reform of the Commons and its procedures, allowing for more effective scrutiny and revision of Bills, could yet render the House of Lords superfluous.

7 Parliamentary Privilege

7.1 Introduction

For a Member of Parliament to carry out his duties to his constituents properly he must be free to raise matters without the fear of being sued for slander or libel. Parliamentary privilege allows him to do so within the confines of Parliament itself. There is, of course, the risk of abuse and, in any event, the counter argument that those attacked may not have a chance to defend themselves.

It is sometimes said that the rules of parliamentary privilege constitute a clear case of 'power without responsibility', but it has to be accepted that over the years parliamentary privilege has been essential to the exposure of injustices and malpractices which the restrictive English libel laws might otherwise have allowed to continue unchecked.

As with most of constitutional law it is a matter of striking the right balance; in this area the need for freedom of speech in Parliament has to be respected and, perhaps, all that needs to be changed to achieve the balance is for Parliament itself to be much more willing to impose heavy penalties on those members who are deemed to have abused this privilege.

7.2 Key points

It is important that students understand the following issues regarding parliamentary privilege:

a) *Definition*

Parliamentary privilege is defined by Erskine May in *Parliamentary Practice*, 21st edition, as:

' ... the sum of the peculiar rights enjoyed by each House collectively as a constitutional part of the High Court of Parliament and by members of each House individually, without which they could not discharge their functions, and which exceed those possessed by other bodies or individuals.'

b) *Privileges of the House of Commons*

i) 'Ancient and undoubted rights and privileges'

At the opening of each Parliament, the Speaker formally claims from the Crown for the Commons 'their ancient and undoubted rights and privileges'. These are:

- Freedom of Speech in Debate

  The right is guaranteed in art 9 of the Bill of Rights 1689 which provides:

'the freedom of speech and debates or proceedings in Parliament ought not to be impeached or questioned in any court or place out of Parliament.'

Thus the basic rule is that no MP may be made liable in the courts for words spoken in the course of parliamentary proceedings – what is said in Parliament cannot be used to support a cause of action in defamation: *Church of Scientology of California* v *Johnson-Smith* [1972] 1 QB 522. Whilst this protects MPs as defendants it also has the effect of preventing them from putting in evidence things said in Parliament in order to bring defamation actions as plaintiffs. This aspect of the law has now been amended with the enactment of s13(1) of the Defamation Act 1996 which provides:

'Where the conduct of a person in or in relation to proceedings in Parliament is in issue in defamation proceedings, he may waive for the purposes of those proceedings, so far as concerns him, the protection of any enactment or rule of law which prevents proceedings in Parliament being impeached or questioned in any court or place out of Parliament.'

Note also that in *Pepper* v *Hart* [1993] 1 All ER 42 the court held that account could be taken of extracts from *Hansard* to assist in statutory interpretation. Emphasis was, however, made of the need to give effect to Parliament's intentions, rather than to undermine the independence of MPs.

As indicated in section 8.4 (below), a likely point for consideration in the examination question is what constitutes 'proceedings in Parliament'. Remarks made in debate, discussions in committee, parliamentary questions and answers, and votes are clearly within the definition. Other words spoken within the precincts of Parliament unconnected with parliamentary proceedings are not protected: *Rivlin* v *Bilainkin* [1953] 1 QB 485. Students should note the following statement from Viscount Radcliffe in *Attorney-General for Ceylon* v *De Livera* [1963] AC 103 in which he was considering what was meant by a proceeding in Parliament:

'... the answer given to that somewhat more limited question depends upon the following consideration, in what circumstances and in what situations is a member of the House exercising his "real" or "essential" function as a member? The most that can be said is that, despite reluctance to treat a member's privileges as going beyond anything that is essential, it is generally recognised that it is impossible to regard his only proper functions as a member as being confined to what he does on the floor of the House.'

Particular problems have frequently arisen regarding the status of communications between MPs and ministers: *Case of GWR Strauss MP* (1957–58) HC 227. Such communications may only enjoy qualified privilege under the law of defamation: *Beach* v *Freeson* [1972] QB 14. Letters from members of the public to MPs enjoy only qualified privilege under the law of defamation: *R* v *Rule* [1937] 2 KB 375. Communications between MPs and the Parliamentary Commissioner for Administration are accorded absolute privilege in the law of defamation: Parliamentary Commissioner Act 1967, s10(5). It is instructive to note that s13(5) of the Defamation Act 1996 envisages parliamentary proceedings as encompassing:

1. the giving of evidence before either House or a committee;
2. the presentation or submission of a document to either House or a committee;

3. the preparation of a document for the purposes of or incidental to the transacting of any such business;
4. the formulation, making or publication of a document, including a report, by or pursuant to an order of either House or a committee; and
5. any communication with the Parliamentary Commissioner for Standards or any person having functions in connection with the registration of members' interests.

At common law the fair and accurate reporting of parliamentary proceedings is protected by qualified privilege at common law: *Wason* v *Walter* (1869) LR 4 QB 73; *Cook* v *Alexander* [1974] QB 279. The defence now has a statutory basis: see s15 Defamation Act 1996. Fair and accurate extracts from, or abstracts of, papers published under the authority of Parliament enjoy qualified privilege in the law of defamation: Parliamentary Papers Act 1840.

- Freedom from arrest

  The immunity only applies to civil arrest and extends while Parliament sits and for 40 days before and 40 days after: *Stourton* v *Stourton* [1963] P 302.

  The immunity does not protect members from arrest on criminal charges.

- Freedom of access to Her Majesty whenever occasion shall require; and that the most favourable construction should be placed upon all their proceedings.

ii) Other privileges

The other privileges of the House of Commons, not expressly claimed by the Speaker include:

- The right of the House to regulate its own composition

  The House retains the exclusive right to determine by resolution when a writ for the holding of a by-election shall be issued.

  The House maintains the right to determine whether a member is qualified to sit in the House and can declare a member's seat vacant on grounds of legal disqualification or for any other reason it thinks fit.

  The House may expel a member whom it considers unfit to sit: the *Case of Gary Allighan MP* (1947) HC 138.

- The right to take exclusive cognisance of matters arising within the precincts of the House

  The House maintains the right to control its own proceedings and regulate its internal affairs without interference from the courts: *Bradlaugh* v *Gossett* (1884) 12 QBD 271.

  If a statute is to bind the House it must do so clearly: *R* v *Graham-Campbell, ex parte Herbert* [1935] 1 KB 594.

iii) The right to punish both members and non-members for breach of privilege and contempt

The House has the power to maintain its privileges and to punish those who break or commit contempt of the House.

Contempt of the House is a very wide concept. Erskine May describes it as:

> '... any act or omission which obstructs or impedes either House or Parliament in the performance of its functions, or which obstructs or impedes any member or officer of such House in the discharge of his duty, or which has a tendency, directly or indirectly, to produce such results may be treated as a contempt even though there is no precedent of the offence.'

Thus while the House cannot create new privileges, except by statute, there is no complete list of behaviour which constitutes contempt.

Complaints of breach of privilege may be raised by a member or in the House by the Speaker. If the Speaker rules that a prima facie case has been made out a motion is proposed that the matter be referred to the Committee on Standards and Privileges.

The Committee comprises 15 senior members of the House. It is the master of its own proceedings. It can compel the attendance of witnesses and the production of documents; failure to comply being a contempt. There is no requirement of legal representation.

The Select Committee on Parliamentary Privilege in 1967 recommended that persons directly concerned in the Committee's investigations should have the right to attend its hearings, make submissions, call, examine and cross-examine witnesses, and be legally represented and apply for legal aid.

Offenders may be reprimanded or admonished or committed to prison. Members may be suspended or expelled from the House.

iv) The right of impeachment (now obsolete).

c) *The courts and parliamentary privilege*

The House of Commons claims to be the absolute and sole judge of its own privileges and maintains that its judgment cannot be called into question by any other court. The courts do not agree. They maintain the right to determine the nature and extent of parliamentary privilege when adjudicating upon the rights of individuals outside the house. This disagreement has given rise to constitutional conflict: *Stockdale* v *Hansard* (1839) 9 Ad & E 1; *Case of the Sheriffs of Middlesex* (1840) 11 Ad & E 273.

d) *MPs as representatives of outside interests*

If a member agrees to represent an outside interest group in Parliament, is a threat by that group to remove support from the member a breach of privilege?

i) It is improper for a member to enter into any arrangement fettering his complete independence by undertaking to press some particular point of view on behalf of an outside interest whether for reward or not: *Case of WJ Brown MP* (1947).

ii) It is improper to attempt to punish a member financially because of his actions as a member: *Case of the Yorkshire Area Council of National Union of Mineworkers* (1975).

e) *Privileges of the House of Lords*

The privileges of the House of Lords are similar to those enjoyed by the House of Commons.

f) *The Nolan Report*

The Nolan Report (see comment in Chapter 6) recommended that the House should:

i) require agreements and remuneration relating to parliamentary services to be disclosed;

ii) expand the guidance on avoiding conflicts of interests;

iii) introduce a new code of conduct for members;

iv) appoint a Parliamentary Commissioner for standards;

v) establish a new procedure for investigating and adjudicating on complaints in this area about members.

Controversy has arisen amongst Members of Parliament as to:

i) the extent to which Parliamentarians should enjoy outside interests; and

ii) whether consultancies and other paid work should be reviewed by a body other than Parliament.

7.3 Recent cases

In *R* v *Parliamentary Commissioner for Standards, ex parte Al Fayed* [1998] 1 All ER 93 the Court of Appeal held that the Parliamentary Commissioner for Standards was not amenable to judicial review. Unlike the Ombudsman, who was concerned with the administrative process *outwith* Parliament, the Parliamentary Commissioner for Standards was concerned with the activities and events *within* Parliament. Thus the matters with which the Ombudsman dealt were very much the staple fare of judicial review. By contrast, the courts had always been careful not to trespass on the jurisdiction of Parliament to regulate its own procedure where the subject matter was something wholly concerned with proceedings in Parliament. Lord Woolf MR was further encouraged to this conclusion by the fact that the Parliamentary Commissioner for Standards operated within a framework that included the Committee on Standards in Public Life, and the Select Committee on Standards and Privileges, thus indicating that the way in which he discharged his functions was a matter for scrutiny by Parliament rather than the courts.

7.4 Analysis of questions

This is an important subject and a question on this area in nearly every examination paper can be expected. The question can either be a general essay question requiring a critical discussion of the topic or a problem solving exercise; if the latter, the popular question requires you to consider whether what a particular MP has said about someone comes within the meaning of a 'proceeding in Parliament' so as to be protected by parliamentary privilege and/or whether what a particular newspaper writes about an MP comes within the meaning of qualified privilege so as, once again, to be protected from attack.

7.5 Questions

QUESTION ONE

The House of Commons has too wide a jurisdiction to punish contempts and breaches of privilege.

Discuss.

University of London LLB Examination
(for External Students) Constitutional law June 1984 Q5

General Comment

This is a straightforward essay question requiring the student to show the relationship of Parliament to the courts as regards parliamentary privilege.

Skeleton Solution

Parliamentary privilege:

- courts decide what privileges exist;
- Parliament deals with breaches of such privileges.

Suggested Solution

Parliamentary privilege is part of the law and custom of Parliament evolved by the two Houses in order to protect their freedom to conduct their proceedings without improper interference by the sovereign, the courts, or the public. The privileges enjoyed by the House of Commons include those 'ancient and undoubted privileges' claimed by the Speaker at the beginning of each new Parliament such as freedom of speech in debate, freedom from civil arrest and freedom of access via the Speaker to the sovereign. There are also those privileges enjoyed by the House in its corporate capacity such as the right to regulate its own composition and the right to regulate its own proceedings. These special rights, powers and immunities conferred by parliamentary privilege are justified as being essential for the conduct of the business and the maintenance of the authority of the House.

Parliamentary privileges are part of the common law in so far as their existence and validity are recognised by the courts. But they are enforced not by the courts but exclusively by Parliament. By virtue of its inherent right to control its own proceedings and maintain its dignity, the House of Commons in protecting its privileges may punish those who violate them or commit contempt of the House. Breach of privilege consists of either an abuse of a particular privilege by a member or any conduct which interferes with one of the privileges of Parliament. Contempt is a much wider concept and consists of any conduct which tends to bring the House into disrepute or detract from its dignity. No matter whether the offence is styled a breach of privilege or a contempt, or both, the penal powers of the House are the same. Offenders may be reprimanded or admonished by the Speaker. Members may be suspended or expelled. Officials of the House may be dismissed and any member or stranger may be committed to prison for the duration of the Parliamentary session. However, in discussing the jurisdiction of the House to punish for breach of privilege and contempt a distinction must be drawn between the two.

In the past questions of privilege have been a source of considerable conflict between the Commons and the courts. Indeed, the House still asserts that it is the absolute and sole judge of the extent of its own privileges and has invoked its historical status as part of the High Court of Parliament in claiming that its judgments are not examinable by any other court. But this is a claim to which the courts do not fully accede. While the courts recognise the control which the House has over its own proceedings, in *Stockdale* v *Hansard* (1839) the court maintained the right to determine the nature and the limits of parliamentary privilege when adjudicating upon the rights of individuals outside the House. The court also affirmed that the Commons cannot create new privileges by resolutions of the House, only by statute. Therefore, while the jurisdiction of the House of Commons to punish for breaches of privilege is wide, in the sense that the privileges are enforced exclusively by the House, nevertheless there are limitations, notably the court's power to determine whether the privilege arises and if so its scope and effect. In such cases privilege forms a part of the common law and is subject to it.

But while the House cannot by resolution enlarge the scope of its own privileges, it has not closed the categories of contempt. Therefore, while the courts may assert their jurisdiction to decide the existence and extent of privileges of the House, what constitutes a contempt of the House is essentially a matter which only the House can decide. If a contempt issue arises relating to the internal proceedings of the House, the courts will decline to interfere, and whether in relation to matters inside or outside the House, the courts have always recognised the power of the House to imprison for contempt. It is accepted today that where the cause of committal stated in the return to the writ is insufficient in law, the court may review. But if no cause for committal other than the simple statement of contempt of the House is shown in the return, the court will not make further inquiry into the reasons for the committal. Therefore the jurisdiction of the House of Commons to punish for contempt is very wide. The House has power to commit persons for contempt for whatever conduct it adjudges to amount to contempt, provided that the cause of the contempt is not stated.

QUESTION TWO

Jones is an MP for the constituency of Westhampton which for some time has suffered from a deterioration in relations between the police and the immigrant community. Recently Jones received a letter from a constituent complaining that he had been beaten up by one PC Plod for no reason whatsoever other than the fact that he was black. (This allegation was completely untrue.) Jones decided this was an opportunity to get to grips with the race relations problem and wrote three letters: one to a minister in the Home Office; one to the Westhampton Weekly; and one to the Community Relations Officer of the Local Authority. All the letters repeated the allegation as if it was pure fact. Jones also repeated the allegation in a question to the Secretary of State for the Home Office made during parliamentary question time and the question was reported in the Daily Garble the next day. Jones has also recently been offered a post with the Equality for Immigrants Association in which he is to be paid £5,000 per annum and he is expected to always support measures furthering the interests of the Association.

PC Plod has recently issued writs against the constituent, the Daily Garble and Jones complaining he has been libelled. Furthermore, the Speaker of the House has become aware of the offer of employment made by the EIA.

Discuss the foregoing in the light of the law relating to parliamentary privilege.

Written by the Editors

General Comment

A typical question on the major aspect of parliamentary privilege, namely freedom of speech, requiring a discussion of the relationship of the privilege with the tort of defamation.

Skeleton Solution

Introduction

- Outline nature and basis of parliamentary privilege.
- State types of privilege raised by question, ie freedom of speech, freedom from interference.
- State that the question raises following:

  Is letter from constituent privileged?

  Are letters from Jones privileged?

  Is report by Daily Garble protected by qualified privilege?

  Is employment with EIA against freedom from interference?

Letter from constituent

- Probably not absolutely privileged: *Rivlin* v *Bilainkin* (1953).
- May attract qualified privilege – *R* v *Rule* (1937) – but is he acting maliciously?

Letters from Jones – which ones fall within meaning of 'proceeding in Parliament'?

- Question in house – yes: *Church of Scientology* v *Johnston-Smith* (1972); *Case of GWR Strauss MP* (1957–58).
- Letter to Home Office – yes: *Attorney-General for Ceylon* v *De Livera* (1963).
- Letter to Westhampton Weekly – no.
- Letter to Community Relations Officer – no.

Daily Garble report

- Probably attracts qualified privilege: s7 Defamation Act 1954; *Cook* v *Alexander* (1974); *Beach* v *Freeson* (1972).

The offer of employment

- Jones is restricted in how he can act and also is receiving a payment. Accordingly this offer probably does interfere with his freedom as an MP and would be a contempt: *Case of DFS Henderson MP* (1945); *Case of WJ Brown MP* (1947).

Suggested Solution

In order for MPs to function properly they must be able to carry out their duties freely and without fear of being sued for defamation. Such protections come within the ambit of parliamentary privilege. This question raises two particular privileges as far as Jones is concerned: freedom of speech and freedom from interference. It is also in the public interest that constituents in their complaints to Members of Parliament and newspapers reporting parliamentary matters should also receive a degree of protection from the possibility of being sued for libel. This question also demands a discussion of the extent to which such persons are protected by qualified privilege.

Turning firstly to the letter to Jones from the constituent, in *R* v *Rule* (1937) the appellant wrote a letter to the MP containing defamatory statements about a police officer and a magistrate. It was held that such a letter may attract qualified privilege, ie so long as the author was not motivated by malice he could not be sued for defamation. Further in *Rivlin* v *Bilainkin* (1953) it was suggested that if such a letter concerned matters currently being discussed by Parliament it might be absolutely privileged. On the facts of the instant case since the allegation by the constituent is completely untrue it is difficult to see how he can be said not to be acting maliciously and, therefore, he is likely to be held liable to PC Plod.

As regards the actions by Jones, whether he is absolutely privileged depends on whether they fall within the meaning of 'proceedings in Parliament'. Clearly the question raised in the House of Commons must be a 'proceeding in Parliament' and would be privileged: *Church of Scientology* v *Johnston-Smith* (1972). In the *Attorney-General for Ceylon* v *De Livera* (1963) Viscount Radcliffe stated that it was not only proceedings on the floor of the House that were covered by the expression 'proceedings in Parliament'. His Lordship considered that an MP was protected whenever he was carrying out his 'real' or 'essential' functions as an MP.

It would seem that the letter to the Minister for the Home Office would come within the 'real' or 'essential' functions of Jones and, therefore, be privileged. Support for this can be found in the *Case of GWR Strauss MP* (1957–58). In this case Strauss wrote to the Paymaster General about a nationalised industry. The Select Committee held this letter to be privileged although the matter was then referred to the full House of Commons which decided it was not privileged. However, it is now felt that it would be deemed to be privileged.

On the basis of the above, however, it is doubtful whether the letters to the Westhampton Weekly and the Community Relations Officer can be deemed 'proceedings in Parliament' and would not, therefore, be privileged.

The Daily Garble has reported a 'parliamentary proceeding' namely the question in the House. The Defamation Act 1954 preserves the right of newspapers to accurately and fairly report such proceedings. Such reporting attracts qualified privilege and, since there is no suggestion of malice by the Daily Garble, it will be protected from the defamation action by PC Plod: *Cook* v *Alexander* (1974).

Finally the offer of employment by the Equality for Immigrants Association has to be considered. Jones is to be paid £5,000 for always supporting measures that further the interests of the Association. Two cases fall to be considered in deciding whether this arrangement would be in breach of the privilege against interference.

In the *Case of DFS Henderson* (1945) Henderson asked an MP for help in his negotiations with the Ministry of Agriculture. He offered to pay 100 guineas to the MP's local association if the negotiations were successful. Was this a bribe and, therefore, a contempt of Parliament? It was held that since the payment was not to the MP personally and also because the MP's permission to make such a payment was sought beforehand that there was no contempt. However, such a practice was deemed to be generally objectionable. And in the *Case of WJ Brown* (1947) the MP had been elected General Secretary of the Civil Service Union on condition that it did *not* affect his political independence and that he did *not* have to represent the views of the union. Brown fell out with the Union who voted to remove him as its General Secretary. Brown complained that the Union was trying to interfere with his independence as an MP and was, therefore, in contempt. It was held that Brown had voluntarily placed himself in his position and the actions of the Union could not amount to a contempt.

In Jones' case he clearly is receiving a direct payment and, further, is limiting his political independence because he would have to vote in support of measures in the interests of the EIA whether he agreed with them or not. It is likely, therefore, that the Speaker would report him to the Committee on Standards and Privileges if he accepted the employment and that he would be held to be in contempt. Whilst the Committee has powers to expel and fine Members of Parliament it is often the case that MPs are let off with little more than a stern warning.

QUESTION THREE

Bulldog is a Member of Parliament. He received unsolicited mail from several constituents alleging that a company operating in the constituency had been guilty of gross negligence resulting in financial loss to those constituents. Bulldog raised the matter with the company but received no satisfactory response. He then raised the question of the company's negligence during a debate in the House of Commons. He also sent copies of the letters of complaint to the responsible Minister and had a meeting with that Minister at the Minister's private home during which Bulldog again accused the company of negligence. Bulldog also raised the matter at a public meeting in his constituency. He has since found out that the allegations were not true and has received a letter from the company's solicitors alleging defamation.

To what extent will the doctrine of parliamentary privilege protect him against the threatened defamation action?

Written by the Editors

General Comment

A question requiring the student to identify whether each of the three situations in which Bulldog makes the false allegation against the company can be deemed a 'proceeding in Parliament' so as to come with the parliamentary privilege of freedom of speech and, accordingly, amount to a full defence to an action for defamation.

Skeleton Solution

- Open by explaining what parliamentary privilege is and its legal effect, dealing in particular with the particular privilege of freedom of speech.
- Explain the importance and meaning of 'proceeding in Parliament'.
- Go on to consider each of the situations in which the alleged defamatory remarks have been made and conclude whether or not they are covered by privilege.

Suggested Solution

At the beginning of a parliamentary session the Speaker of the House of Commons claims for Parliament and all its members all those 'ancient and undoubted rights and privileges' that Parliament has traditionally enjoyed. These privileges include such matters as freedom from civil arrest and freedom to regulate Parliament's internal affairs (eg the ordinary licensing laws of the country do not apply inside Parliament: see *R* v *Graham-Campbell, ex parte Herbert* (1935). However the most important of these privileges is freedom of speech in debates and other 'proceedings in Parliament'. What is covered by the privilege cannot be called into question in any court outside Parliament. Parliament itself has its own Committee on Standards and Privileges which can take its members to task if the privilege is abused. But no-one outside Parliament can bring an action for defamation against a Member of Parliament if what he says comes within the ambit of a 'proceeding in Parliament'. This has been defined as applying whenever a Member of Parliament is carrying out his 'real or essential functions' as an MP (see *Attorney-General for Ceylon* v *De Livera* (1963)). This question demands an examination of each of the occasions that Bulldog made the false allegation in order to see whether all or any of those occasions can be properly regarded as 'a proceeding in Parliament' so as to attract the defence of parliamentary privilege.

As regards the letters from the constituents it appears from the case of *Rivlin* v *Bilainkin* (1953) that since the letters do not concern parliamentary proceedings they cannot attract absolute privilege but they can attract qualified privilege (see *R* v *Rule* (1937)). Accordingly unless the company can show malice then the writers are protected from an action of defamation against them for passing the accusation on to Bulldog and, further, Bulldog would be protected when passing the accusation on by sending the letters to the Minister.

Bulldog raises the matter again on the floor of the House during a parliamentary debate. This is clearly 'a proceeding in Parliament' and would be absolutely privileged: see *Church of Scientology* v *Johnson-Smith* (1972). But what about the repetition of the allegation outside Parliament at the Minister's house? As indicated above the case of *Attorney-General for Ceylon* v *De Livera* makes it clear that the privilege is not confined to proceedings within the House of Parliament. Since he is reporting a matter of public concern to the responsible minister I consider that it would be held to be a situation where Bulldog is carrying out his 'real' or 'essential' role as an MP, and would be deemed a 'proceeding in Parliament' and, therefore, absolutely privileged.

Lastly we have to consider the repetition of the allegation at the public meeting in Bulldog's constituency. It is extremely doubtful that such meeting could be described as a 'proceeding in Parliament'. His remarks would, therefore, attract neither absolute nor qualified privilege. He may have the defence of fair comment but I would advise him to offer a public apology to the company as soon as possible in the hope that a financially damaging action for defamation may thereby be avoided.

QUESTION FOUR

'The sole justification for the present privileges of the House of Commons is that they are essential for the conduct of its business and the maintenance of its authority.' (Sir Barnett Cocks)

Discuss.

University of London LLB Examination
(for External Students) Constitutional Law June 1989 Q3

General Comment

An essay question requiring a critical discussion of how far parliamentary privileges are justified today.

Skeleton Solution

- Introduction – original necessity for privilege and examples of privileges.
- Examine privileges in detail pointing out whether they remain essential – freedom of speech,

freedom from civil arrest, right to regulate composition and proceedings and to punish those in contempt or breach of privilege.
- Conclusion.

Suggested Solution

Many of the privileges of Parliament have their origins in the sixteenth and seventeenth centuries at a time when the House of Commons was striving to prove its independence and to prevent interference with its members and proceedings by the Monarch and others outside Parliament. The privileges were originally developed to safeguard the position of MPs individually and that of the House as a whole. Today the privileges established during these centuries still exist but a select committee in 1967 commented that some were no longer required as they had become obsolete and suggested reforms, which have still not been implemented.

At the beginning of each new Parliament the Speaker claims 'ancient and undoubted privileges' which consist of freedom of speech in debate, freedom from civil arrest and freedom of access via the Speaker to the sovereign. The Commons also enjoys privileges in its corporate capacity such as the right to regulate its own composition, the right to take exclusive cognisance of matters arising within the precincts of the House and the right to punish both members and non-members for breach of privilege and contempt.

Perhaps the most important of the privileges of the Commons is that of freedom of speech. It was enshrined in the Constitution by art 9 of the Bill of Rights 1689 and provides 'The freedom of speech and debates or proceedings in Parliament ought not to be impeached or questioned in any court or place out of Parliament.' Practically this means that no criminal prosecution can be launched nor can any civil action for defamation be commenced in respect of words uttered or written during 'debates and proceedings in Parliament.' There is debate over the meaning of the phrase 'proceedings in Parliament' (*Strauss* case (1957–58)) but it seems that for anything said in the House in the course of Parliamentary business (such as debates or committee hearings etc) the MP has immunity. Potentially MPs could abuse this privilege by knowingly making false statements in the House but it was considered that this danger was outweighed by the public interest in ensuring that MPs could speak freely when carrying out Parliamentary business. It should be noted that if an MP does abuse his privilege it is open to the House itself to punish him for contempt of Parliament or to expel him from the House as unfit (*Allighan* (1947)).

The privilege of freedom of speech also prevents those outside Parliament attempting to dictate to MPs how they should speak in debate and/or vote. Although it is acknowledged that MPs may maintain business and other interests outside Parliament there is a Register of Members' Interests in which each MP is supposed to declare his other activities. Article 9 has been used to stop such outside commitments being used to force an MP into a particular course of action in the Chamber (*Yorkshire Area Council of the National Union of Mineworkers* case (1975)).

In these ways the privilege of freedom of speech remains important to the Houses of Parliament.

By contrast the privilege of freedom from civil arrest is obsolete and is long overdue for repeal. It provides that for the forty days before, during a session and for the forty days after it an MP may not be subject to civil (not criminal) arrest. Although this was needed when the usual method of enforcing a debt was to incarcerate the debtor in a debtors' prison which, in the absence of the immunity, could have effectively disenfranchised large numbers of voters it is no longer required when arrest in civil proceedings is rare indeed.

Freedom of access via the speaker to the sovereign is today merely a formality but the Common's powers to regulate its own composition and internal proceedings remain relevant. Election petitions are no longer determined by the Commons itself, but by an election court made up of High Court judges, but the Commons still determines when to move a writ for a by election to fill any vacancies which arise. It may also declare that a member is unfit and expel him from the House. The House regulates its own proceedings and the courts will not take cognisance of these procedures even when these conflict with statute as in *Bradlaugh* v *Gossett* (1884), where an MP was refused permission by the Commons to make his oath of allegiance in a form permitted by statute. The court's refusal to interfere in Parliament's internal procedure is exemplified in *Pickin* v *British Railways Board* (1974) where the fact that notices had apparently not been given by promoters of a private Bill so as to satisfy orders of the House of Lords did not lead to the invalidity of the Act of Parliament subsequently passed. This attitude is one aspect of the doctrine of parliamentary sovereignty and there has been criticism of the fact that the courts do not intervene in such cases.

One aspect of Parliament's right to regulate its own conduct is its jurisdiction to punish breach of privilege and contempt of Parliament. Breach of privileges, consists of abuse of privilege by a member or of any conduct by any one MP or non member which interferes with one of the privileges of Parliament. Contempt is a wider concept and consists of conduct which tends to bring the House into disrepute or detract from its dignity. Whether the offence is breach of privilege or contempt, the penal powers of the House are the same. Members may be reprimanded or admonished by the Speaker or Members may be suspended or expelled. Officials of the House may be dismissed or a Member or stranger may be committed to prison for the duration of the Parliamentary Session. The Select Committee on Parliamentary Privileges recommended that the punitive powers of the Commons and Lords be curtailed and although no such reform has been formally made, in practice the Commons seems reluctant to do more than give a reprimand to outsiders found to be in contempt (even where as in 1986 the then Committee of Privileges had recommended that a lobby correspondent be expelled for six months with his paper, *The Times*, being allowed no substitute for that period). The most severe penalty it uses in respect of MPs is suspension.

The procedure by which complaints of breach of privilege or contempt of Parliament are made is open to criticism. At present a member may complain to the Speaker and the Speaker may refer the matter to the Committee on Standards and Privileges. This committee can compel attendance of witnesses and production of documents. Failure to comply is a contempt. The Select Committee on Parliamentary Privileges in 1967 recommended that persons directly concerned in the Committee's investigation should have the right to attend the hearings, make submissions, call and examine witnesses. Also legal aid, with leave of the Committee, should be granted. These recommendations were not implemented.

Furthermore even when the Committee on Standards and Privileges has reached its conclusion on the evidence that decision is not binding on the House which may reject it (eg *Strauss* (1957–58)). This state of affairs can hardly be justified in cases where the Commons might take a harsher point of view without hearing the evidence. However normally the Commons as a whole take a more lenient view than the Committee.

It does seem that this area is ripe for reform but such reform is unlikely to materialise in the near future as it is not seen by political parties as a priority.

QUESTION FIVE

What reforms, if any, should be made to the privileges of the House of Commons?

University of London LLB Examination
(for External Students) Constitutional Law June 1991 Q5

General Comment

It is desirable to set out the main privileges and then deal with the more significant privileges in detail. Most of the answer will be concerned with the privilege of free speech as this is currently the most contentious. In some cases it is desirable to point out that privileges need not be reformed because they are not being abused in practice.

Skeleton Solution

- List the main privileges.
- Explain freedom of speech, possible abuses, reform of its scope.
- Consider freedom from arrest; little need for this any more.
- Other privileges considered briefly.

Suggested Solution

The principal privileges claimed from the Crown for the Commons are freedom of speech in debate, freedom from arrest, freedom of access to Her Majesty whenever occasion shall require, the right to have the most favourable construction placed upon all their proceedings, the right of the House to regulate its own composition, the right to take exclusive cognisance of matters arising within the precincts of the House, the right to punish both members and non-members for breach of privilege and contempt, and the right of impeachment.

a) *Freedom of speech*

Freedom of speech is of fundamental importance to the freedom and indeed the power of Parliament. If members could be attacked by the public or the executive for speaking their minds they might be so intimidated as not to be able to carry out their deliberative and legislative functions properly. The right is guaranteed in art 9 of the Bill of Rights 1689 which provides:

'The freedom of speech and debates or proceedings in Parliament ought not to be impeached or questioned in any court or place out of Parliament.'

The effect of art 9 is that no member may be made liable in the courts for words spoken in the course of parliamentary proceedings. If a member were to be sued for defamation in respect of something said during the course of parliamentary proceedings, the writ should be struck out as declaring no cause of action. If the matter did come to trial the court must hold that the member is protected by absolute privilege in the law of defamation. This protection extends to both civil and criminal liability. Nor can what is said in Parliament be used to support a cause of action in defamation where the MP is a defendant (see further *Church of Scientology* v *Johnson-Smith* (1972)). But, as a result of the enactment of s13 of the Defamation Act 1996, an MP can now waive parliamentary privilege and pursue an action in defamation that requires him or her to adduce as evidence statements made during proceedings in Parliament.

It has not been seriously suggested that the parliamentary privilege of free speech be removed, otherwise than at the behest of the member in question, but reliance upon it by members has from time to time been criticised. The danger is that members will make statements in the House under the cloak of privilege that they would not dream of repeating outside. The reputations of others can be damaged without any right of compensation. The MP Geoffrey Dickins was heavily criticised when he threatened to reveal the name of a doctor who had allegedly raped an eight year old girl, but against whom the police had declined to take proceedings due to lack of evidence. As was pointed out, the danger in such cases is that the individual named may have his career ruined by such statements, without ever having been convicted of the alleged offence in a court of law. It is submitted that such abuses of privilege are best dealt with, not by reforming the scope of the privilege, but by relying upon the Speaker of the House to properly regulate the conduct of debate in the House. It is conceded, however, that one aspect of this privilege that could be clarified is the scope of the expression 'proceedings in Parliament'. Remarks made in debate, discussions in committee, parliamentary questions and answers, and votes are clearly within the definition. Other words spoken within the precincts of Parliament unconnected with parliamentary proceedings are not protected. There are 'grey areas' however, as illustrated by the so-called *Strauss* affair (1957–58), which concerned a letter written by Strauss, a Labour MP, to the Paymaster General complaining about the way in which the London Electricity Board disposed of their scrap cable. The Paymaster General denied responsibility on the ground that the matter concerned day to day administration rather than policy, and he passed the letter to the Board. The Board took exception to Strauss' allegations and threatened to sue him for libel unless he withdrew and apologised. Strauss raised the threat as a question of privilege and the matter was referred to the what was then the Committee of Privileges. The Committee reported that in writing his letter Strauss was engaged in a proceeding in Parliament for the purposes of art 9 and that the Board, in threatening to sue, were in breach of parliamentary privilege. However when the Report of the Committee was debated in the House, on a free vote it rejected the findings of the Committee. The House resolved that Strauss' letter was not a proceeding in Parliament. See further *Rost* v *Edwards* (1990).

b) *Freedom from arrest*

Immunity from arrest is now of little importance and in 1967 the Committee on Parliamentary Privilege appointed to review the law of parliamentary privilege recommended its abolition. The immunity only applies to civil arrest and extends not only while Parliament sits, but also for 40 days before and after. The immunity does not protect members from arrest on criminal charges, nor from detention under regulations made under the Defence of the Realm Acts in time of war. In 1940, for example, the Commons Committee of Privileges was of opinion that there had been no breach of privilege when Captain Ramsay, a member, had been detained under regulations made under the Emergency Powers (Defence) Act 1939. There is little basis for the continued existence of the privilege.

c) *The right of the House to regulate its own composition*

Within the scope of this privilege fall a number of matters which are important as matters of principle, but which are of little significance in everyday terms. The privilege, which encompasses the right to determine disputed elections, the right to determine by resolution when a writ for the holding of a by-election shall be issued, the right to determine whether a member is qualified to sit in the House, and the right to expel a member whom it considers unfit to sit, has been used sparingly. Provided these powers are not used oppressively, it is submitted that they are not in need of any substantive reform.

d) *The right to punish for breach of privilege and contempt*

The House has the power to maintain its privileges and to punish those who break them or commit contempt of the House. All breaches of privilege are contempts of the House but not all contempts involve the infringement of the existing privileges of the House. Contempt of the House is a very wide concept. Perhaps the most questionable aspect of this system is the fact that the House sits as victim, prosecutor and judge when dealing with offenders. It is noteworthy that in proceedings before the European Commission on Human Rights it was held that the jurisdiction of the Maltese House of Representatives, to punish those alleged to have been in breach of its privileges, contravened art 6(1) of the European Convention on Human Rights.

QUESTION SIX

Critically assess the respective roles of the House of Commons and the courts in regulating Parliamentary privilege.

University of London LLB Examination
(for External Students) Constitutional Law June 1993 Q8(b)

General Comment

A wide-ranging question, requiring the examinee to look at privilege from the angles of the House of Commons (by character prejudiced angles) and of the courts (by character independent angles). But assessment of those angles should take place in the context of the historical development of privilege, which at least gives a kind of rational basis to Parliament's exclusive claims in several important areas. Critical analysis should be supported by reference to appropriate academic research.

Skeleton Solution

- Definition of parliamentary privilege and problems of control.
- Internal proceedings of the House and risk of abuse of collective power.
- Roles of Speaker and Standards and Privileges Committee.
- Manner of hearing for alleged contemnors.
- Scope of privilege of free speech under art 9 Bill of Rights 1689.
- Internal discipline and absence of judicial review.
- Vagueness of concept of 'proceedings in Parliament' and case for and against codification.

(Other reform proposals are considered at appropriate points during the solution.)

Suggested Solution

Parliamentary privilege is part of the common law which grants certain exemptions from the law to MPs in order that they may perform their functions. By its nature privilege is difficult to subject to normal processes of parliamentary and judicial review. There is the added complication that parliamentary privilege was won after an historic conflict between the legislature and an absolute monarchy (the latter at times supported by the judges). This explains the traditional sensitivity of the relationship between the legislature and the judiciary on the matter of privilege, raising fears for the Rule of Law.

Dicey argued for equality under the law, but the internal proceedings of the House of Commons are not subject to judicial review. Control, if any, must be exercised by the Commons itself, principally through the Speaker and the Select Committee on Standards and Privileges. The danger is that the House, collectively, may act as judge and jury in its own cause on a matter concerning an individual MP's rights to represent the constituency which elected him, eg as in the House's expulsion for political reasons of the radical Charles Bradlaugh: *Bradlaugh* v *Gossett* (1884). Since no judicial review is available over such a decision, the only remedy for an expelled member is to petition the House which expelled him: *Case of the Sheriffs of Middlesex* (1840).

The House also claims exclusive rights to punish 'strangers' (non-MPs) for breaches of MPs' individual privileges and for contempt of the whole House. These are dealt with either by rulings from the Speaker or by reference to the Committee on Standards and Privileges, consisting of 15 MPs from all parties chosen for their expertise in parliamentary law and their long experience of the life of the Commons. But MPs not on the Committee as well as academic observers, have expressed fears about the degree of discretion delegated to the Speaker and the Committee by the whole House. The methods used to deal with 'offenders' are far removed from 'due process of law'.

For example, the accused may be arrested by the Sergeant-at-Arms (the enforcement officer of the House) and brought before a private hearing of the Committee. The accused has no right to legal representation and may be cross-examined by a panel of QCs. The accused has no right to call evidence or to cross-examine the witnesses against him. The Committee reports to the whole House on whether the offence is proven and, if so, what penalty (including, in theory, imprisonment) should be imposed. There is no right of appeal to the courts against conviction or sentence and no opportunity for judicial review over the way the decision was reached.

It is not surprising that authorities such as the late Professor de Smith condemned privilege hearings as a 'travesty of justice' in which biased MPs acted as judges in their own cause. He argued cogently that, with a modern independent judiciary, such privileges were not necessary and that the House's jurisdiction over punishable contempts and breaches of privilege should be transferred to the courts so that these matters are subject to due process of law.

Similarly it has been argued that the House no longer needs the absolute rights to freedom of speech granted in respect of 'proceedings in Parliament' by art 9 of the Bill of Rights 1688. Such freedom has the potential to become a licence to defame, to be used irresponsibly by publicity-seeking members. Whilst the House, through the Speaker, has the power under its internal standing orders to discipline members who abuse the right, it appears that the House has been very reluctant to exercise such discipline, at least over an MP who criticises the conduct of outsiders. When an MP criticises the behaviour or integrity of a fellow MP this is usually taken more seriously and the speaker will demand a retraction and issue warnings about the need for 'parliamentary language in respect of the honourable members of this House'. Some MPs, eg Labour MPs Brian Sedgemore and Tam Dalyell in the 1980s, were suspended from sittings of the House because of their refusals to retract accusations against particular MPs (who were also Government Ministers).

Patricia Leopold ([1981] PL 30) suggests that the House should introduce new safeguards on this matter, eg new conventions which oblige MPs to give advance notice to the person they intend to criticise, and to use all other methods to establish the truth of particular rumours/allegations before ventilating them under the cover of privilege. Others have argued that the absolute privilege under art 9 should be replaced by the defence of qualified privilege, giving MPs the same degree of protection as given to everyone else by the law of defamation.

The fact that MPs can now waive parliamentary privilege in order to pursue actions for defamation where they seek to adduce as evidence their statements made during the course of parliamentary proceedings (see s13 Defamation Act 1996) has also been criticised. Opponents of the change have warned against upsetting the delicate balance of the unwritten constitution, and have pointed out that it might result in Parliament surrendering its collective privilege at the behest of one member. It was also envisaged that conflicts between Parliament and the courts could arise where it was alleged in the course of an MP being cross-examined that he or she had lied to the House of Commons. The contrary view, expressed by Lord Hoffman during the passage of what became the 1996 Act, is that, whilst there is an obvious public interest in maintaining absolute privilege in respect of proceedings in Parliament, there is (arguably) no obvious corresponding public interest in allowing absolute privilege to those commenting upon the way in which members discharge their functions in the House.

Further difficulties remain in respect of determining the scope of the concept of 'proceedings in Parliament': see the inability of the Judicial Committee of the Privy Council to reach a decided view on this point in the reference arising from the *Strauss* case (1957–58). Only a bold judge would feel able to give the benefit of any doubt to the citizen when faced with a claim to privilege, eg Popplewell J in declaring that the Register of MPs' Interests was not privileged in *Rost* v *Edwards* (1990). Miss Leopold ([1990] PL 475) commends this 'robust' attitude but argues that the matter is too important to be left to haphazard development of the common law, contending that the area of privilege requires codification on lines of Australia's Parliamentary Proceedings Act 1987.

In this regard it should be noted that s13(5) of the Defamation Act 1996 does attempt such a codification for the purposes of that provision and defines proceedings in Parliament as encompassing:

a) the giving of evidence before either House or a committee;

b) the presentation or submission of a document to either House or a committee;

c) the preparation of a document for the purposes of or incidental to the transacting of any such business;

d) the formulation, making or publication of a document, including a report, by or pursuant to an order of either House or a committee; and

e) any communication with the Parliamentary Commissioner for Standards or any person having functions in connection with the registration of members' interests.

8 The Executive

8.1 Introduction

The executive includes the monarchy, ministers, central government, the civil service, armed forces and the police. The monarchy is bound by convention and executive functions are largely exercised by ministers. With the advent of the Cabinet, policies decided by government form the basis of legislation passed by Parliament. The Prime Minister enjoys enormous powers because of his position as head of the Cabinet.

8.2 Key points

a) *The Prime Minister*

i) Formal position of the Prime Minister

- The office of Prime Minister is a de facto institution recognised by statute but governed mainly by convention.
- The office of Prime Minister is invariably held together with the office of First Lord of the Treasury: Ministerial and Other Salaries Act 1975.
- On the creation of the Civil Service Department in 1968 the Prime Minister became Minister for the Civil Service.

ii) Choosing a Prime Minister

- The choice of Prime Minister is a matter for the Queen alone in the exercise of the sovereign's personal prerogative.
- By convention however the Queen should choose that person who is able to command the support of the majority in the House of Commons.

iii) Functions of the Prime Minister

- Formation of the government: Ministers are appointed by the Queen on the advice of the Prime Minister. All ministers must be or become members of one or other House of Parliament. There may be up to 95 holders of ministerial office in the House of Commons: House of Commons Disqualification Act 1975.
- Formation of the Cabinet: The choice of a Conservative Cabinet is a matter entirely in the Prime Minister's discretion, although his choice will be influenced by political expediency. The Labour Shadow Cabinet is elected.
- Presiding over Cabinet meetings: The Prime Minister presides over full Cabinet meetings and also over meetings of the most important committees of the Cabinet.

The Prime Minister decides the agenda for Cabinet meetings and controls discussion within the Cabinet. At the conclusion of a Cabinet meeting no formal vote is taken on the policy decided; it is for the Prime Minister to sum up the consensus opinion. The Cabinet Secretariat is directly responsible to the Prime Minister and the allocation of functions between Cabinet, committees of the Cabinet and individual departments is controlled by him.

- The organisation and control of central government: The Prime Minister decides how government functions should be allocated between departments and may create, amalgamate or abolish government departments. The Prime Minister may also take an interest in the affairs of particular departments and intervene personally in major issues and take decisions without consulting Cabinet.
- Powers of patronage: By convention the Prime Minister advises the Queen on the granting of peerages and other honours and on appointments to certain high offices of state.
- Advising the Sovereign: The Prime Minister is the main channel of communication between the Cabinet and the sovereign, and it is his duty to keep the Queen informed on matters of state.
- Presentation and defence of government policy: Prime Minister's interventions in debate always attract media attention. The Prime Minister also controls government communications and the dissemination of information.

b) *The Cabinet*

i) Composition of the Cabinet

The number of ministers in the Cabinet is the sole choice of the Prime Minister. Usually it comprises between 18 and 23 members. The composition of the Cabinet is also a matter for the Prime Minister's discretion. However by convention and custom certain ministers are always members of the Cabinet.

ii) Conventions relating to Cabinet government

- The Queen must act on the advice of her ministers.
- The Cabinet must always tender unanimous advice.
- The Cabinet must obtain and maintain a majority in the House of Commons on all major matters of policy.
- The Cabinet must produce a 'Queen's Speech' at the opening of each session of Parliament, stating the legislation which it proposes during that session.
- The 'mandate' doctrine requires the government's statement in the Queen's speech to be consistent with the policy on which they were elected.

iii) Cabinet committees

A complicated system of Cabinet committees exists to facilitate the discussion and formulation of policy options and to co-ordinate the activities of the various government departments, with regard to policy.

iv) The Cabinet Secretariat

In 1917 a Secretary to the Cabinet was appointed to service Cabinet and Cabinet committee meetings, take minutes and circulate details of conclusions reached in

Cabinet. The Secretariat is headed by the Permanent Secretary to the Cabinet Office who is directly responsible to the Prime Minister.

v) Prime Minister's Policy Unit

The Prime Minister maintains a Policy Unit in Downing Street, independent of the Cabinet Office.

vi) Cabinet secrecy

As all ministers must support government policy it is desirable that the process by which such policy decisions are made be kept secret, unless the Prime Minister decides otherwise, therefore secrecy is attached to discussions in Cabinet, Cabinet papers and the proceedings of Cabinet committees.

c) *Prime Ministerial or Cabinet government?*

i) The Cabinet is the engine house of government. Administrative action is co-ordinated and legislative initiatives sanctioned in the Cabinet. Cabinet can therefore exert significant control over Parliament.

However, the special position enjoyed by the Prime Minister has led some authorities to the conclusion that Cabinet government has now given way to Prime Ministerial government.

A Prime Minister is, however, dependent on the support of Cabinet members which once withdrawn makes continued office untenable. This was the position when Margaret Thatcher resigned following the party vote on the leadership contest. It had originally been her intention to continue to the final ballot but she was advised against this action by ministers.

ii) The power of Prime Minister relative to the Cabinet depends upon several factors:

- The personality of the particular Prime Minister.
- The standing of the Prime Minister both in Parliament and in the Party.
- Whether the Prime Minister is minded to take full advantage of the conventional powers available to the holder of the office.

d) *Collective responsibility*

The doctrine of collective responsibility involves two rules:

i) The rule that the government must resign if it loses the support of the House of Commons.

The Prime Minister and his ministers are collectively responsible to Parliament for the conduct of national affairs. If the Prime Minister loses support in Parliament he must resign or seek a dissolution of Parliament.

ii) The rule that the government must speak with one voice.

- All members of the government share in the collective responsibility of the government, and ministers may not publicly criticise or dissociate themselves from the government policy.
- A Cabinet minister who feels unable to agree with his colleagues should resign.
- The rule is closely related to that of Cabinet secrecy. As all ministers must support

government policy it is desirable that the process by which such policy decisions are made be kept secret.

- The rule increases party discipline and unity within the government and also serves to strengthen the authority of the Prime Minister in relation to his colleagues.

e) *Agreements to differ*

Occasionally it may be politically impossible for the Cabinet to maintain a collective front.

i) The National government 1932: The Liberal members of the National government only agreed to remain in the government on condition that they were allowed to speak and vote against it on the question of the imposition of tariffs.

ii) The Labour government 1975: The Labour Cabinet 'agreed to differ' on the question of the United Kingdom's continued membership of the European Community.

f) *Individual responsibility*

Ministers are responsible to Parliament for their own actions, omissions and mistakes as well as for those of the officials in their departments. Normally criticism should be directed at the minister rather than at any civil servant who may be at fault. This principle is said to help preserve the anonymity, and therefore the objectivity and efficiency, of the Civil Service.

i) Ministerial responsibility for departmental maladministration

Two questions arise from the minister's departmental responsibility:

- Is the minister obliged to accept responsibility for every piece of maladministration within his department?
- If maladministration is found to have occurred is the minister under a duty to resign?

ii) Situations in which a minister must accept responsibility

In a debate on the Crichel Down Affair 1954, the Home Secretary stated his views as to when a minister must accept responsibility and not blame his civil servants:

- A minister must protect a civil servant who has carried out his explicit orders.
- A minister must defend a civil servant who acts properly in accordance with the policy laid down by the minister.
- Where an official makes a mistake or causes some delay, but not on an important issue of policy and not where a claim to individual rights is seriously involved, the minister acknowledges the mistake and he accepts the responsibility although he is not personally involved.
- Where action has been taken by a civil servant of which the minister disapproves and has no previous knowledge, and the conduct of the official is reprehensible, there is no obligation on a minister to endorse what he believes to be wrong or to defend what are clearly shown to be errors of his officers. He remains, however, constitutionally responsible to Parliament for the fact that something has gone wrong, but this does not affect his power to control and discipline his staff.

iii) Is there a duty to resign?

There is no suggestion that a minister has to resign if he does accept responsibility.

Whether a minister has to resign or not depends upon a variety of political factors including:

- the temperament of the minister;
- the attitude of the Prime Minister; and
- the mood of the party and the tone of the Opposition.

Note the recent tendency to confine responsibility to 'policy' rather than 'operation' of policy.

g) *The courts and ministerial responsibility*

While the courts cannot enforce the convention of ministerial responsibility they are prepared to acknowledge its existence: *Carltona Ltd* v *Commissioners of Works* [1943] 2 All ER 560.

8.3 Recent developments

An up-to-date knowledge of political affairs as they affect the role of the Prime Minister and government ministers is important.

In August 1997 a revised version of the code of practice *Questions of Procedure for Ministers* was promulgated by Prime Minister Blair. The code reflect issues raised in the Nolan Report and also the Scott Report on the 'Arms to Iraq' affair. Ministers are expected to comply with both the letter and the spirit of the code.

The code expressly states that ministers must 'give accurate and truthful information to Parliament, correcting any inadvertent error at the earliest opportunity', and makes clear that 'ministers who knowingly mislead Parliament will be expected to offer their resignation to the Prime Minister'.

The code also provides that ministers should:

a) uphold the political impartiality of the Civil Service, and not to ask civil servants to act in any way which would conflict with the Civil Service Code – in particular ministers should not ask civil servants to attend part conferences or policy groups of any parliamentary party;

b) give fair consideration and due weight to informed and impartial advice from civil servants, as well as to other considerations and advice, in reaching decisions;

c) comply with the law, including international law and treaty obligations, and to uphold the administration of justice;

d) make efficient use of official cars and other publicly funded travel arrangements – air miles and other benefits earned whilst travelling on government business should be forgone or used against official travel;

e) be scrupulous in avoiding any apparent conflict of interest between their private affairs (or those of a spouse) and their public duties, particularly in relating to financial matters.

f) report all gifts to the permanent secretary – those exceeding £140 in value should not be accepted.

Ministers should not:

a) use public resources for party political purposes – in particular ministers should not use government property in connection with constituency work;

b) accept payment (other than donations to an agreed charity) for public speeches of an official nature;

c) take any active part in the affairs of any union of which he might be a member.

The revised code also reinforces the Prime Minister's control over his Cabinet colleagues by providing that the assignment of duties to junior ministers outside the Cabinet will have to have Prime Ministerial approval, as will the appointment of special advisers to Cabinet ministers. The importance of ensuring a co-ordinated presentation of government policy is also underlined by the requirement that all major interviews and media events, and the content of key policy speeches and press releases, should be agreed first with the Prime Minister's office.

The Nolan Committee's first report on *Standards in Public Life* dealt in particular with the growing criticism directed at ministers taking up lucrative posts in industry immediately following resignation from ministerial office. As a result ministers are now subject to restrictions similar to those imposed on senior civil servants who resign to take up private sector employment. The code provides that ministers wishing to take up paid employment within two years of leaving office should seek guidance from the Advisory Committee on Business Appointments. It is perhaps significant that the matter could not be left to the common sense of the ministers concerned.

8.4 Analysis of questions

Questions are essay type and often test students' knowledge of the conventions of ministerial responsibility. A good understanding of the function of Parliament and accountability of government is required.

8.5 Questions

QUESTION ONE

'Parliamentary experience of recent years has demonstrated that collectively Members (of the House of Commons) can exercise the political will necessary to provide the parameters within which the Government can govern, albeit of necessity in a limited and generally negative way.' (Norton)

Discuss.

University of London LLB Examination
(for External Students) Constitutional Law June 1990 Q1

General Comment

A difficult question that requires students to identify ways in which MPs can influence and hold to account the government.

Skeleton Solution

- Parliamentary accountability – the extent to which government is truly accountable for its actions: conventions of accountability; committee system; ombudsman; debate, question time.
- Conclusion: separation of powers; legislature's control over the executive.

Suggested Solution

The starting point of the constitution is the representation of the electorate in Parliament, which is the supreme and sovereign law maker. Developed from this is the notion that the electorate thereby makes its preferred choice of government. However, for obvious practical reasons, elections cannot be held every year, nor can referendums be held on all points of importance that arise during a government's term of office. Thus, the accountability of government directly to the electorate is only periodic and it is this situation that gives rise to the fear of the possibility of an 'elective dictatorship', with a carte blanche to govern in whichever way it pleases for the term of its office.

To a certain extent this is an ill founded fear since the final reckoning will ultimately come with the dissolution of Parliament. Of more concern, however, is the situation that arises where, for the most part, a government's policies and style of government finds general approval, but where particular measures are potentially constitutionally threatening.

In such circumstances, government becomes indirectly accountable to the representatives of the electorate in Parliament and as such Parliament is termed the 'watchdog' of executive action. Since the Commons is the elected chamber and the focus of most political activity, without dismissing the important work of the Lords, it must clearly be the area where the ground rules of governmental activity are laid down.

Thus in purist theory, the political arm of the executive is collectively responsible to Parliament in general and to the House of Commons in particular. The idiomatic traditions of Parliament provide the forum for the supervision of government. The experience of recent years has brought much attention to bear on how effective these complex constraints and restrictions are when the Commons is effectively dominated by the party that holds office.

Before considering in detail the general parliamentary restrictions on government activity, it must be made clear that the mere fact that a party commands a majority in the House does not guarantee a majority of votes. Even where the whip system that urges members to comply is in strict operation, a member cannot be forcibly compelled to vote with the government. Although the price of such rebellion might be suspension from the parliamentary party, such defiance often has a profound political consequence and may be the prompt for revision of legislation when the action is taken in concert.

As well as such purely political considerations, the application of conventions relating to the accountability individually and collectively of ministers establishes a further set of checks which are enforced through Parliament. The intense political embarrassment caused by ministerial or departmental misfeasance usually finds its focus in parliamentary questions or debates, where, on serious issues, the choice of either a convincing explanation or resignation is expected to be forthcoming.

Similarly, where decisions are made at Cabinet level, ministers are held collectively to account to Parliament. As De Smith observes, if a minister dissents he should resign first, and then publicly distance himself from the subject in contention. However, the purist theory lacks a little in substance, since a suspension of the convention is possible and the government attitude seems to be enshrined not a little in Mr Callaghan's remark that 'I certainly think the doctrine should apply, except in cases where I announce that it does not.' This indeed indicates the extent of the 'flexibility' of our unwritten constitution.

Parliament, if it feels so inclined, may censure the government with a motion of no confidence where the government is held to be collectively responsible. Of convention, such a motion, if it were successful, would prompt the resignation of the government. In recent years, however, Mrs Thatcher was censured on specific issues without subsequently leaving office. Once again it is the 'flexible' constitution at work. The significance of such a motion is to be viewed more in terms of a political tactic and a method of attracting media attention.

A more direct and effective control of government is the need for parliamentary approval for the financing of government initiatives. Since Parliament holds the country's purse strings, the government must inspire enough confidence in the Commons, at least to provide funding for new policies. The structure of government finance is necessarily complex, but the parliamentary system is structured so as to cope with these rigours. Central to this system is the Public Accounts Committee, which, although reflecting the parliamentary representation of the parties, has such a non-partisan reputation that it is, by convention, chaired by a member of the opposition. Although it primarily seeks out financial irregularities, it also monitors extravagant spending and imprudent contractual transactions.

Extensive powers of discovery and enquiry were conferred on the Treasury and Civil Service Committee, which was set up in 1979, to the extent that scrutinising Treasury policy is within the Committee's brief. In such ways Parliament tacitly defines the parameters within which the executive can finance its policies.

Aside from these financial controls, the standing orders and procedures of the Commons provide adequate opportunities for confrontation of the government by the opposition and their own back benchers on contentious issues. Debating opportunities on the Queen's speech, budget and on opposition days, motions of censure and others and emergency debates take on more significance with the eye of the country fixed on television.

The committee system now mirrors the departmental organisation of central government with the setting up of select committees to examine the expenditure, administration and policy of various designated government departments. Their powers are the same as those of the Treasury and Civil Service Committee and are brought together under the auspices of the Liaison Committee. The force of the House's authority and powers to punish for contempt are behind these committees.

The teeth of the Defence Select Committee were tested during the 'Westland Affair' (1986) when it sought to discover the names of civil servants who were responsible for the leaking of a letter from the Solicitor General. Although the government achieved a compromise, the Committee never conceded that in law there were any governmental restraints on the exercise of its functions.

The departmental select committee system is generally regarded as a forum for more in-depth and informed discussion than is available elsewhere in Parliament. Furthermore, their unanimous, but often powerfully critical reports, such as that of the Foreign Affairs Committee on government proposals to raise fees for overseas university students, have certainly had effects on executive policy. However, the paucity of free debating time means that only a handful of the reports have had full discussion on the floor of the House of Commons.

Parliament's role as the arena for airing criticism of the government has been significantly augmented by the advent of television cameras. Certainly the parliamentary proceeding that most captivates the imagination of the electorate is Question Time, when the government at least appears to be under the most stringent attack. The extent to which the request for oral or written answers to questions to any minister is actually laying down the parameters of government, rather than political point scoring, is somewhat questionable. However, it is clear that the electoral fortunes of a party or MP may be decided in the cut and thrust of these brief sessions, something of which the government is clearly aware. However, De Smith's view that 'a question to a minister is rather a method of ventilating a grievance than of securing a remedy' is perhaps the most realistic approach.

In addition to the practical limitations of parliamentary questions as a method of scrutinising the government, certain questions may be refused if they lie outside the sphere of competence of a minister. Answers may not be forthcoming if the matter is sub judice, or simply because an answer would cost more than £250, the current ceiling for expenditure on parliamentary answers.

A final method available to members to ensure the maintenance of the standards of government is by directing the Parliamentary Commissioner for Administration to investigate alleged maladministration. However, this function is one that is seldom exercised collectively, and therefore merits no detailed discussion.

Thus, having explored the way in which members might scrutinise the executive, we must assess the truth of Norton's assertions. In our parliamentary system, strong reliance is placed upon adherence to conventions. The effect of disapproving motions relating to conventions of responsibility cannot be denied; resignations in the 1988–89 parliamentary session underline this. However, the change in attitude towards, for example, the motion of censure, demonstrates that reliance on convention as a method of executive control is unsatisfactory, particularly when a government commands a sizeable majority in the Commons.

Equally, there are limits on the extent to which control of the government can be exercised by intermittent rebellions of back bench members, who stand to lose their status within the parliamentary party and with the electorate.

Financial control holds out the most practical promise as delineating the parameters of government, but once again is subject to the control of the majority party in the House, which is almost always subject to strict party discipline.

It is therefore in the arena of the debating floor and during Question Time, which, due to its high media profile, is of great significance in terms of public opinion, that the democratic check on the executive finds its strongest weapon. Where MPs collectively know that public opinion supports them against government policy, even back benchers of the party in power may find a reservoir of courage to criticise and rebel.

Conversely, the committee system is increasingly being regarded as the part of the Commons where much of the serious work goes on. With its smaller and more informed membership, and its greater opportunities for detailed and lengthy scrutiny, as well as the tendency of committees to be less partisan or concerned with political point scoring, this forum has become in many ways a powerhouse of the democratic process. Opportunities exist not only to criticise, but to make searching enquiries of the way in which the process of government is carried on.

It is difficult to envisage, however, what Norton's conception of a positive way of providing the parameters within which government can govern would amount to. Obviously, the doctrine of the separation of powers prevents excessive interference by the legislature in executive functions. Thus, the positive function of members must be to maintain and enforce the constitutional safeguards against abuse of executive power. Since these safeguards are largely in the nature of conventions, then following the general view that they are adhered to since their breach would result in political embarrassment, Parliament's only significant function is to heighten the electorate's awareness of government threats to the constitution. It is arguable that this role is better performed by the media, although it cannot compel ministers to account.

More importantly parliamentary committees can extract information in a way that need not be as self-consciously populist as the methods employed on the floor of the House of Commons.

In the final analysis, any weaknesses or limitations in the methods available to members who wish to lay down the parameters for good government have to be put down to the inherent weaknesses of our constitution. Additionally, it must be remembered that excessive interference in executive functions by the legislature is constitutionally undesirable.

QUESTION TWO

To what extent, if at all, is it true to say that the conventions of individual and collective ministerial responsibility are twins and yet incompatible?

University of London LLB Examination
(for External Students) Constitutional Law June 1986 Q6

General Comment

This question involves discussion of the conventions of collective and individual responsibility and comment upon the inter-relationship between them, in particular the overlaps which seem to exist in their application.

Skeleton Solution

- Introduction – the doctrine of responsible government.
- Collective responsibility; the content and application of, and the justification for, the convention.
- Individual responsibility; the content and application of, and the justification for, the convention.
- The possibility for conflict in the application of collective and individual responsibility.

Suggested Solution

Democracy requires that those who govern should be responsible to those whom they govern. The convention of ministerial responsibility seeks to achieve this aim. It has two aspects. Firstly, the collective responsibility of the government as a whole to Parliament and, secondly the individual responsibility of ministers to Parliament for decisions, taken in their departments, whether by themselves or by their civil servants.

The doctrine of collective responsibility involves two rules. Firstly, it is accepted that the government must resign if it loses the support of the House of Commons. The Prime Minister and his ministers are collectively responsible to Parliament for the conduct of national affairs. If the Prime Minister loses support in Parliament he must resign or seek a dissolution of parliament. The rule does not mean that the government must resign whenever it is defeated on any issue. There has to be a clear-cut defeat for the government on a matter of policy.

Secondly, the doctrine of collective responsibility involves the rule that the government must speak with one voice. All members of the government share in the collective responsibility of the government, and ministers may not publicly criticise or dissociate themselves from government policy. The essence of collective responsibility is that the Cabinet should be seen to be in agreement: a Cabinet minister who feels unable to agree with his colleagues should resign. The constitutional justification for the rule is that the answerability of the government to Parliament would be severely impaired if individual ministers were able to say that they personally did not agree with decisions taken in Cabinet. Ministers, including non-Cabinet members, are normally bound therefore not to differ publicly from Cabinet decisions nor to speak or vote against the government in Parliament. The rule increases party discipline and unity within the government, strengthens the government in Parliament and reinforces the secrecy of decision making within the Cabinet thereby minimising public disagreement between both ministers and departments of state. It also serves to strengthen the authority of the Prime Minister in relation to his colleagues.

The convention of individual responsibility requires that ministers are responsible to Parliament for their own actions, omissions and mistakes as well as for those of the officials in their departments. This principle is said to help preserve the anonymity and therefore the objectivity and efficiency of the civil service. Thus, government Bills are introduced into Parliament by the departmental ministers, who are responsible for the proposals they contain. In debates concerning the work of individual departments, the minister concerned is expected to reply to the criticisms raised and usually seek to defend the department. Ministers are also expected to meet the reasonable requests of members for information concerning their departments and answer questions relating to their departments at question time.

It can be seen therefore that in many respects the relationship between individual and collective responsibility is very close and to this extent they may be viewed as twins. However, there is also in some respects a high degree of incompatibility between the two. For instance, if responsibility for making of policy decisions lies collectively with the whole government, is it not inconsistent to hold the departmental minister individually responsible for the implementation of that policy? Many of the decisions announced by a minister will have been taken or approved in Cabinet or by Cabinet committees and to this extent the doctrine of collective responsibility will attach to them. Similarly, while a departmental minister may have the authority to make decisions relating exclusively to the sphere for which he is responsible, on many matters he may have to consult with other departments, for example the Treasury. Should that minister then be held responsible for the consequences? Conversely, if a minister is facing censure in Parliament as a result of his departmental policies, he may be individually responsible and accountable to Parliament, but he can nevertheless expect to receive the support of his governmental colleagues by bringing collective responsibility into play.

Of course, both individual and collective responsibility are rules of convention governed largely by political expediency and in consequence their practice may bear little relation to their theory. While their theory therefore may give an impression of incompatibility, the practical application of these conventions, looked at in their political context and judged on their particular facts, may explain the apparent incompatibility.

QUESTION THREE

'If a mistake is made in a government department the minister is responsible even if he knew nothing about it.' 'A minister cannot be blamed for a mistake made if he did not make it himself.'

Consider these contrasting views.

University of London LLB Examination
(for External Students) Constitutional Law June 1989 Q4

General Comment

A straightforward question on individual responsibility.

Skeleton Solution

- Discuss individual responsibility giving examples which are relevant.
- A lot depends on the attitude of PM of the day.
- Contrast Crichel Down criteria with recent examples of resignations.

Suggested Solution

In any democratic state it is a requirement that the people who govern should be responsible to those whom they govern. In the UK, for instance, responsibility is collective ie the government as a whole is responsible to Parliament and responsibility is individual ie individual ministers are responsible to Parliament for decisions taken by them or their civil servants in their departments. The principle of individual ministerial responsibility developed historically before the doctrine of collective responsibility. Collective and individual responsibility are rules of convention and as such are flexible concepts since conventions are rules of political practice regarded as binding by those to whom they apply but everyone recognises that they are subject to exceptions. Neither of the two quotations is an accurate statement of the requirements of individual ministerial responsibility, which it is wellnigh impossible to formulate in a way which indicates in every case what the outcome will be for a minister who has made a mistake or whose department has in some way failed.

A minister is responsible for his or her personal acts whether or not he or she is a member of the Cabinet. Responsibility will also include general conduct in the relevant department and any acts or omissions done in the name of the department. The responsibility may be legal or political or a combination of these. It seems that the meaning of responsibility and the persons or bodies to whom it is owed will vary according to the circumstances.

One of the practical expressions of individual ministerial responsibility is that a minister is required to answer questions in Parliament with regard to the conduct of officials in his department although questions may be disallowed because of the sub judice rule or because of national security. It is true that a minister need not accept responsibility if an official has committed a dishonest act, exceeded his authority or disobeyed instructions. He cannot, however, totally absolve himself and he will be required to explain in public what has happened. In this sense the minister will – whether he is to blame or not – have to 'carry the can'. The minister must also, of course, when required, explain government policy in relation to his department. In the event that the minister's replies fail to satisfy MPs or the Lords a motion to reduce the minister's salary or to censure him may result, but because of party discipline these are rare. In order to consider the truth or otherwise of the quotations it is now necessary to consider some precedents in detail categorising them, if possible, under one of the quotations.

Perhaps one of the clearest examples of a minister resigning because of a mistake, even though he knew nothing of it at the time it occurred, is that of Sir Thomas Dugdale who resigned as Minister of Agriculture as a result of the Crichel Down Affair in 1954: In doing so he took responsibility for alleged maladministration by senior civil servants without his knowledge. Some commentators have sought to explain this resignation on the basis that compulsory purchase was involved, (a matter about which the electorate were extremely sensitive at the time) but it certainly stands as a most stringent example of the 'rule' in force, particularly since the maladministration affected only one family and was a matter of embarrassment rather than one where severe loss either financial or in terms of physical wellbeing was concerned.

Lord Carrington's resignation in 1982 as Secretary of State for Foreign Affairs together with those of the other Foreign Office ministers who resigned with him can also be seen as an example of the first quotation in that it could be argued that Lord Carrington was poorly advised during the negotiations with Argentina over the Falkland Islands but personally made no mistake. On the other hand one could argue that he himself was culpable in that the department's failure to predict the invasion was an indication that it was inefficient or ill run and that in his position he should himself have been better informed and better able to foresee the invasion.

In recent times a rather different attitude has been taken in relation to mistakes by civil servants; whereas formerly the minister maintained the anonymity of the civil servant and would take responsibility in certain recent cases the blame has been laid squarely at the feet of civil servants (who have sometimes been disciplined) whilst ministers have felt no compunction to resign. An example of the 'rule' set out in the second quotation is the Maze Prison breakout which was followed by resignation of civil servants but no ministerial departures.

If the first quotation is correct then a fortiori it would be expected that any minister himself making a mistake would have to take responsibility for it and very likely resign. If one examines some recent resignations and calls for resignation one can see that ministerial mistakes do not necessarily result in resignation.

The second quotation also tends to imply that a minister who personally makes a mistake will be 'blamed'; and the concomitant of this would very likely be resignation. If one examines recent cases one can see that there is no hard and fast rule. Some mistakes by ministers lead to resignations others merely to calls by the Opposition for resignation. Whether a minister survives a mistake seems to depend upon factors such as whether he nevertheless retains the confidence of the Prime Minister and the Cabinet, the view of the backbenchers of his own party and the level of public outcry. For instance Sir Leon Brittan initially survived calls for his resignation as Secretary of State for Trade and Industry over allegations that he had misled the Commons about a letter from British Aerospace to the government during the Westland Helicopter Affair in 1986. His survival was due to the continued support of Prime Minister and Cabinet. However when his behaviour (in authorising a leak to the press of a letter sent by the law officers to Michael Heseltine and then arguably covering up what had been done) came to light, several weeks later not even the Cabinet's support could protect his position when the Conservative backbenchers withdrew their support from him and he was forced to resign. In December 1988 Edwina Currie resigned as a Health Minister after over enthusiastic and somewhat misleading comments on the level of salmonella infection in poultry production. Her fault was to alienate poultry producers who had suffered severe financial loss and the government was forced to mount a costly compensation scheme. The remarks cost Mrs Currie her job but was she simply unlucky? Had there been some other important news story on the day of her remarks perhaps the media and the public would have overlooked them entirely – they would not then have been a 'mistake' and there would have been no resignation.

A further issue to consider in relation to both quotations is the increasing agensificisation of the work of government, which results in the distancing of ministers from the execution of policy. For example, the Home Secretary has increasingly refused to take responsibility for failures within the prison system following the creation of the Prison Service, which was set up as an executive agency to run prisons in the late 1980s. Following a number of high-profile prison escapes, including escapes from Parkhurst, there were calls for the then Home Secretary, Michael Howard, to resign. He, however, argued that the running of prisons was now chiefly the responsibility of the Prison Service, and duly sacked its chief executive Derek Lewis, pointing out that the escapes in question were not the direct result of any Home Office policy for which the Home Secretary was responsible. It is significant that between 1945 and 1995, only five Cabinet ministers have resigned because of the way in which they have discharged their ministerial functions. Much depends on the attitude of the Prime Minister of the day, the Cabinet and backbenchers and the attitude of the public to the particular mistake. The two contrasting views expressed in the question, are neither taken singly nor together a sufficient explanation of the difficult and subtle convention of individual ministerial responsibility.

QUESTION FOUR

'There are no conventions about ministerial responsibility. Ministers simply do what they, or the Prime Minister, want to do.'

Discuss.

Written by the Editors

General Comment

A difficult question to answer well. Students need not only to give an account of the conventions of individual and collective responsibility, but also to have a good understanding of developments in British politics in the last 15 years, and then be able to give examples to show that much depended on the Prime Minister's attitude.

Skeleton Solution

- The conventions of individual and collective responsibility to Parliament – a statement of the traditional position with examples.
- An analysis of the more recent tendency for ministers to resign dependent on the factors such as the mood of the country, the support of the PM and the attitude of the minister concerned, with examples.

Suggested Solution

Democracy requires that those who govern should be answerable to those whom they govern. The convention of ministerial responsibility seeks to achieve this aim. It has two aspects. Firstly, the collective responsibility of the government as a whole to Parliament and, secondly the individual responsibility of ministers to Parliament for decisions taken in their departments whether by themselves or by their civil servants.

The doctrine of collective responsibility involves two rules. Firstly, it is accepted that the government must resign if it loses the support of the House of Commons. The Prime Minister and his ministers are collectively responsible to Parliament for the conduct of national affairs. If the Prime Minister loses support in Parliament he must resign or seek a dissolution of Parliament. The rule does not mean that the government must resign whenever it is defeated on any issue. There has to be a clear cut defeat for the government on a matter of policy or a vote of no confidence.

Secondly, the doctrine of collective responsibility involves the rule that the government must speak with one voice. All members of the government share in the collective responsibility of the government, and ministers may not publicly criticise or dissociate themselves from government policy. The essence of collective responsibility is that the Cabinet should be seen to be in agreement. A Cabinet minister who feels unable to agree with his colleagues should resign. The constitutional justification for this rule is that the answerability of the government to Parliament would be severely impaired if individual ministers were able to say that they personally did not agree with the decision taken in Cabinet. Ministers, including non-Cabinet members and parliamentary private secretaries are normally bound therefore not to differ publicly from Cabinet decisions nor to speak or vote against the government in Parliament. The rule increases party discipline and unity within the government, strengthens the government in Parliament and reinforces the secrecy of decision making within the Cabinet thereby minimising public disagreement between both ministers and the departments of State. It also serves to strengthen the authority of the Prime Minister in relation to his Cabinet colleagues.

The convention of individual responsibility requires that ministers are responsible to Parliament for their own actions, omissions and mistakes as well as for those of their officials in the department. This principle is said to help preserve the anonymity and therefore the objectivity and efficiency of the civil service. Thus, government Bills are introduced into Parliament by the departmental ministers, who are responsible for the proposals they contain. In debates concerning the work of individual departments the minister concerned is expected to reply to the criticisms raised and usually seeks to defend the department. Ministers are also expected to meet the reasonable requests of members for information concerning their departments and answer questions relating to their departments at question time.

Both individual and collective ministerial responsibility are rules of convention governed largely by political expediency. It may therefore be true to observe that as regards responsibility, ministers simply do what they, or the Prime Minister, want to do. So long as they do not get into political difficulty no other sanction is available to compel compliance. The whole purpose of conventions is to introduce flexibility into the constitution and ministerial responsibility, particularly individual responsibility, is perhaps one of the best examples of conventional flexibility in contemporary constitutional practice.

If one were to start with the classic exposition of individual ministerial responsibility stated by Maxwell-Fyfe in the Crichel Down debate and then contrast it with modern practice it is quite obvious that a fundamental change has taken place regarding the situations in which the minister must accept responsibility and not publicly blame the civil servant. For example, the Secretary of State for Northern Ireland distinguished between defects of policy for which he was responsible and defects in the operation of that policy for which he was not when IRA prisoners broke out of the Maze Prison. The minister escaped political difficulties so one must assume that this now represents the current conventional practice.

One can of course defend this change on the grounds that as the minister within the new super departments relies more upon the expertise of his civil servants, the increased profile of the civil servants in decision-making should be reflected in the civil servant accepting more public responsibility when things go wrong. Convention is merely adapting itself and evolving to meet this change.

One can also identify a change to the concept of ministerial responsibility arising from the increase in the use of agencies to discharge what would, in the past, have been departmental functions. Hence the Home Secretary refused to take responsibility for failures within the prison system following the creation of the Prison Service, which was set up as an executive agency to run prisons in the late 1980s. Following a number of high-profile prison escapes, including escapes from Parkhurst, there were calls for the then Home Secretary, Michael Howard, to resign. He, however, argued that the running of prisons was now chiefly the responsibility of the Prison Service, and duly sacked its chief executive Derek Lewis, pointing out that the escapes in question were not the direct result of any Home Office policy for which the Home Secretary was responsible.

One should also be wary of confusing ministerial resignations with the convention of individual responsibility. Resignation has never fallen under the convention and thus has always depended to a large extent upon the attitude of the individual minister and the Prime Minister in particular, but the attitude of fellow ministers and of government backbenchers also plays a role. The position of Leon Brittan, Secretary of State for Trade and Industry, during the Westland Affair in 1986 is an instructive example. Leon Brittan faced criticisms and calls for his resignation on two occasions and was finally forced into resignation. The first criticism was of an alleged breach of collective responsibility when the Secretary of State allegedly indicated to a senior executive of British Aerospace that it would be in the public interest if that company withdrew from the European Consortium (the inference being that it was in the national interest for the rival US rescue by Sikorsky Helicopters to go through) a breach of collective responsibility as the government's declared policy was one of neutrality. A letter was sent by British Aerospace to the Prime Minister to complain and the Secretary of State under close questioning in the House of Commons denied all knowledge of such a letter.

This misjudgment gave rise to calls for his resignation, but the Cabinet closed ranks to protect the minister. Finally, the Secretary of State was forced into resignation when it was discovered that without authority from the law officers he had authorised the leaking to the press of a letter addressed by them to Michael Heseltine, former Secretary of State for Defence. The Prime Minister and Cabinet again tried to close ranks to protect Mr Brittan but the Conservative backbenchers 1922 Committee resolved that it could no longer support his tenure of office and he was thus forced to resign.

Similarly with collective responsibility. Breach usually results in resignation but in some situations a breach will involve no adverse consequence. There may even be waivers of collective responsibility. During the period of the Labour government in the 1970s waivers were granted in respect of the referendum on EC membership in 1975 and the European Assembly elections in 1978. In both cases these were necessitated by the precarious position of the government which was split over the issue. The essence of convention is flexibility and occasional breaches and waivers of collective responsibility do not remove the underlying convention. Its continued existence can be seen in the resignation of Michael Heseltine, Secretary of State for Defence, during the Westland Affair in 1986.

There is in many respects a degree of incompatibility between collective and individual responsibility. For example, if responsibility for the making of policy decisions lies collectively with the whole government, is it not inconsistent to hold the departmental minister responsible for the implementation of that policy? Many of the decisions announced by a minister will have been taken or approved in Cabinet or by Cabinet committee and to this extent the doctrine of collective responsibility will attach to them. So why should the Prime Minister when things go wrong be able to divert attention from the government by passing responsibility to the departmental minister. Undoubtedly this happens and once again it is accommodated within the flexible confines of convention. If the convention of collective responsibility is serving a purpose then some sanction will follow its breach.

Inevitably, however, the only sanction tends to be political embarrassment, which may not be a huge deterrent in some circumstances. To a large extent, therefore, the sentiments expressed in the question are true, but there is evidence that Parliament is aware of the low opinion many members have of the business of politics, and are keen to reassert the conventions that govern its relationships with the executive. Hence, in the wake of the Scott Enquiry Report into the 'Arms to Iraq', which noted that the failure of ministers, when answering parliamentary questions, or taking part in debates in the House of Commons, to advise the House of the liberalisation of the guidelines relating to arm sales to Iraq, amounted to a failure to discharge the duty of ministerial accountability, the House of Commons Public Service Committee has made a number of recommendations. In particular it has suggested that the House of Commons should pass a resolution to the effect that ministers and civil servants should not obstruct the House. The Committee also attempted to redefine ministerial responsibility in terms of ministerial duty to give the House full information and to resign if found to have knowingly misled the House.

QUESTION FIVE

Compare and contrast the effectiveness of judicial and parliamentary controls over the exercise of prerogative executive powers by government ministers.

University of London LLB Examination
(for External Students) Constitutional Law June 1996 Q6

General Comment

The question involves a detailed discussion of the cases involved in examining the exercise of the prerogative. Candidates should be familiar with the decision of the House of Lords in the so-called GCHQ case and its potential as revealed in subsequent cases.

With reference to parliamentary control in this area some of the knowledge in relation to the role of the Attorney-General may be utilised. Candidates should be familiar with the operation of the prerogative in foreign affairs (acts of State) and how these are or are not controlled by Parliament.

Skeleton Solution

- Definition of royal prerogative.
- Who exercises it?
- The attitude of the courts to its exercise: *Council of Civil Service Unions* v *Minister for the Civil Service*.
- *Ex parte Everett*.
- *Ex parte Bentley*.
- Prerogative and statutory authority.
- Parliamentary control.
- The role of the Attorney-General.
- The prerogative in foreign affairs.
- Conclusion.

Suggested Solution

The royal prerogative consists of those powers which are unique and inherent to the Crown. These powers are in the majority of cases exercised by the Crown in an executive capacity, by which is meant the government. The prerogative is a non-statutory power which may be described as having a common law source, or recognised by the common law. Its extent is finite and since the seventeenth century it is clear from judicial pronouncements that it cannot be extended. In the words of Lord Diplock in *BBC* v *Johns* (1965): 'It is 350 years and a civil war too late for the Queen's courts to broaden the prerogative.'

The seminal case which defined the attitude of the courts to the attempt by the Crown to extend the prerogative is the *Case of Proclamations* (1611). James I sought to create a new offence without seeking parliamentary approval. The court was robust in quashing such a use or misuse of the prerogative. Coke CJ held that: 'the King hath no prerogative, but that which the law of the land allows him'.

Since the *Case of Proclamations* it has become clear that the Crown cannot create a new offence or in other ways punish its subjects except by an Act of Parliament.

The seventeenth-century pronouncement by Coke CJ in relation to the courts determining the extent of the prerogative has survived intact, and if the British constitution has any fundamentals then this might be one of them. It was not, however, until relatively recently that the courts felt confident enough to challenge the exercise of the prerogative by the executive. Dicey (*Law of the Constitution* (10th edn, 1959)) argued that the prerogative may be seen as an arbitrary power in the sense that once the courts have determined its existence they will no longer utilise their jurisdictional powers to examine the adequacy of the grounds upon which it has been exercised. A change in judicial attitudes was foreshadowed by Lord Denning in *Laker Airways* v *Department of Trade* (1976) and was expanded upon by the House of Lords in the leading case of *Council of Civil Service Unions* v *Minister for the Civil Service* (1984).

This latter case centres around the government intelligence institution known as GCHQ, a public service institution under the Foreign and Commonwealth Office. As a result of civil service industrial action the government, acting under an Order in Council issued by virtue of the prerogative, sought to ban trade union membership for those working at the institution. This was done without any prior consultation. The prerogative power involved was the power to regulate the Home Civil Service.

The House of Lords was presented with the question as to whether the exercise of the prerogative could be examined in the courts. The Lords answered in the affirmative though this did not apply to all the prerogative powers and not under all circumstances. Lord Diplock held that judicial review had developed to a stage where one could classify under three heads the grounds upon which administrative action was subject to control by judicial review: (a) illegality; (b) irrationality; and (c) procedural impropriety. There was in this case procedural impropriety as the unions had not been consulted before the ban was imposed. Their Lordships were, however, agreed, following earlier precedents, that procedural impropriety must give way to national security.

The importance of the case lies not, however, upon its particular facts but rather its potential. The House of Lords was unanimous in holding that the prerogative is capable of judicial review in its exercise; the difference of opinion centred around how the courts were to determine which prerogatives were so capable. Lord Scarman emphasised the subject matter, while Lord Roskill argued that certain prerogatives, such as the making of treaties and the defence of the realm, were not in their nature amenable to judicial review.

The decision in the GCHQ case has been followed by other judgments, for example, rendering the issuance or non-issuance of passports subject to judicial review (*R* v *Secretary of State for Foreign and Commonwealth Affairs, ex parte Everett* (1989)), and even a willingness to urge the Home Secretary to 'think again' in his refusal to exercise his prerogative of pardon (*R* v *Secretary of State for the Home Department, ex parte Bentley* (1994)). Nor will the courts refrain from holding a minister of the Crown to be personally liable in his official capacity for contempt of court: *M* v *Home Office* (1993).

The courts have also been active in examining the relationship between the prerogative and statutes as a source of power. In *Attorney-General* v *De Keyser's Royal Hotel Ltd* (1920) the House of Lords emphasised that the courts will not permit the use of the prerogative when a statute covers the same area. The Crown is obliged to use the statute even if the terms are less advantageous to it. What exactly happens to the prerogatives in these circumstances is unclear, but Lord Atkinson was of the opinion that the prerogative went into abeyance. A statute may of course abolish the prerogative, as with the Crown Proceedings Act 1947, rather than just covering the same area. The case of *De Keyser's Royal Hotel* presumes that the Crown has a monopoly of power. In an area where this is not the case, the Court of Appeal has been willing (*R* v *Secretary of State for the Home Department, ex parte Northumbria Police Authority* (1988)) to hold that a statutory power and a prerogative power may co-exist covering the same subject matter (the issuance of riot gear to the police) but only where they are exercised by separate bodies – the police authority and the Home Secretary.

The courts have taken a more robust attitude when discussing this relationship in other areas. In *R* v *Secretary of State for the Home Department, ex parte Fire Brigades Union* (1995), the Home Secretary had attempted to use the prerogative to amend the workings of the Criminal Injuries Compensation Scheme, which had itself been set up under the royal prerogative. By a majority the House of Lords ruled that this was unlawful. There was an alternative scheme from the Criminal Justice Act 1988 already on the statue book (but not yet in force), and the Home Secretary could neither abuse his power to introduce that by deciding never to do so, nor could he frustrate the will of Parliament by introducing a scheme so different to that which they had approved.

Parliamentary control over the governmental exercise of the prerogative varies in effectiveness depending upon the subject matter. As has been mentioned, the signing of treaties is a prerogative act and whether they are ever discussed or approved by Parliament often depends upon the will of the executive. If, however, a treaty is to have domestic effect (as with European Community and Union treaties), then an Act of Parliament must be passed. A declaration of war is also a prerogative power and, for instance, the declaration of war against Germany in 1939 was carried out without parliamentary approval. The Crown does not, however, have any independent source of revenue, and if Parliament were to oppose the military action then the government would run out of money.

Individual office holders in the exercise of their prerogative functions are not in some cases answerable to the courts but are answerable to Parliament. The Attorney-General in performing his role as a quasi-judicial officer of the Crown is not answerable to the courts, but is answerable to Parliament, and theoretically could be asked to resign after a vote of no confidence. Similarly, moves by the court notwithstanding (see the discussion of *ex parte Bentley* above), the Home Secretary is answerable to Parliament for his acts or omissions in not granting a prerogative of mercy or pardon.

The above is, of course, dependent upon the workings of the House of Commons, and if the government of the day can maintain a majority in any vote of confidence then the office holder will survive. Other prerogatives, such as the granting of honours, are not open to parliamentary scrutiny nor any prerogative functions involving defence of the realm.

One may conclude that while the courts are now robust in examining the prerogative, and more particularly its exercise, parliamentary control is hindered by the impact of the party system upon the workings of the House of Commons in particular. There is a word of warning, though. One should not draw far-reaching conclusions from particular events. On the facts of the GCHQ case the trade unions failed in their case but the potential of the House of Lords' decision was there for all to see. Similarly, the perceived weakness of Parliament in controlling the prerogative exercise by ministers could be reversed if minority governments were to become the norm rather than the exception.

9 Judicial Review of Administrative Action

9.1 Introduction

Far from being a separate subject, administrative law is a key aspect of constitutional law. At its core is the role played by the judiciary in ensuring that the executive – for these purposes comprising in its 'narrow' sense government ministers, local authorities, tribunals and other statutory bodies – stays within the limits of its powers. The basis of administrative law is the ultra vires doctrine – the common law notion that a public body should not be permitted to exceed the limits placed on its powers either by statute or common law. In this sense it becomes possible to see administrative law for what it really is – a vital aspect of two key constitutional principles: the separation of powers whereby the judiciary can act as a check and balance on the powers of the executive; and the rule of law doctrine whereby no body should be above the law.

The application for judicial review is the means by which administrative law is brought into effect. Any body with sufficient interest in the matter concerned can apply to the courts to have the legality of the executive action tested. Where it is found to be unlawful it can, at the court's discretion, be struck down by means of an order of certiorari – the effect is that the decision in question becomes a nullity.

In the latter part of the twentieth century the judges have grown more confidant in their application of the principles of administrative law, however. The scope of judicial review has been extended to subjectively worded powers vested in ministers and to the exercise of prerogative power. The scope of judicial review has also been extended by the courts adopting a creative approach to the concept of what constitutes a 'public' body. That term is no longer limited to statutory bodies but has been extended to encompass any organisation or person exercising a significant power that affects the public at large, particularly where those affected by the exercise of the power would have no other means of seeking legal control of the way in which the power has been exercised.

9.2 Key points

a) *The ultra vires principle*

The essence of the High Court's jurisdiction is that it has the power to review the actions of an executive or public law body to determine whether or not that body has acted within the scope of its powers (ie acted 'ultra vires'). In general terms action can be ultra vires because it is incompatible with the express limits laid down in an enabling Act or because it is incompatible with the implied limits that attach to the power provided for in the enabling Act. Of the implied limits there are some that relate to the way in which a decision is made (ie the procedure leading up to the decision) and others that relate to the actual decision itself (ie the reasonableness of the decision), although it would be inaccurate to suggest that the two types of implied limit were mutually exclusive.

b) *Breach of natural justice*

Where a statute lays down a procedure that a public body must follow before exercising its discretion the courts will ensure that such requirements are complied with, to the extent that they are seen as being mandatory. In many cases there is no statutory procedure, or the statute does not cover all aspects of the procedure. Where the statute is silent the courts will look to the common rules of natural justice to determine what is required.

As a general principle *Ridge* v *Baldwin* [1964] AC 40 provides that the extent to which the common law will require procedural safeguards to be complied with will in turn depend upon the nature of the interest at stake. The more significant the rights affected, and the more significant the impact of the decision on the applicant, the more that will be required in the way of fairness at common law. For these purposes interests are not just traditional property rights: see *Leech* v *Deputy Governor of Parkhurst Prison* [1988] 1 All ER 485. The courts are less likely to intervene on behalf of an applicant who merely seeks a privilege: *R* v *Gaming Board for Great Britain, ex parte Benaim and Khaida* [1970] 2 QB 417.

c) *Legitimate expectation*

Today the courts will often assess the applicant's entitlement to protection by the rules of natural justice by asking whether or not he has a 'legitimate expectation' of fairness. Four different bases for legitimate expectation can be identified.

i) Where the litigant asserts a substantive right, in the form of an entitlement that should not be denied him: see *R* v *Secretary of State for the Home Department, ex parte Khan* [1985] 1 All ER 40.

ii) Where the applicant's interest lies in some ultimate benefit that he hopes to attain or, possibly, retain. This classification can be traced back to decisions such as *Schmidt* v *Secretary of State for Home Affairs* [1969] 2 Ch 149.

iii) Where the legitimate expectation is used to refer to the fair procedure itself, ie the applicant claims to have a legitimate expectation that the public body will act fairly towards him.

iv) Where a particular procedure, not otherwise required by law, has to be followed as a result of a previous promise or course of dealing: see *Attorney-General of Hong Kong* v *Ng Yuen Shiu* [1983] 2 All ER 346.

d) *Aspects of a fair procedure*

There are no set rules on what constitutes a fair procedure at common law – much depends upon the context within which the decision-making process is being conducted. The following points frequently arise, however.

i) Notice of the hearing should be given: see *Glynn* v *Keele University* [1971] 1 WLR 487. Clearly the more that is at stake for the applicant, the greater the obligation to give notice of the case to be met: see *R* v *Secretary of State for the Home Department, ex parte Mohammed Al Fayed* [1997] 1 All ER 228.

ii) A hearing need not entail an oral hearing: see *Lloyd and Others* v *McMahon* [1987] 2

WLR 821 and *R* v *Secretary of State for the Home Department, ex parte Doody and Others* [1993] 3 WLR 154.

iii) Fairness may require that the applicant is permitted the right to cross-examine witnesses if a hearing is held: see *R* v *Army Board of the Defence Council, ex parte Anderson* [1991] 3 All ER 375 and *University of Ceylon* v *Fernando* [1960] 1 All ER 631.

iv) Legal representation should normally be permitted if a hearing is held, but is not always required in order to satisfy the requirements of natural justice. Again much depends on whether the hearing is disciplinary in nature, and the consequences for the applicant if the hearing goes against him: see *R* v *Secretary of State for the Home Department, ex parte Tarrant* [1984] 1 All ER 799.

v) There is no absolute duty to provide reasons for decisions at common law, however the courts increasingly regard the giving of reasons as an aspect of good administrative practice: see *R* v *Secretary of State for the Home Department, ex parte Doody and Others* (above). A useful summary of the current law was provided by Sedley J in *R* v *Higher Education Funding Council, ex parte Institute of Dental Surgery* [1994] 1 All ER 651.

e) *The rule against bias*

The rule against bias is a common law doctrine that provides that no man should be a judge in his own cause. Where an applicant can provide the court with evidence of actual bias, the court should be willing to quash the decision in question, subject to any statutory considerations. Apart from actual bias, two types of apparent bias can occur:

i) Financial interest – *Dimes* v *Grand Junction Canal Proprietors* (1852) 3 HL Cas 759 provides that anything other than a remote and negligible financial interest in the subject matter of a dispute will always disqualify the decision-maker.

ii) Apparent bias – this can be based on arrange of matters such as political interest, family links, business connections, avowed prejudices etc: see *R* v *Sussex Justices, ex parte McCarthy* [1924] 1 KB 256 and *R* v *Bow Street Metropolitan Stipendiary Magistrate, ex parte Pinochet Ugarte* [1998] 4 All ER 897.

Whether or not such connections or interests will disqualify a decision-maker on the grounds of bias will depend upon the application of the test for bias: see *R* v *Gough* [1993] 2 WLR 883. The court should ask whether or not there was a real danger of bias, the test being seen as equally applicable to arbitrators and members of inferior tribunals. The term 'real danger' was preferred to 'real likelihood' because of the desire to emphasis that the possibility of bias should be enough to impugn the validity of proceedings, as opposed to proof of probability.

f) *Reasonableness*

A decision may be ultra vires because it is in itself unreasonable. This is a broad concept covering decisions that are so wrong-headed that no sane person could have arrived at the conclusion (eg *Williams* v *Giddy* [1911] AC 381 and *Backhouse* v *Lambeth London Borough Council* (1972) 116 SJ 802), decisions based on irrelevant considerations, decisions where relevant considerations have not been taken into account and, increasingly, decisions that are ultra vires on the grounds of proportionality.

The modern basis for the test for reasonableness in English administrative law is derived from the Court of Appeal's decision in *Associated Provincial Picture Houses Ltd* v *Wednesbury Corporation* (1948) – the test to be applied is whether or not the public body has acted in a manner that no reasonable authority would have. Lord Diplock, in the course of his speech in *Council of Civil Service Unions* v *Minister for the Civil Service* [1984] 3 All ER 935 preferred to use the term 'irrationality' to describe what had hitherto traditionally been regarded as *Wednesbury* unreasonableness. He stated (at p951):

'By "irrationality" I mean what can by now be succinctly referred to as "*Wednesbury* unreasonableness"... It applies to a decision which is so outrageous in its defiance of logic or of accepted moral standards that no sensible person who had applied his mind to the question to be decided could have arrived at it. Whether a decision falls within this category is a question that judges by their training and experience should be well equipped to answer, or else there would be something badly wrong without judicial system ... "Irrationality" by now can stand on its own feet as an accepted ground on which a decision may be attacked by judicial review.'

i) The doctrine of proportionality provides that action will be unlawful if it is disproportionate in its effect, or relative to what is required. The doctrine might, for example, be invoked where a punishment is out of all proportion to the wrongdoing alleged: see *R* v *Barnsley Metropolitan Borough Council, ex parte Hook* [1976] 1 WLR 1052. In *R* v *Chief Constable of Sussex, ex parte International Trader's Ferry Ltd* [1999] 1 All ER 129 Lord Slynn noted that even if the Chief Constable's decisions survived scrutiny on the basis of the domestic law concept of *Wednesbury* reasonableness, it was not necessarily the case that they would also be lawful within the context of Community law, where a key question was whether they were proportionate to the problem they sought to deal with.

ii) Proportionality is also a feature of the jurisprudence of the European Court of Human Rights and will increasingly be a feature in applications for judicial review when the Human Rights Act 1998 comes fully in to force. Public bodies will be under a duty to comply with the terms of the European Convention on Human Rights as enacted in the 1998 Act. Hence it will be possible to apply for judicial review on the basis of non-compliance.

iii) The courts will intervene if a public body fails to take into account relevant considerations prior to exercising a statutory discretion: see the key case of *Padfield* v *Minister of Agriculture* [1968] AC 997 where the Minister was held to have abused his discretion by not acting in accordance with the aims and objects of the parent Act, the Agricultural Marketing Act 1958. Similarly, if there is evidence that a public body has taken irrelevant considerations into account the courts can strike the decision down: see *Sydney Municipal Council* v *Campbell* [1925] AC 388, *R* v *Hillingdon London Borough Council, ex parte Royco Homes Ltd* [1974] QB 720 and *R* v *Ealing London Borough Council and Others, ex parte Times Newspapers Ltd* (1986) 85 LGR 316. Public bodies such as local authorities have to exercise care regarding the extent to which the exercise of discretion can be impugned on the basis that it is motivated by political dogma or even political correctness: see *R* v *Somerset County Council, ex parte Fewings* [1995] 3 All ER 20, where the Court of Appeal held (by a majority) that a resolution passed by the respondent authority prohibiting stag hunting on certain land within its ownership was unlawful.

iv) A public body must have regard to its financial resources when exercising discretion, but only to the extent that resources were intended by Parliament to be a relevant consideration – determining whether or not this is the case can be extremely complex. Compare *R* v *Gloucestershire County Council, ex parte Barry* [1997] 2 WLR 459 with *R* v *East Sussex County Council, ex parte Tandy* [1998] 2 All ER 769.

g) *The application for judicial review*

The procedure for an application for judicial review is as laid down in RSC O.53 and s31 of the Supreme Court Act 1981. The following points should be noted:

i) Is the respondent a public law body?

In *O'Reilly* v *Mackman* [1983] 2 AC 237 the House of Lords held that if the applicant sought to challenge the decision of a public body on an issue of public law the challenge would have to proceed as an application for judicial review – to proceed by way of action would be an abuse of process causing the action to be struck out. A public law body would typically be one that derived its powers from statute – but not necessarily. In *R* v *Panel on Take-overs and Mergers, ex parte Datafin plc* [1987] 2 WLR 699 – the court held that the Panel could be reviewed even though it exercised no statutory or prerogative powers, and was not even based on a private contract or constitution. What mattered was that it wielded enormous *de facto* power to take decisions affecting the public and, significantly, there was no other means by which those affected by the decisions could have challenged them in the courts.

ii) Is the issue a public law issue?

Davy v *Spelthorne Borough Council* [1984] AC 262 – it will not be an abuse of process to proceed by way of action in respect of a private law issue provided the public law issue was merely tangential to the main purpose of the litigation. There are signs that the courts are taking a more flexible approach to the issue: see *Roy* v *Kensington and Chelsea and Westminster Family Practitioner Committee* [1992] 1 AC 624 and *Trustees of the Dennis Rye Pension Fund and Another* v *Sheffield City Council* [1997] 4 All ER 747.

iii) Does the applicant have locus standi?

See *Inland Revenue Commissioners* v *National Federation of Self-Employed and Small Businesses* [1982] AC 617 – whether or not an applicant seeking judicial review has sufficient interest is to be regarded as a mixed decision of fact and law for the courts to decide on legal principles – should be considered when the application for leave to apply for judicial review is made and, if granted, reconsidered when the actual hearing of the application takes place. There is increasing evidence that the courts are coming to value the role played by certain pressure groups in making applications for judicial review: see *R* v *Secretary of State for Foreign and Commonwealth Affairs, ex parte World Development Movement Ltd* [1995] 1 WLR 386 where significant matters included the need to uphold the rule of law, the fact that no other organisation was likely to launch such a challenge, and the key role played by the applicants in giving advice, guidance and assistance regarding aid.

iv) Is the application out of time?

Applications for judicial review must be made without delay, and at any rate within three months of the action complained: see RSC O.53 r4. Section 31(6) of the Supreme Court Act 1981 provides that the court may refuse an application for judicial review if there has been undue delay, particularly if permitting the application would be likely to cause substantial hardship to, or substantially prejudice the rights of, any person or would be detrimental to good administration. See further *R* v *Stratford-upon-Avon District Council, ex parte Jackson* [1985] 1 WLR 1319.

v) What remedies are available?

- Certiorari – effect is to quash the decision of an inferior body.
- Prohibition – an order directed at an inferior body, compelling it to refrain from a course of action, in effect the public law equivalent of an injunction.
- Mandamus – an order directed at an inferior body, compelling it to act in accordance with duties to which it is subject.

An applicant for judicial review can also apply for the 'private' law remedies of injunction, declaration and damages. All remedies are at the discretion of the court, and regard will be had to the conduct of the applicant, the availability of other remedies, and the consequences of granting the remedy sought.

9.3 Recent cases

O'Rourke v *Camden London Borough Council* [1997] 3 All ER 23 House of Lords – reaffirmation of the notion that in areas of welfare provision the courts will be slow to recognise any private law right to sue for breach of statutory duty.

R v *Chief Constable of Sussex, ex parte International Trader's Ferry Ltd* [1999] 1 All ER 129 – House of Lords applying the doctrine of proportionality to judge the legality of action taken by the Chief Constable in policing animal rights protests.

R v *East Sussex County Council, ex parte Tandy* [1998] 2 All ER 769 – resources not relevant in determining what was a 'suitable education' for an individual pupil.

R v *Gloucestershire County Council, ex parte Barry* [1997] 2 WLR 459 – relevance of resources in determining the needs of a chronically sick and disabled persons – statute permitted reference to resources.

R v *Pierson* [1997] 3 All ER 577 – Home Secretary's decision to increase tariffs for life-sentence prisoners quashed by the courts because it contravened the principles of legal certainty and non-retrospectivity.

9.4 Analysis of questions

Questions tend to be of the two types. Examiners may set essay-style questions asking candidates to reflect on the nature and purpose of administrative law and its significance within the United Kingdom constitution. In answering such questions it is important to bring out the connection with key constitutional principles such as the rule of law and the separation of powers. Problem questions will require the candidate to adopt a methodical approach to be sure of picking up all the relevant issues. In simple terms one should consider: the grounds for review (ie has there been ultra vires action); whether or not the decision-making body is amenable to judicial review; whether or not the issue is one of public law; whether or not the applicant has locus standi; and the remedies that might be sought.

9.5 Questions

QUESTION ONE

'Recent suggestions that the courts are engaged in a strategy of "judicial supremacism" are quite misguided. Rigorous judicial review of executive action enhances rather than undermines the sovereignty of Parliament.'

Discuss.

University of London LL.B Examination
(for External Students) Administrative Law June 1997 Q1

General Comment

The proposition invites detailed critical analysis of the modern constitutional purposes of judicial review. Traditional thinkers can be expected to take a 'purist' view of the constitutional limits upon judicial review, leading to what has become known as the 'green light' theory of administrative law. Against this view may be set the 'red light' theory which puts the emphasis on protecting human rights against the ever-growing power of the centralised state. The red light theory supports the view that the judges 'share' sovereignty with Parliament in calling the executive to account. Illustrations can be given from recent case law to show how these competing theories can affect the practical outcome of vital decisions involving the most vulnerable members of the community.

Skeleton Solution

- Definition of 'red light' theory.
- Definition of 'green light' theory.
- Case law illustrations of differing judicial approaches: *R* v *Cambridge District Health Authority, ex parte B*; *R* v *Gloucestershire County Council, ex parte Barry*.
- Conclusion and evaluation of the debate.

Suggested Solution

The proposition in question reflects the 'red light' theory of administrative law by contending that it is the judicial function to put a stop to the misuse of executive power on the ground that Parliament would not have intended delegated discretions to be abused in such a way as to interfere with basic human rights. 'Red light' theorists applaud those judges who are prepared to take a 'hard look' at the exercise of executive discretion that impinges upon such rights. The 'hard look' approach enables the judge to require from the public body under scrutiny a substantially rational decision based on ethical and moral values. In this way, it is said, the 'true intentions' of the legislature are enforced.

However, those who subscribe to the 'green light' theory of administrative law would dispute these arguments on the ground that Parliament entrusted the executive, not the judiciary, with the final say on the merits of administrative policy. If the judges become too bold in the exercise of judicial review they endanger their impartiality and independence by appearing to undermine the separation of powers and the supremacy of Parliament. 'Green light' theorists contend that judicial review must take account of the need for public authorities to enjoy a sufficient amount of discretion (a 'margin of appreciation') so as to govern efficiently and effectively, as Parliament intended. (The 'red light' and 'green light' theories were conceived by Harlow and Rawlings, *Law and Administration* (2nd ed, 1997), Chapters 1 and 2.)

The tension between the 'red light' and 'green light' approaches to judicial review is well illustrated in the tragic case of *R* v *Cambridge District Health Authority, ex parte B* (1995). A girl of ten suffering from leukaemia was refused further medical treatment on the grounds that the likelihood of a successful recovery was very small (less than 10 per cent), that the treatment itself would cause her great suffering, and that the total cost of the treatment was £75,000, which was too much for the Health Authority to bear in the light of other demands on its medical services.

At first instance Laws J granted judicial review and quashed the Authority's decision. He adopted a 'red light' approach by emphasising the need to protect fundamental human rights, in this case the right to life. Where such a right was at stake 'the responsible authority had to do more than toll the bell of tight resources'. However, on the appeal the Court of Appeal quashed this decision. Sir Thomas Bingham MR (as he then was) gave a 'green light' judgment in which he expressed sympathy for the 'difficult and agonising' judgments that medical authorities had to make in such cases. The cost factor, he said, was a very relevant consideration which the Authority had been right to take into account; in an imperfect world of finite resources priorities had to be set and it was not for courts of to substitute their views on such questions for those of the responsible authority He stated:

'The courts are not ... arbiters as to the merits of cases of this kind. Were we to express opinions as to the likelihood of the effectiveness of medical treatment, or as to the merits of medical judgment, then we would be straying far from the sphere under which our constitution is accorded to us. We have one function only, which is to rule upon the lawfulness of decisions. That is a function to which we would strictly confine ourselves.'

A similar difference of judicial opinion on the relevance of financial considerations can be found in the recent case of *R* v *Gloucestershire County Council, ex parte Barry* (1997). The applicant, B, was an 80-year-old heart-attack victim for whom the local authority had provided community care support, including a cleaning and laundry service. Citing a lack of funds the authority had decided to withdraw these services. B sought a declaration to the effect that, in assessing the needs of a disabled person under the Chronically Sick and Disabled Persons Act 1970, a local authority was not entitled to take into account its financial resources. At first instance the declaration was refused, but the Court of Appeal allowed the appeal and granted relief on the ground that, once an assessment had determined that certain needs should be met, an absolute duty to provide those services arose. The authority could not simply decide that it could not afford such provision.

The Court of Appeal decision was based upon a strict interpretation of the relevant statute law and may or may not have been influenced by 'red light' considerations involving the need to protect vulnerable citizens from oppressive use of public powers. Nevertheless, that was the view of many of those who applauded the decision, such as Stephen Cragg of the Public Law Project, who described the Court of Appeal ruling as a 'wonderful victory' for disabled people.

However, on the further appeal to the House of Lords, the decision of the Court of Appeal was reversed. By a three to two majority (Lords Nicholls, Hoffmann and Clyde; Lords Lloyd and Steyn dissenting) the House held that, on a true construction of the relevant statute, the criteria for assessing need had themselves to be set by taking into account the relative cost weighed against the relative benefit and the relative need for that benefit. The majority found that the local authority had therefore acted lawfully in taking account of the cost factor. Further, the local authority's consequent decision on the merits was not so unreasonable or irrational as to justify judicial interference.

Who can say with confidence whether the eventual outcome in this case reflects the true intentions of the legislature? Judicial review of administrative decisions has been generally welcomed as a desirable evolutionary development – a necessary check upon the centralisation of power. So long as judges enforce good government by policing the constitutional correctness of executive decisions there can be surely no objection on grounds of principle to 'rigorous' judicial review of executive action. But if judges ignore the constitutional imperative of judicial self-restraint when exercising judicial review they will risk being accused of 'judicial supremacism' by crossing the boundary between law and politics – a view expressed by the present Lord Chancellor, Lord Irvine (Lord Irvine, 'Judges and Decision-Makers: The Theory and Practice of *Wednesbury Review*' [1996] PL 59 (at the time of this article Lord Irvine was Shadow Lord Chancellor)), though one not necessarily shared by the governed.

QUESTION TWO

Section 1 of the (fictitious) Education (Standards) Act 1998 empowers a local authority to close any of its schools which, in its opinion, are failing to deliver a 'satisfactory educational product to their consumers'. The Act does not provide any mechanism for any person to appeal against such a closure, but requires the council to consult parents of children at the school before deciding to close it.

In May 1999, Ashtown Council decides to close Thistledown Primary School, which, the council claims, has performed poorly according to a recent (unpublished) government report. A research study by the local university suggests, in contrast, that the school is performing at a commendable level given its low level of resources.

No parents at the school wish to challenge the closure, apparently because they all hope that the council will open a new school in the near future.

You are approached by the following organisations/individuals who wish to challenge the council's decision.

i) The National Union of Teachers, several of whose members work at the school.

ii) The local pack of the Brownies, which uses the school's facilities for its activities. The Brownies have recently donated £1,000 to the school to pay for redecoration of its sports hall.

iii) Bill and Betty Bennet, who had hoped that their daughter would begin to attend the school in September 1999.

Advise your clients if they would be granted locus standi in these circumstances.

Adapted from the University of London LL.B Examination
(for External Students) Administrative Law June 1997 Q7

General Comment

It is important not to fall into the trap of discussing at length the merits of this problem question. Whilst grounds for review (eg natural justice) need to be touched on so as to assess the issue of locus standi, the emphasis of the question is on the procedural case law concerning the way in which the concept of legal standing has been developed from one of purely personal standing to embrace representative standing, though not, as yet, associational standing. Clear advice needs to be offered on the locus standi of the three specified classes of applicant.

Skeleton Solution

- Definition of modern locus standi requirement.
- The inter-relationship between sufficient interest and the merits of the application: *IRC* v *National Federation of Self-Employed and Small Businesses.*
- The merits (in outline only).
- Historical development of test of locus standi.
- Definition of representative standing – cases involving reputable pressure groups.
- Definition of associational standing and the problem of capacity facing an unincorporated association.
- The concept of legitimate expectation – can it be equated with the concept of locus standi?
- Mere 'hopes' distinguished from legitimate expectations.

Suggested Solution

Supreme Court Act 1981, s31(3) and RSC O.53 r3 provide that no application for judicial review shall be made unless the leave of the court has been obtained, and that such leave shall be refused unless the applicant has 'sufficient interest in the matter to which the application relates'. The commentary to O.53 states that the issue of locus standi is a mixed question of fact and law, that it is a question of fact and degree, and will depend on the relationship between the applicant and the matter to which the application relates, having regard to all the circumstances of the case. Consequently it has been held that it will be necessary for the single judge at the leave stage to take a 'bird's eye view' of the merits of the application in order to decide the issue of legal standing: *IRC* v *National Federation of Self-Employed and Small Businesses* (1981).

In regard to the merits of the present case there would appear to be grounds for arguing that the Ashtown Council made an ultra vires decision when deciding to close Thistledown Primary School. These grounds are:

a) *Wednesbury* unreasonableness (*Associated Provincial Picture Houses Ltd* v *Wednesbury Corporation* (1948)) – arguably the local university research study shows that there may be no sufficient evidence to support the council's view that the school was performing poorly. An application for judicial review might at least ensure that the council publishes its own evidence to support its view; and

b) procedural impropriety – arguably the council acted in breach of natural justice by failing to consult interested parties (eg the teachers at the school) before reaching its closure decision.

The question then becomes one of procedure – does each potential applicant for judicial review have sufficient interest in these particular aspects of apparent administrative failings?

At one time the common law took a very strict approach to the issue of standing apparently from a desire to safeguard public bodies from being harassed by 'mere busybodies' interfering in matters that did not concern them. But in more recent times the common law has developed a more relaxed approach on the ground that preserving access to justice is an essential safeguard for individual rights as well as a precondition for the proper development of administrative law principles. As Lord Diplock observed in *IRC* v *National Federation*:

'It would be a grave lacuna in our system of public law if a pressure group ... or even a single public spirited taxpayer were prevented by outdated technical rules of locus standi from bringing the matter to the attention of the court to vindicate the Rule of Law and to get unlawful conduct stopped.'

However, Lord Diplock was speaking in the context of alleged flagrant and serious breaches of the law, or exceptionally grave widespread illegality, and his dictum could not be appropriately applied to the present case, where an applicant for review would need to show more than 'public spirit' or a genuine concern to prevent an apparent injustice. Each of the three classes of applicant in the present case therefore needs to be examined to establish their exact relationship to the alleged ultra vires decision:

i) The National Union of Teachers would appear to have a sound claim to 'representative standing' as it has a contractual relationship with teachers at the school and those teachers will be directly affected by the school's closure. It may well be that the individual teachers do not have the resources to bring applications for review as individuals and hence a well established pressure group, such as a trade union, would be better placed, with its particular expertise in employment law, to mount a relevant and well argued challenge on behalf of its members. This basis for representative standing has been recognised in the case of non-union pressure groups: *R* v *Secretary of State for Social Services, ex parte Child Poverty Action Group* (1989), *R* v *Inspectorate of Pollution, ex parte Greenpeace Ltd (No 2)* (1994) and *R* v *Secretary of State for Foreign and Commonwealth Affairs, ex parte World Development Movement Ltd* (1995).

   However, it is by no means certain that the NUT will be recognised as having sufficient interest since the *Federation* case, above, is authority for rejecting an application based on 'associational standing', ie the mere fact that the applicant is a body claiming to act on behalf of its individual members is not sufficient to give it locus standi. The NUT will need to convince the single judge at the leave stage that the individual teachers are genuinely unable to bring an application themselves and that it would serve the administration of justice for the NUT to be granted standing. Further, there is at least one authority which suggests that an unincorporated association lacks capacity to seek judicial review in its own name, whether or not it has sufficient interest under the ordinary tests of standing: *R* v *Darlington Borough Council, ex parte Association of Darlington Taxi Owners and Darlington Owner Drivers Association* (1994).

ii) The Brownies, as an unincorporated association, may lack capacity to seek judicial review and, as explained in (i) above, mere associational standing will not be sufficient to enable the organisation to obtain leave to apply for judicial review. The donation of £1,000 to the school to pay for redecoration may be sufficient to give rise to a legitimate expectation that the Brownies would be consulted about the closure decision and, if so, such a legitimate expectation may be enough to constitute sufficient interest in the way the closure decision was taken. It would then be possible for the Brownies to argue at the merits stage that there had been a breach of natural justice and to require the council to think again, this time after consulting the Brownies and hearing representations from them. Certainly cases involving recognised legitimate expectations seem to have come close to equating a legitimate expectation with a sufficient interest, eg *Attorney-General of Hong Kong* v *Ng Yuen Shiu* (1983).

iii) Since they had only a hope that their daughter would be attending the school from September 1997, Bill and Betty Bennet cannot claim a 'legitimate expectation' of the sort enjoyed by the Brownies, above, who actually used the school facilities and had a direct link with the school's activities. At one time a mere hope of obtaining a place at a public educational institution was not enough to require such an institution to grant a hearing to those who had applied and been refused a place: dicta of Megarry V-C in *McInnes* v *Onslow-Fane* (1978). However, in more recent times a rapid expansion in the protection offered by the doctrine of legitimate expectation has led some judges to suggest that even a 'bare applicant' is entitled to fair play: see per Simon Brown LJ in *R* v *Devon County Council, ex parte Baker* (1995). That case involved a council decision to close an old peoples' home and, although the residents were not in the position of being licensees, it was held that they had a legitimate expectation of consultation before the closure decision was taken.

If Bill and Betty Bennet's daughter had actually been attending the school they would have had a statutory right of appeal under the (fictitious) Education (Standards) Act 1995 *and* the opportunity to apply for judicial review on the basis of legitimate expectation, since the statutory right does not automatically preclude the remedy of judicial review: *R* v *Devon County Council,* above. But since their daughter was not attending the school, but had only a hope of doing so, it would appear that they have very flimsy grounds for establishing sufficient interest and it must be very doubtful whether the single judge would apply Simon Brown LJ's dictum, above, so as to allow the Bennets to contest a full hearing on the merits.

QUESTION THREE

'Administrative law is the law relating to the control by the courts of the actions of administrative bodies.'

Consider this statement.

Written by the Editors

General Comment

The statement you are asked to consider is particularly bland and open, leaving you with a great deal of scope as to how to approach the answer. The important points are to start with a general explanation of the purpose of administrative law, and then give specific examples to show how it works in practice.

Skeleton Solution

- Dicey's view of administrative law.
- The constitutional framework.
- Bodies subject to review.
- Grounds for review.
- Extension of review to ministers and prerogative power.
- Academic views.
- Conclusion.

Suggested Solution

It is sometimes said that administrative law has never fully recovered from Dicey's denial of its existence; to some extent this is true, in that it has had to strive to establish itself as a readily recognisable branch of English law over the past thirty years or so. That we have a discipline which can be described as 'administrative law' is in many ways a tribute to the work of the judiciary, who, coming to terms with the massive increase in administrative agencies in the post-war period, have developed a coherent body of legal rules that can be applied to administrative bodies in order to keep them within the legal limits of their power.

Before any discussion of the nature of administrative law can be undertaken some illustration of its setting must be considered. Parliament is obviously the supreme power, in the exercise of which it creates administrative agencies to carry out various tasks, or grants new powers, and imposes duties on bodies already in existence. Many of these powers are capable of having a far-reaching effect on individual liberty, ownership and use of property, and opportunity to earn livelihood.

Obviously they need to be kept in check and this should be the role performed by the courts. The traditional view is that this triangular relationship is at the heart of administrative law. Such a view does, however, presuppose a clear idea of what an administrative agency is. Regarding some bodies there would seem to be no doubt, eg statutory tribunals, local authorities. Others are less clearly defined, eg public corporations, universities, Benchers of the Inns of Court. If one adopts a traditional narrow view, then administrative law concerns the control of those bodies amenable to control by the prerogative writs – as to which see *O'Reilly* v *Mackman* (1983) – but this would be to ignore the true ambit of the subject. This point is further developed below.

The grounds upon which the courts will exercise their power of judicial review, as the process is known, are now reasonably clear. An administrative body must not exceed the express limits laid down in its enabling statute, or the implied limits laid down by the courts themselves. In connection with the latter the courts have developed a test for 'reasonableness' by which administrative actions are judged, and also developed a sophisticated set of rules in order to determine the 'fairness' of various procedures otherwise known as natural justice. Again, caution must be exercised here because cases concerning natural justice frequently involve so called 'domestic' bodies, such as the British Board of Boxing Control – see *McInnes* v *Onslow-Fane* (1978) – and it would be inaccurate to describe such bodies as 'administrative'. Further, the actions of some administrative bodies are seen as being beyond the reach of the normal rules of natural justice, eg those that are acting in a 'purely administrative' capacity, eg *Norwest Holst* v *Secretary of State for Trade* (1978), although even in these cases a minimum standard of fair behaviour is imposed, eg to act without bias and without caprice: *McInnes* v *Onslow-Fane*. The development of the doctrine of legitimate expectation has resulted in very few 'no-go' areas remaining so far as judicial review is concerned: *R* v *Devon County Council, ex parte Baker* (1995).

The way in which administrative law operates can be determined by consideration of the various administrative bodies to which it is applied.

With the massive increase in state intervention in public life over the last 50 years, there has been a large growth in the use of tribunals as a means of adjudication upon disputes between the individual and the administration. In addition to the controls outlined above, the courts can also review the decisions of such bodies for 'errors of law on the face of the record', even though such a body may not have acted in excess of its limited powers. The Tribunals and Inquiries Act 1992 increases the controls by the courts over such bodies even further.

Local authorities, being creatures of statute, are subject to similar controls by the courts. The ultra vires principle being frequently invoked to invalidate such things as overspending by councils, (see *Roberts* v *Hopwood* (1925); *Bromley London Borough Council* v *Greater London Council* (1983)) and ultra vires contractual dealings (see *Hazell* v *Hammersmith and Fulham London Borough Council* (1991) and *Credit Suisse* v *Allerdale Borough Council* (1996)).

One of the most significant developments in administrative law has been the application of the above principles to government ministers, despite their being vested with subjectively worded powers by statute. Examples are *Padfield* v *Minister of Agriculture* (1968); *Congreve* v *Home Office* (1976). In both of these cases the courts had no hesitation in declaring the powers of such ministers to be subject to certain implied limits, such as, ministerial discretion having to be exercised in accordance with the policy of the enabling Act, and not for some ulterior motive.

It should be noted, however, that such decisions can sometimes give the illusion of control. The sequel of the *Padfield* case, for example, was that the Minister considered the inquiry's report, but declined to act upon it.

To give a more complete picture it must be added that there are certain administrative agencies and procedures that are beyond the principles of administrative law. When ministers are exercising powers traditionally regarded as being part of the Crown prerogative, the courts are usually unwilling to intervene, although they do state what the limits of prerogative power are. In rare cases judicial review may be granted for error of law in the exercise of prerogative powers: *R* v *Secretary of State for the Home Department, ex parte Bentley* (1994) (prerogative of mercy), though in general the prerogative of mercy is non-reviewable: *Reckley* v *Minister of Public Safety* (1996).

Public corporations do not really fall within the scheme of control provided by Administrative Law as already discussed. They are public bodies closely controlled by central Government but not part of any government department: see *Tamlin* v *Hannaford* (1950). For many, their legal powers and duties are so vaguely drawn as to make the application of the prerogative writs impossible. Similarly, the police, obviously an important administrative agency, are not really controlled by the principle of administrative law. In a number of decisions the courts have purported to review the exercise of discretion by chief constables, but no satisfactory explanation of the grounds upon which certiorari would be available have ever been given (see *R* v *Metropolitan Police Commissioner, ex parte Blackburn* (1968)), and even if the courts do review the actions of chief constables, the remedies available are limited, the courts being reluctant to direct them as to how they should exercise their discretion: see *Chief Constable of North Wales* v *Evans* (1982).

Even where there is no sound constitutional basis for the courts to exercise their inherent common law power of review, they have stepped into control the actions of administrative agencies that make decisions affecting the public. An early example being the control exercised over the Criminal Injuries Compensation Board as shown in *R* v *Criminal Injuries Compensation Board, ex parte Lain* (1967). Another example of this approach is provided by *R* v *Panel on Take-overs and Mergers, ex parte Datafin plc* (1987). Arguably, one of the most exciting developments in recent years has been the extension of judicial review to so-called self-regulatory, 'private law' bodies: see *R* v *Advertising Standards Authority, ex parte The Insurance*

Service (1989). This has led some to question whether the ultra vires rule is still the basis of judicial review: see eg Dawn Oliver [1987] PL 543.

From the above it will be seen that administrative law is essentially concerned with the problem of ensuring that power given to public bodies by Parliament is exercised within the proper legal limits. The courts, ever conscious of their role in this regard, have staunchly resisted attempts by Parliament to exclude their power of review, see *Anisminic* v *Foreign Compensation Commission* (1969), realising that if the courts are unable to perform their task of reviewing the exercise of power by administrative agencies, the rules referred to as 'administrative law' become redundant. In rejecting such attempts to thwart the control of administrative bodies by the courts, Wade argues that the judiciary have discovered a deeper constitutional logic than that of crude Parliamentary supremacy: (1969) 85 LQR 198.

In conclusion, therefore, the statement in question must be regarded as being correct, even though it gives no indication of the complexities involved. It should be added that administrative law as such is largely remedial, being applied to curb excesses of jurisdiction. There are many undesirable aspects of administrative action which it is unable to deal with simply because they do not involve ultra vires, or errors of law. These may come within the province of the Parliamentary Commissioner for Administration, who can investigate aspects of bad administration not at present covered by the traditional heads of ultra vires, eg incompetence, rudeness, delay.

QUESTION FOUR

'The appreciation of the distinction in substantive law between what is private law and what is public law has been a latecomer to the English legal system' – Lord Diplock in *O'Reilly* v *Mackman*.

What is the distinction? What is its significance for administrative law?

Written by the Editors

General Comment

Given the controversy in recent years regarding the distinction between private and public law, this was a predictable question. A question that defies any definite answer but one for which recent case law provides some clues.

Skeleton solution

- Origins of the public/private dichotomy.
- Situations where it can be of significance.
- Consequences in terms of remedies.
- How the courts identify public bodies.
- How the courts identify public law issues.
- Extent to which the courts are resiling from the *O'Reilly* v *Mackman* orthodoxy.

Suggested Solution

i) *The distinction between public and private law*

The distinction between public and private law in England has never been as clear as that which exists in some other legal systems, notably of France. The views of Dicey, that there was no separate system of rules for public bodies in English law, have been credited with hampering the development of a coherent body of rules recognisable as administrative law. It is just because there is no separate system of rules dealing with the legal liability of public bodies that the judiciary, among others, labour under some difficulty in identifying 'public law issues'. The hesitation implicit in Lord Diplock's statement has been lately echoed by another of his brethren; Lord Wilberforce, in *Davy* v *Spelthorne Borough Council* (1984) seriously questioned the extent to which public and private law issues could be differentiated.

At a simplistic level one could draw the distinction that private law governs relations between individuals, and public law relations between individuals and the state. Further, one could look at the differences between the remedies available in private law and those available under public law. Under the former, remedies frequently provide for personal compensation (ie common law damages); whereas under the latter remedies are principally concerned with ensuring that public bodies are prevented from acting ultra vires, by means of prerogative orders of certiorari and prohibition, or compelled to perform their public functions by means of orders of mandamus. Note that damages are only available under an application for judicial review, if they would have been available in an action started by writ. The Privy Council's decision in *Dunlop* v *Woollahra Municipal Council* (1982) further underlines the point that a public law action is not primarily concerned with the compensation of individuals who suffer financial loss resulting from ultra vires administrative action. The only 'public law tort' which gives rise to compensation is the tort of misfeasance in public office (deliberate and dishonest abuse of public power): *Three Rivers District Council* v *Bank of England* (1996).

The distinction between private and public law is significant in the consideration of liability in tort especially for negligence. It may be that a body classified as 'public' gains the protection of the 'policy/operation' distinction enunciated by Lord Diplock in *Home Office* v *Dorset Yacht Co* (1970) or because it would not be fair, just and reasonable at common law to find a breach of an operational duty: *Stovin* v *Wise* (1996). But by far the most important and difficult questions of differentiation arise in applications for judicial review under the new O.53.

Broadly stated the position is that if a dispute concerns a public law issue, and the respondent is a public law body then its actions must be contested by way of the application for judicial review, this much is the effect of Lord Diplock's speech in *O'Reilly* v *Mackman* (1983). This ruling of course highlights the very problem with which this essay is concerned: how does one identify bodies as 'public'? Similarly with 'issues'.

In *O'Reilly* v *Mackman* his Lordship classified the legitimate expectations of those prisoners appearing before prison boards of visitors as public law rights – but it is submitted that an argument could be sustained that individual liberty is a very private right.

Case law subsequent to the above decision reveals the problem. An action by a nursing officer for unfair dismissal by a health authority is a private law matter in the eyes of Donaldson MR: see *R* v *East Berkshire Health Authority, ex parte Walsh* (1984). Conversely the dismissal of a prison officer comes under public law issues, being regulated by statute: see *R* v *Secretary of State for the Home Department, ex parte Benwell* (1985). Whichever decision is correct, they illustrate the difficulty in trying to make a public/private law distinction. The task appears almost pointless in the light of such decisions as *An Bord*

Bainne v *Milk Marketing Board* (1984), wherein the Court of Appeal held that the plaintiffs (the Irish Dairy Board) were correct to proceed, by way of a private action at law, in their claim for damages arising out of the alleged failure of the respondents to comply with certain EC regulations. The deciding factor for the Master of the Rolls was that the plaintiffs could make good their case on the facts and in private law, so that there was no discretion in the court to prevent the claim from proceeding. The determining factors in *ex parte Benwell* (above) were the absence of any private law right that the applicant could have invoked and the statutory underpinning of his status or office.

Part of the problem arises from Lord Diplock's obiter statement in *O'Reilly* v *Mackman* (above) that an action could proceed by way of writ, if the public law issues involved arose as being merely collateral to the main point in the litigation. The difficulties this gives rise to can be further seen in *Davy* v *Spelthorne Borough Council* (1984), *Wandsworth London Borough Council* v *Winder* (1984) and *Lonrho* v *Tebbit* (1992).

Identifying a 'public body' may not be too difficult. Characteristics such as the fact that it was statutory, created under royal prerogative (Criminal Injuries Compensation Board), or by charter (Universities, BBC), would be highly persuasive. The source of power, whilst a relevant factor, is also no longer the sole test for determining public or private status; the 'functions' test has indicated that a body exercising 'governmental' powers may be treated as a public body: *R* v *Chief Rabbi, ex parte Wachman* (1992).

This approach builds on earlier decisions such as *R* v *Panel on Take-overs and Mergers, ex parte Datafin plc* (1987), the classification of a body as 'public law' in nature, should be based on the functions it performs, rather than the source of its powers. Such a view is certainly borne out by some subsequent decisions, such as *R* v *Advertising Standards Authority, ex parte The Insurance Service plc* (1989), but not by all: see *R* v *Disciplinary Committee of the Jockey Club, ex parte The Aga Khan* (1993), where Sir Thomas Bingham MR laid emphasis on the source of the Jockey Club's powers.

ii) *Significance for administrative law*

It follows from the last point that one possible consequence is the emergence of an 'Administrative Court', ie one dealing almost exclusively with public law matters. By studying the 'type' of case regarded by the judiciary as suitable for judicial review one may be able to piece together a picture of what is meant by the expression public law in English administrative law.

A second possible significance is that cases may be forced into the O.53 procedure, for which it is not suitable, ie those where there is little agreement as to fact, and much examination and cross-examination is called for. (The usual procedure under O.53 is by affidavit only.)

It has to be questioned whether the creation of an exclusive procedure for dealing with public law issues was intended by the authors of the Law Commission's report on *Remedies in Administrative Law* published in 1976.

The comments of Lord Lowry in *Roy* v *Kensington and Chelsea and Westminster Family Practitioner Committee* (1992) express a preference for the 'broad' view that an aggrieved person should apply by way of judicial review when there are no private law rights at stake, and this may signal a general relaxation of the previously strict exclusivity principle created by *O'Reilly* v *Mackman*. In its 1994 report on *Judicial Review*, the Law Commission recommended retention of the exclusivity principle of *O'Reilly* v *Mackman* (above) but to be operated in the 'broad' way expounded by Lord Lowry in *Roy*'s case, above. The 'broad' approach was developed still further by the House of Lords in *Mercury Communications* v *Director-General of Telecommunications* (1996), where the House appeared to favour a choice of proceedings provided that use of private law procedures would not amount to an 'abuse of process'.

The courts are still keen to employ the dichotomy, however, where welfare benefit claims are concerned; see *O'Rourke* v *Camden London Borough Council* (1997).

It is clear from these decisions that the public/private dichotomy remains a live and complex issue for litigants to deal with.

QUESTION FIVE

The Secretary of State has statutory powers to provide financial assistance for correspondence colleges. The Allpass College applies for assistance. In view of press reports throwing some doubts on the College the Secretary of State appoints Pry to inquire into the College and its work.

Pry is a recently retired General Secretary of a teachers' trade union which has strong views about the support of private education out of public funds. He first interviews tutors employed by the College and comes to the provisional view that the College ought not to be supported. A former student tells him that the proprietor had been convicted of having falsely claimed to have a PhD degree of London University. Pry then interviews the proprietor, but refuses his request to be accompanied by a lawyer. Pry submits a report highly critical of the College. A summary of the report made by a civil servant is put before the Secretary of State.

In due course the Secretary of State informs the College that in accordance with his current policy of not supporting correspondence colleges, assistance is refused. He states that the reasons for his policy are current financial stringency, and his preference for students to attend classes in local education authority colleges.

Advise the College as to whether there are any grounds on which it might successfully challenge the Secretary of State's decision.

Written by the Editors

General Comment

A detailed natural justice question, requiring some knowledge of investigatory processes, and the rule against bias. In addition the validity of policy needs to be discussed. Best approached on a point-by-point basis.

Skeleton Solution

- Consideration of natural justice rules.
- The right to no the case to be met.
- Denial of legal representation.
- Problems of bias.
- Tackling the policy issue.

Suggested Solution

There are a number of incidents leading up to and including the decision by the Secretary of State to refuse financial assistance, to which the Allpass College (the College) would raise legal objection, some of these being more powerful than others.

Firstly, the Secretary of State used his discretionary powers to appoint Pry. It could be argued that there was no evidence upon which this decision could be based – applying principles developed in *Coleen Properties* v *MHLG* (1971) and *Secretary of State for Education and Science* v *Tameside Metropolitan Borough Council* (1977). It seems unlikely that the courts are likely to interfere at this stage however.

Secondly, the College might wish to challenge the conduct of the investigation. The actual decision to investigate would appear to be what the courts have come to classify as a preliminary matter, and as such may not attract the rules of natural justice or the duty to act fairly. In *Norwest Holst* v *Secretary of State for Trade* (1978), for example, it was held that the appointment of inspectors to investigate a company's affairs was purely administrative and there was consequently no requirement at that stage to allow the company an opportunity to answer allegations made about it. In the present case, there is no requirement at the outset that the minister give the College an opportunity to answer the press reports.

The College might further object to the manner of the investigation, in particular that evidence was collected from tutors without informing the College of its nature. The courts are unlikely to invalidate any such process. It was held in *R* v *Pergamon Press Ltd* (1971) that inspectors appointed to investigate a company could obtain information in any way that they thought best. A body, such as Pry, who is required to make an investigation and form an opinion must act fairly however: see *Selvarajan* v *Race Relations Board* (1976). Pry has collected damaging evidence concerning the College's proprietor; the College may be able to show that Pry acted unfairly in the way he interviewed this person.

Natural justice requires that the proprietor at least be given an outline of the charge against him. In *Maxwell* v *Department of Trade and Industry* (1974) the Court of Appeal held that it was enough that inspectors put to a witness any prejudicial point of substance against him, so as to give him a chance to explain it. Failure to inform the proprietor of the allegation could, therefore, be a breach of natural justice.

The failure to provide legal representation at the interview is not a breach of natural justice – in fact it is only necessary to ensure fairness in exceptional cases, such as those where serious charges are involved, or potential loss of property: see *R* v *Secretary of State for Home Department, ex parte Tarrant* (1984).

Thirdly, the College might argue that the whole inquiry by Pry is void because of bias. His 'strong views' on private education may mean that he is prejudiced against such institutions. Preconceived opinions will not per se disqualify Pry from acting provided he can still listen fairly to the evidence. For example, a licensing justice is not disqualified simply because he is a teetotaller (see *R* v *Nailsworth Licensing Justices, ex parte Bird* (1953)), but one who refused to grant a liquor licence on principle would be. The success of this ground of attack depends very much, therefore, on the nature and degree of bias. The College will have to show that there is a 'real danger' that Pry is biased; this is a higher standard of proof than the old 'reasonable suspicion' test, and is roughly equivalent to the 'real likelihood' of bias test of *Hannam* v *Bradford Corporation* (1970), though the emphasis is not on the probability of bias but on a degree of sufficiency to impugn the decision: per Lord Goff in *R* v *Gough* (1993). The real danger of bias test is applicable to all kinds of decision-making, including purely administrative decision-making: per Sedley J in *R* v *Secretary of State for Environment, ex parte Kirkstall Valley Campaign* (1996). However, one further difficulty on this point is the decision in *R* v *Secretary of State for Trade, ex parte Perestrello* (1981), where it was held that inspectors investigating a company's affairs had to act fairly, but that bias, as that concept was used in cases such as *Metropolitan Properties Co Ltd* v *Lannon* (1968), was not an appropriate ground on which to attack their actions. Further, the College may object to the inspector's report being summarised by a civil servant, but provided it is a fair and balanced summary that does not pre-judge the issue it cannot be challenged: see *Selvarajan* v *Race Relations Board* (above). These cases probably remain good law even after Sedley J's 'red light' extension of the real danger of bias test to administrative decision-making, since Sedley J himself made it clear that whilst the test for bias should be constant the question of whether or not apparent bias has been established would depend on the proximity of the interest to the issue being decided.

There is probably insufficient proximity in the present case, which involves preliminary investigations.

Finally, the College might challenge the minister's policy of not supporting correspondence colleges. Arguably it is not in keeping with the granting to him of a power to help such colleges, and could be further attacked on the grounds that it places undue emphasis on the government's overall spending policy, and that it reflects the minister's admitted preference for public sector education. Even if this is not enough to invalidate the policy upon which the refusal of assistance was based, the College could go further and show that in applying the policy, the minister failed to consider anything new that the College might have had to say: see *British Oxygen Co Ltd* v *Minister of Technology* (1971). The College will be able to establish illegality if it can be shown that the minister deliberately closed his ears to anything new it might have had to say that might have persuaded him to depart from his policy: see *R* v *Port of London Authority, ex parte Kynoch* (1919) and *R* v *Secretary of State for the Environment, ex parte Brent London Borough Council* (1982).

10 The European Convention on Human Rights

10.1 Introduction

The civil liberties enjoyed by citizens of the United Kingdom have, traditionally, been described as 'residual'. What is meant by this is that citizens have been free to do as they please provided their actions have not contravened the law. This position can be contrasted with the position in countries with a written constitution where individual freedoms are usually 'positive', ie defined and protected in a Bill of Rights.

Legislation which curtails freedom includes, for example, public order legislation, laws on obscenity, laws to protect national security and so on. By the same token some legislation confers rights, eg race relations and sex equality. Traditionally the courts have viewed their role as being to protect liberty. Note, however, that under the doctrine of parliamentary sovereignty the government is often able to pass primary legislation that cannot be challenged by the courts. Civil liberties groups complain from time to time that such measures make significant inroads into traditional freedoms.

The incorporation of most aspects of the European Convention on Human Rights in the form of the Human Rights Act 1998 looks set to change the whole philosophy of civil rights in the United Kingdom. For the first time there will be directly enforceable legal rights to privacy, family life, freedom of expression and public association.

10.2 Key points

a) *Why is a Bill of Rights important?*

The common law is inadequate to protect human rights; it lays down negative as opposed to positive rights. For example, there is no positive common law right to freedom of speech but merely a number of rules about what cannot be said, ie defamation, obscenity etc.

Whilst rights are given to the individual by the common law and statute, an individual would have to search through a host of cases and statutory provisions to find out what his civil rights were; much better for such rights to be contained in one document which would be fixed in the mind of each citizen, eg the basic rights contained in the American constitution are known by most United States' citizens.

The United Kingdom lacks a written constitution. In countries with such a written constitution the courts are free to strike down legislation which is in breach of the constitution. In the United Kingdom the concept of parliamentary sovereignty means that Parliament can do no wrong; so long as an Act receives the approval of both Houses of Parliament and the assent of the Monarch the courts are bound to apply it even if it does interfere with what elsewhere would be basic civil liberties.

The apparent reluctance of the courts to trespass on the right of Parliament to enact any such legislation as it sees fit further suggests that Parliament ought to be constrained by a document that sets out and protects basic human rights.

b) *The European Convention on Human Rights*

The United Kingdom was one of the original signatories to the European Convention on Human Rights in 1953, but it was not until the Human Rights Act 1998 was enacted that the Convention became directly enforceable as part of the United Kingdom's domestic law.

i) The rights protected are:

Article 2: Right to life

Article 3: Prohibition of torture

Article 4: Prohibition of slavery and forced labour

Article 5: Right to liberty and security

Article 6: Right to a fair trial

Article 7: No punishment without law

Article 8: Right to respect for private and family life

Article 9: Freedom of thought, conscience and religion

Article 10: Freedom of expression

Article 11: Freedom of assembly and association

Article 12: Right to marry

There are a number of protocols to the European Convention on Human Rights that states can sign up to as they see fit. The First Protocol, to which the United Kingdom is a signatory, provides for peaceful enjoyment of possessions. A number of articles contain express exemption provisions. For example, arts 11(2), 8(2), 9(2) and 10(2). States can apply for a derogation in time of war or public emergency – the United Kingdom applied for a derogation in respect of art 5(3) in the light of the terrorist problem in Northern Ireland: see *Brannigan and McBride* v *United Kingdom* (1993) 17 EHRR 539.

ii) Enforcing these rights at Strasbourg

At present applications are to the European Commission on Human Rights by United Kingdom Citizens alleging that their rights under the European Convention on Human Rights have been violated by the United Kingdom. If the application is found to be substantiated the Commission attempts to secure a friendly settlement between the parties. If this cannot be achieved it refers the matter to the European Court of Human Rights. Such has been the increase in the number of cases being brought before the

Commission and the European Court of Human Rights that serious backlogs have built up, with delays stretching to several years. As a result a new procedure has been agreed for handling cases at Strasbourg and is likely to come into operation on 1 January 2000. The new procedure will involve an applicant submitting his application with the Court's registry, which assigns it to a Chamber and a judge rapporteur who has responsibility for overseeing the progress of the application. A committee, or tribunal, of judges considers the admissibility of the application and, provided at least one of the three considers it to be admissible, the ruling is communicated to the member state against whom the application has been made. If a friendly settlement cannot be reached the Chamber (seven judges) will give its judgment. The procedure also applies to applications between states. The authors of these reforms envisage that an application will only need to be referred to the Grand Chamber in exceptional cases, and a panel of five Grand Chamber judges will decide whether there are grounds for re-examination, unless the case is one where the Chamber itself has relinquished jurisdiction. It may be a number of years before this new single-tier system becomes operational. The Committee of Ministers becomes responsible for overseeing the enforcement of the Court's rulings.

c) *How the Convention will be enforced in the United Kingdom*

i) How will Convention issues be brought before the courts?

The 1998 Act does not expressly create a new procedure for raising alleged violations of Convention rights. Section 7(1) envisages that individuals will be able to bring proceedings (or a counterclaim) against a public body in the appropriate court or tribunal 'as may be determined in accordance with rules' (s7(2)). Section 7(9) provides that these rules are to be made by the Lord Chancellor. Alternatively, litigants will be allowed to 'rely on the Convention right or rights concerned in any legal proceedings' (s7(1)(b)), legal proceedings including, for these purposes, 'proceedings brought by or at the instigation of a public authority; and ... an appeal against the decision of a court or tribunal' (s7(6)(a) and (b)). Only the 'victim' of the alleged unlawful act is permitted to bring proceedings or rely on the Convention in legal proceedings (s7(1)). It is clear that many of the cases involving reliance on Convention rights will take the form of applications for judicial review, given that the Act is of direct application to public bodies (see below). The result is that a narrower test for locus standi will be applied in applications alleging a breach of Convention rights, as compared to applications for review generally.

ii) Who can be the subject of these proceedings?

By virtue of s6(1) it becomes unlawful for a public authority to act (or fail to act – see s6(6)) in a way which is incompatible with a Convention right. A public body for these purposes includes a court or tribunal, and 'any person certain of whose functions are functions of a public nature, but does not include either House of the [United Kingdom] Parliament or a person exercising functions in connection with proceedings in the [United Kingdom] Parliament' (s6(3)). The term 'Parliament' as used in s6(3) does not include the House of Lords in its judicial capacity. By contrast the Scottish Parliament and the Welsh Assembly, as subordinate legislatures, are bound by the 1998 Act. A 'person is not a public authority by virtue only of subsection (3)(b) if the nature of the act is private.' It seems likely that the courts will be influenced by the jurisprudence built up in relation to applications for judicial review in determining whether non-statutory bodies can be regarded as public authorities for these purposes: see for example *R* v *Panel on Take-overs and Mergers, ex parte Datafin plc* [1987] 2 WLR 699. It is possible that bodies such as the BBC, the Church of England and other religious bodies, universities, the governing bodies of various sports associations, self-regulatory bodies, and any organisation that has taken over what was previously a public law function, such as running prisons, could come within the scope of 'public authority' for the purposes of the Act, as regards their public law functions. The press will presumably not come within the scope of the Act, raising the possibility of different approaches being taken to the right to privacy under art 8 depending on whether it is a television broadcast or newspaper article that is complained of.

iii) How should the courts approach a Convention claim?

A court or tribunal called upon to do so, must interpret primary legislation and subordinate legislation 'in a way which is compatible with the Convention rights' (s3(1)). This duty applies whether the legislation was enacted before or after the coming into force of the Human Rights Act 1998. Section 2(1) of the 1998 Act makes it clear that any court or tribunal determining a question arising in connection with a Convention right *must* take into account: any judgment, decision, declaration or advisory opinion of the European Court of Human Rights; any opinion of the Commission given in a report adopted under art 31 of the Convention; any decision of the Commission in connection with art 26 or 27(2) of the Convention, or any decision of the Committee of Ministers taken under art 46 of the Convention, 'whenever made or given, so far as, in the opinion of the court or tribunal, it is relevant to the proceedings in which that question has arisen.'

iv) What remedies will be available?

A court dealing with an application for judicial review of subordinate legislation would be able to declare it to be ultra vires if it was found to incompatible with the Convention rights. The courts have no such power in relation to primary legislation, however. Indeed s3(2)(b) expressly provides that the section 'does not affect the validity, continuing operation or enforcement of any incompatible primary legislation'. Further the section cannot be relied upon to invalidate incompatible subordinate legislation if '(disregarding any possibility of revocation) primary legislation prevents removal of the incompatibility' (s3(2)(c)). Where an irreconcilable issue of compatibility arises before the House of Lords, the Judicial Committee of the Privy Council, the Courts-Martial Appeal Court, or the High Court or the Court of Appeal, that court will be empowered to grant a declaration of incompatibility. In relation to subordinate legislation the power to make such declarations will arise provided (disregarding any possibility of revocation) the primary legislation concerned prevents removal of the incompatibility. Where such a declaration is made it does not 'affect the validity, continuing operation or enforcement of the provision in respect of which it is given; and ... is not binding on the parties to the proceedings in which it is made' (s4(6)). Whilst the 1998 Act does not provide for any new judicial remedies (other than the declaration of incompatibility), a court finding that a public authority as acted unlawfully within the terms of s6 'may grant such relief or remedy, or make such order, within its powers as it considers just and appropriate' (s8(1)).

v) Remedial action by ministers

Where a declaration of incompatibility has been made and rights of appeal have been exhausted, abandoned or become time-barred, or it appears to a minister that (in the light of a finding of the European Court of Human Rights) a provision of legislation is incompatible with obligations under the Convention, a minister may, if he considers that there are compelling reasons for so doing, make orders to amend the relevant legislation to the extent that considers necessary to remove the incompatibility: see s10(1) and (2).

vi) Pre-enactment procedures

Section 19 of the 1998 Act places the relevant minister in charge of a Bill under a duty to 'make a statement to the effect that in his view the provisions of the Bill are compatible with the Convention rights', or to make a statement to the effect that 'although he is unable to make a statement of compatibility the government nevertheless wishes the House to proceed with the Bill.' Such statements must be made before the Second Reading of a Bill, must be in writing and should be published in such manner as the minister considers appropriate.

d) *Is the European Convention on Human Rights the most desirable Bill of Rights?*

The European Convention on Human rights is over 45 years old. It was mooted and designed in the years immediately following the end of the Second World War. Can it really be said to be relevant to what is today a very different world?

It is drafted in very general terms. United Kingdom judges are used to specifically worded statutes that they can and do interpret literally. Will United Kingdom judges be able to deal with such generally worded provisions that will require more than a mere literal interpretation? Even if they are will they be accused of 'making' law and thereby come into conflict with the legislature?

The nature of the rights protected under the Convention is open to question. For example the right to 'liberty and security of the person' (art 5) is expressly subject to a number of exceptions allowing, for example, the lawful detention of persons for the prevention of infectious diseases, of persons of unsound mind, of alcoholics, of vagrants and of drug addicts. Article 11 which protects the 'right of freedom of assembly' etc is subject to restrictions – in particular governments can argue 'national security' as a legitimate reason for denying such a freedom. Finally, art 15 allows a government in time of war or other public emergency to ignore certain of the Convention's provisions. What is a public emergency can be a very subjective matter!

e) *Should the Human Rights Act 1998 have been protected by entrenchment?*

Given the doctrine of parliamentary sovereignty entrenchment of domestic legislation in the United Kingdom is problematic. Generally Parliament cannot bind its successors. Accordingly it cannot pass 'unrepealable' Acts: see *Vauxhall Estates* v *Liverpool Corporation* [1932] 1 KB 733 and *Ellen Street Estates Ltd* v *Minister of Health* [1934] 1 KB 590. Thus, in theory, it would be impossible to pass a Bill of Rights which could be 'entrenched' for evermore.

The courts could have been given the express power to disapply legislation found to be incompatible with Convention rights, but this would have represented a constitutional resettlement for which the Labour government responsible for the Human Rights Act 1998 had no political mandate. See as an example of this approach the Canadian Charter of Rights and Freedoms whereby the Canadian courts have been given the power to disapply incompatible legislation, unless the legislation in question expressly states that it is to apply notwithstanding any such incompatibility. The Labour government opted not to copy the approach taken following the incorporation of the Treaty of Rome (as it then was), whereby the European Communities Act 1972 operates to make certain aspects of European Community law directly part of domestic law, as this was a prerequisite of EU membership whilst becoming a signatory to the European Convention on Human Rights created no such obligations.

10.3 Recent cases

A v *United Kingdom* Case 100/1997/884/1096 (1998) The Times 1 October European Court of Human Rights – beating of child by parent amounted to violation of art 3 – the existing state of English criminal law, which permitted a defence of law reasonable chastisement, did not provide adequate protection for children.

D v *United Kingdom* (1997) The Times 12 May – deportation could amount to a breach of art 3 the applicant having reached a stage in his illness where the removal of care would have catastrophic personal consequences for him, and the real possibility of his dying in the most distressing circumstances.

Halford v *United Kingdom* (1997) The Times 3 July – interception of calls by employer could amount to a violation of the right to privacy – it extended to calls made from the workplace if no warning was given by an employer that calls would be monitored.

Steel and Others v *United Kingdom* (1998) The Times 1 October – United Kingdom law on breach of the peace could amount to a violation of art 10 where it prevented peaceful demonstrations from continuing.

Tinnelly and Sons Ltd and Others v *United Kingdom; McElduff and Others* v *United Kingdom* (1998) The Times 16 July – suppression of evidence in the public interest – could amount to an infringement of the right of access to the courts – art 6.

10.4 Analysis of questions

Where questions have arisen on the European Convention on Human Rights, or in relation to the adoption of a Bill of Rights for the United Kingdom, they have done so in the context of the United Kingdom merely being a signatory to the Convention, as opposed to the Convention being part of domestic law. Naturally once the Human Rights Act 1998 comes fully into force in early 2000, the type of question set will change dramatically, probably centring on the operation of the 1998 Act. Although the questions and answers that follow are still, as of December 1998, relevant and legally correct, they will quickly become redundant with the passage of time – the issues they raise having been overtaken by events. For the present they should be read as a guide to the background to the debate over incorporation of the European Convention on Human Rights, and as a guide to the effect such a measure is likely to have in terms of the separation of powers, the rule of law and parliamentary sovereignty.

10.5 Questions

QUESTION ONE

Why has the European Convention on Human Rights been incorporated into domestic law?

Written by the Editors

General Comment

This question requires a good knowledge of the arguments for and against the adoption of the European Convention on Human Rights as a Bill of Rights.

Skeleton Solution

- Introduction: the existing constitutional safeguards for protecting human rights in the United Kingdom.
- The nature of the European Convention on Human Rights.
- The arguments in favour of adopting the Convention as a Bill of Rights for the United Kingdom.
- The effect of the Human Rights Act 1998.

Suggested Solution

The United Kingdom constitution is unwritten in the formal sense and accordingly lays great emphasis on the virtues of the common law and the legislative supremacy of Parliament. It relies heavily on the political process to ensure that Parliament does not override the basic rights and liberties of the subject, nor remove from the courts the adjudication of disputes between the citizen and the state arising out of the exercise of executive power.

The European Convention on Human Rights, prepared under the auspices of the Council of Europe, entered into force in September 1953. The Convention is a treaty under international law and its authority derives solely from the consent of those states that have become parties to it. The Convention declares certain human rights that should be protected by law in each state and provides political and judicial procedures by which alleged infringements of these rights may be examined at an international level. Every state party to the Convention has a duty to ensure that its domestic law conforms to the Convention, but a state is under no duty to incorporate the Convention itself within its domestic law.

Those who argued in favour of adopting the European Convention as a Bill of Rights for the United Kingdom pointed out that human rights were not adequately protected under then existing United Kingdom law and that further constitutional protection for human rights was therefore necessary. In support of their case they pointed to the ever-increasing role of the state in economic and social affairs and the widespread public disillusionment with the parliamentary process and the 'undemocratic' electoral system which produced a legislature dominated and controlled by the executive. Critics pointed also to the 'incremental' erosion of civil liberties exemplified by measures such as the Criminal Justice and Public Order Act 1994. There was also concern at the record of the United Kingdom under the European Convention on Human Rights and dissatisfaction with the performance of the courts in dealing with disputes between the citizen and the state: see *Malone* v *Metropolitan Police Commissioner* (1979). With the executive every day assuming more statutory powers and in so doing eroding common law liberties, so it was argued that it became more vital to provide safeguards against the abuse of those powers.

This traditional British approach to individual liberties is considered by many to be outdated and incapable of protecting individual rights from executive encroachment. Critics have long advocated the creation of a new Bill of Rights for the United Kingdom. In 1978 a select committee of the House of Lords was established to consider whether a Bill of Rights was desirable and, if so, what form it should take. The committee, while doubting that a Bill of

Rights was desirable, nevertheless held unanimously that if there were to be a Bill of Rights, it should be a Bill to incorporate the European Convention of Human Rights into United Kingdom law. Following the May 1997 general election the Labour government carried out its manifesto promise to incorporate the European Convention of Human Rights into United Kingdom law by enacting the Human Rights Act 1998.

If one accepts that some form of Bill of Rights was needed in the United Kingdom, incorporation of the European Convention offered the easiest and most acceptable option available to the government. There is no dispute as to the rights protected. The Convention omits economic and social rights, over which considerable political controversy might arise, and is confined to certain basic rights and liberties which the framers of the Convention considered would be generally accepted in the liberal democracies of Western Europe. Incorporation of the Convention will also help avoid the frequent humiliations suffered by the United Kingdom before the European Court of Human Rights when, in the glare of international publicity, it is found in breach of its international obligations under the Convention. 'Foreign' judges will no longer be able to pontificate on the acceptability of United Kingdom law, unless an applicant has exhausted all legal remedies available within the United Kingdom.

Many would argue that, to be fully effective, incorporation would have to enable the British courts to apply the Convention if necessary in preference to existing rules of statute or common law and that this would entail grafting onto the present constitution an added power in the courts to give redress to the individual even against an Act of Parliament. Such an approach would raise issues concerning the relationship of the courts to the political process, including the special difficulties inherent in the attempt by a supreme Parliament to bind itself. In the light of this the government has opted for a compromise by providing in s3(1) of the Human Rights Act 1998 that a court or tribunal called upon to do so, must interpret primary legislation and subordinate legislation in a way which is compatible with the Convention rights. This duty applies whether the legislation was enacted before or after the coming into force of the Human Rights Act 1998.

QUESTION TWO

What difference, if any, does incorporation of the European Convention on Human Rights into United Kingdom law make to the United Kingdom's constitution?

Adapted from University of London LLB Examination
(for External Students) Constitutional Law June 1987 Q9

General Comment

Although this question is phrased rather generally students should concentrate on the effects of incorporation on the sovereignty of Parliament and the role of the judiciary in interpreting and enforcing a Bill of Rights in the United Kingdom.

Skeleton Solution

- Introduction.
- The need for a Bill of Rights.
- The Human Rights Act 1998.
- The role of the judges.
- The impact on parliamentary sovereignty.

Suggested Solution

The incorporation into domestic law of the European Convention on Human Rights by means of the Human Rights Act 1998 comes in the wake of increasing demands for better protection for individual rights in the United Kingdom. The Criminal Justice and Public Order Act 1994 was a controversial measure and seen by many as evidence of the further erosion of freedom of expression and protest under the United Kingdom constitution. In most countries there is a written constitution which is not just a 'sacred' piece of paper but a statement that the people are the ultimate source of power, that the state and its legislature and its civil servants and laws are the servants of the people. It was thought by some that the enactment of a Bill of Rights in the United Kingdom would help to reassert the supremacy of the individual over the state. Does the incorporation of the European Convention on Human Rights achieve these ends?

The answer has to be a qualified 'no'. There are a number of reasons for this. First, the 1998 Act only incorporates certain provisions of the Convention. Second, the United Kingdom courts have not been given the power to override statutes found to be incompatible with the Convention.

A court or tribunal called upon to do so, must interpret primary legislation and subordinate legislation 'in a way which is compatible with the Convention rights.' (s3(1)). This duty applies whether the legislation was enacted before or after the coming into force of the Human Rights Act 1998. Section 2(1) of the 1998 Act further makes it clear that any court or tribunal determining a question arising in connection with a Convention right *must* take into account: any judgment, decision, declaration or advisory opinion of the European Court of Human Rights; any opinion of the Commission given in a report adopted under art 31 of the Convention; any decision of the Commission in connection with art 26 or 27(2) of the Convention, or any decision of the Committee of Ministers taken under art 46 of the Convention, 'whenever made or given, so far as, in the opinion of the court or tribunal, it is relevant to the proceedings in which that question has arisen.'

Hence the courts will retain their traditional role of applying the law, rather than ruling on the validity of primary legislation. Indeed s3(2)(b) expressly provides that the section 'does not affect the validity, continuing operation or enforcement of any incompatible primary legislation'. Where an irreconcilable issue of compatibility arises before the House of Lords, the Judicial Committee of the Privy Council, the Courts-Martial Appeal Court, or the High Court or the Court of Appeal, that court will be empowered to grant a declaration of incompatibility. Where a declaration of incompatibility has been made and rights of appeal have been exhausted, abandoned or become time-barred, or it appears to a minister that (in the light of a finding of the European Court of Human Rights) a provision of legislation is incompatible with obligations under the Convention, a minister may, if he considers that there are compelling reasons for so doing, make orders to amend the relevant legislation to the extent that considers necessary to remove the incompatibility: see s10(1) and (2).

It could be argued that the 1998 Act is further evidence of the steady erosion parliamentary sovereignty. Although a declaration of incompatibility does place a minister under a duty to take remedial action (see below), the political pressure to do so will be intense. It suggests more clearly than ever before that it is the judiciary that are to be the protectors of minority groups, not a legislature that represents, by definition, the interests of majority groups.

It seems inevitable that the courts are going to have to adopt a new approach to statutory interpretation where Convention rights are concerned, rather than stick rigidly to the traditional 'rules' of interpretation. The tradition of the European Court of Human Rights is to be more flexible and evaluative in its exercise of its interpretative functions. Thus domestic judges will have a more explicit role in assessing the merits of executive decision-making (ie its legitimacy within the context of the European Convention on Human Rights), whereas their role to date, at least in theory, has been limited to scrutinising the legality of executive action by means of judicial review.

In all of this it should be remembered that the Human Rights Act 1998 is still just a domestic Act. It would be open to any future Parliament to repeal it at will. Parliament can still make or unmake any law. There is still no area or subject matter outside the scope of its legislative powers. Parliament still cannot bind its successors and a later Parliament will remain, in theory at least, able to expressly repeal the legislation made by an earlier Parliament.

It can be seen therefore that so long as Parliament remains sovereign there can be no entrenchment of legislation against future amendment or repeal. Only Parliament can limit its own sovereignty and such limitations must have been enacted in the form of statute. However, the real check upon the sovereignty of Parliament in practice remains public opinion. The government always knows that it will have to face a general election within a few years and this stark reality may have a restraining effect upon their legislative proposals and deter any attempted government tampering with the Bill of Rights. Of course these informal restraints are present and operating already to curtail executive power and in this respect the presence of a Bill of Rights will make little difference.

QUESTION THREE

Critically assess the following statement 'that the case for a Bill of Rights has always rested on the belief that it would make a distinct and valuable contribution to the better protection of human rights'.

Adapted from University of London LLB Examination
(for External Students) Constitutional Law June 1988 Q6

General Comment

Clearly when this question was set the European Convention on Human Rights had not been incorporated in to domestic law. It is still of relevance, however, in that it raises the question as to whether such a move was necessary and what the effect of the incorporation might be.

Skeleton Solution

- Explain the protection offered under English law – statutory provisions – common law decision.
- Shortcomings of both – examples of breaches of human rights under the European Convention on Human Rights by the United Kingdom government.
- Impact of the Human Rights Act.
- Remaining issues of entrenchment and interpretation.

Suggested Solution

The question invites discussion of the merits and demerits of a Bill of Rights being enacted. One could commence by pointing that there has been a Bill of Rights on the statute book since 1689, but of course that legislation was not concerned with the rights of individuals so much as the relationship between Parliament and the Crown. Whilst the Bill of 1689 may have been effective to prevent individuals being subject to arbitrary prerogative power as exercised by the Monarch in person, it did little to protect the individual citizen from the excesses of governmental power exercised under the guise of parliamentary sovereignty; indeed one might well contend that one of the failings of the Glorious Revolution was to place too much power in the hands of the legislature, and thereby the government.

There have been a number of attempts to introduce a Bill of Rights aimed at strengthening the protection of individual rights under English law, notably Lord Lester's Human Rights Bill, which was considered by the House of Lords in February 1995. Matters have moved on, however, and the election of a Labour government in May 1997 led to the enactment of the Human Rights Act 1998 – by which means most of the key provisions of the European Convention on Human Rights have been incorporated into the domestic law of the United Kingdom.

The statement under consideration suggests that a Bill of Rights, such as the European Convention on Human Rights, can make a distinct contribution to the better protection of human rights. This prompts the question, 'better than what?'

Under English law, individual rights are protected by either statute or common law. Examples of statutory protection are provided by the Race Relations Act 1976, Sex Discrimination Act 1975, and the Police and Criminal Evidence Act 1984. At common law decisions such as *Christie* v *Leachinsky* (1947), under which a police officer was required to inform a suspect of the grounds for an arrest, or *Entick* v *Carrington* (1765), under which the courts invalidated the practice of issuing general search warrants, have undoubtedly contributed to the protection of individual rights and liberties. Can it be said that this combined protection is so inadequate that a formal Bill of Rights is needed?

The problem with 'equal rights' or 'civil liberties' legislation is that such measures are always at the mercy of successive Parliaments. The Human Rights Act 1998 is no different. As a consequence of parliamentary sovereignty these Acts can always be amended or repealed. Further, it can be argued that when Parliament places individual liberties on a statutory basis it can draft them in terms that make them more limited in operation than they were at common law. Historically successive Parliaments have fought shy of granting United Kingdom citizens positive statutory rights, such as the right to free expression, the right to information, and the right to privacy. There has always been a residual fear that the creation of positive statutory rights would draw the judiciary into the political arena. With the enactment of the Human Rights Act 1998 that fear may be about to materialise as reality. It seems inevitable that the courts are going to have to adopt a new approach to statutory interpretation where Convention rights are concerned, rather than stick rigidly to the traditional 'rules' of interpretation. The tradition of the European Court of Human Rights is to be more flexible and evaluative in its exercise of its interpretative functions. Thus domestic judges will have a more explicit role in assessing the merits of executive decision-making (ie its legitimacy within the context of the European Convention on Human Rights), whereas their role to date, at least in theory, has been limited to scrutinising the legality of executive action by means of judicial review.

The courts' decisions will be based on a more overtly principled, indeed moral, basis. The court will need to be satisfied that any interference with a protected right is justified in the public interests in a free democratic society.

The key failing of the common law as a means of protecting individual rights is that it is sporadic in nature. The judiciary can only develop individual rights at common law if cases are brought before them. Whether or not this occurs is a haphazard affair, not the best way in which to tackle such a serious matter. In any event, any decision of the courts can be nullified by subsequent parliamentary action in the form of new legislation, which can even be retrospective if necessary. The courts have not always responded when called upon by litigants to defend or develop human rights. Mr Malone's arguments for a right to privacy fell upon deaf ears in *Malone* v *Metropolitan Police Commissioner* (1979), the Vice Chancellor concluding that as there was no English law governing the matter of telephone-tapping, he would be usurping the function of Parliament by holding that such action did amount to an invasion of the plaintiff's right to privacy regarding his communications.

Those who contend that a Bill of Rights is not needed can be referred to the succession of findings against the United Kingdom by the European Court of Human Rights under the European Convention: see *Malone* v *United Kingdom* (1985), *Tyrer* v *United Kingdom* (1978) etc. Matters in relation to which the British government, and by implication the British constitution, has been found wanting are: the law of contempt; the law relating to telephone-tapping; the rights of prisoners to communicate with lawyers; the rights of prisoners to be legally represented in prison disciplinary proceedings; detention without trial under the Prevention of Terrorism legislation; corporal punishment; and restrictions upon adult homosexuals in Northern Ireland.

Whether, by incorporating the European Convention on Human Rights, the government has chosen the most suitable model for its Bill of Rights is debatable. Three matters in particular should be borne in mind. First, the Convention is selective in the rights it seeks to protect, it contains no reference to a right to education, health care, or employment. It reflects a 'Western' view of individual rights, as opposed to a 'Socialistic' view. Second, the Convention includes many limitations upon the rights set forth, and does allow signatory states to derogate from some of its provisions in certain circumstances. For example, the Convention does provide for freedom of association, but goes on to recognise that governments can limit this right if it is in the national interests to do so, thus the Civil Service Unions involved in the GCHQ union ban dispute were not able to pursue their case under the Convention. Third, a Bill of Rights can only be effective if it is protected to some extent from repeal or amendment by subsequent governments, and if subsequent legislation is applied only to the extent that it does not conflict with the Bill of Rights.

The Human Rights Act 1998 is not entrenched. The United Kingdom courts have not been given the power to override statutes found to be incompatible with the Convention. A court or tribunal called upon to do so, must interpret primary legislation and subordinate legislation 'in a way which is compatible with the Convention rights' but cannot disapply incompatible legislation. Certain higher courts will be able to grant declarations of incompatibility, but these will have no coercive force.

QUESTION FOUR

Was incorporation of the European Convention of Human Rights into domestic law really necessary?

Written by the Editors

General Comment

It is tempting to run through all the well rehearsed arguments for and against incorporation of the Convention on Human Rights, but the examiner wishes the student to concentrate on a particular issue: will individual rights in the United kingdom be better protected following incorporation?

Skeleton Solution

- Examination of the common law tradition.
- Lord Lester's critique.
- The case for incorporation.
- Counter arguments.
- The reality of incorporation.
- How the Human Rights Act 1998 will work.
- Conclusion.

Suggested Solution

In Dicey's exposition of the theory of the Rule of Law emphasis was placed on the role of the judge as defender of civil liberties; indeed Dicey went as far as to assert that the British constitution, in its aspects relating to basic rights and freedoms, was a judge-made one. Historically Parliament built on the foundations laid by the common law. Since 1952 successive British governments have ratified the European Convention on Human Rights and since 1965 individual United Kingdom citizens have been permitted to petition the European Court of Human Rights at Strasbourg to obtain remedies for breaches of the Convention by United Kingdom governments. Eventually, in 1998, the Convention was incorporated into domestic law with the enactment of the Human Rights Act.

Why was such incorporation seen as necessary? In a devastating critique, Anthony Lester QC ([1984] PL 46) argued that the United Kingdom had one of the worst records of violations of the European Convention and stated that: 'no other country which belongs to the Convention has been faced with so many cases of such importance'. His catalogue included cases involving inhumane treatment of prisoners generally and of terrorist suspects in particular; inadequate safeguards against invasion of privacy; unfair sex and race discrimination, especially in the fields of employment and immigration law; inhumane punishments for school children (cane in English schools, tawse or strap in Scottish schools); nationalisation without fair compensation; oppressive interference with free speech through the laws of contempt of court and confidentiality; and so the list goes on. In all these examples the government of the day was usually obliged to enact new laws to comply with the rulings of the European Court of Human Rights. As Lester cogently argued, such slow reform could have been avoided if the European Convention on Human Rights had been directly enforceable by United Kingdom judges able (and indeed obliged) to adapt common law and statute law to comply with the jurisprudence of the European Court of Human Rights and the precedents set by that Court.

Although the matter is somewhat academic, given that incorporation of the Convention has now occurred, thought might still be given to whether it was as necessary as Lord Lester and others maintained. At first sight Lester's catalogue of British inadequacies would appear conclusive, but in fact his case is rather misleading. Although it is true that the United Kingdom has the worst record of violations, this should be set in the context that the United Kingdom allowed the right of individual petition as long ago as 1965, whereas others of the 1952 signatories allowed their citizens such access much later, eg France in the early 1980s, so that the inadequacies of the French system are only now coming to light (bearing in mind the typical wait of four to five years before a case reaches judgment at the European Court of Human Rights).

Another factor which could be used to counter Lester's argument is that United Kingdom judges were already taking account of the Convention when interpreting ambiguous common law and statute law: see *Derbyshire County Council* v *Times Newspapers Ltd* (1993). In the *Derbyshire* case both the Court of Appeal and the House of Lords held that local authorities could not sue for libel in respect of their reputation for administration because otherwise such a right of action would stifle legitimate public criticism of their activities and impose an unnecessary restriction on freedom of expression in a democratic society. Lord Keith, in the leading judgment, managed to reach his conclusion without finding the need to rely upon the European Convention: 'I find it satisfactory to be able to conclude that the common law of England is consistent with the obligations assumed by the Crown under the treaty in this particular field.' Was incorporation of the Convention really necessary when the common law was capable of responding to the challenges placed before it? As Lord Denning often said in his career on the bench, common law is capable of evolving from precedent to precedent so as to move with the times and to meet the needs of society.

Will rights be any better protected following incorporation? The answer must be in the affirmative given that it will be so much easier for litigants to raise arguments related to Convention rights. Instead of taking a case to the Commission in Strasbourg a litigant will be able to bring proceedings (or a counterclaim) against a public body in the appropriate court or tribunal. Alternatively litigants will be allowed to 'rely on the Convention right or rights concerned in any legal proceedings' (s7(1)(b)). By virtue of s6(1) it becomes unlawful for a public authority to act (or fail to act – see s6(6)) in a way which is incompatible with a Convention right. A public body for these purposes includes a court or tribunal, and 'any person certain of whose functions are functions of a public nature'.

Section 6(1), therefore, effectively creates a new 'head' of ultra vires as regards applications for judicial review of public bodies. If a public body fails to pay due regard to the terms of the Convention, or indeed the jurisprudence of the European Court of Justice, in exercising its discretion, prima facie grounds for review will exist. In particular the notion of proportionality as developed by the European Court of Human Rights becomes a facet of domestic law to which reviewing courts will now be obliged to have regard.

The enforcement of rights will be made more effective by virtue of the fact that a court or tribunal called upon to do so, will have to interpret primary legislation and subordinate legislation 'in a way which is compatible with the Convention rights' (s3(1)). This duty will apply whether the legislation in question was enacted before or after the coming into force of the Human Rights Act 1998. Although the courts will not be able to disapply legislation that conflicts with the Convention rights where an irreconcilable issue of compatibility arises before the House of Lords, the Judicial Committee of the Privy Council, the Courts-Martial Appeal Court, or the High Court or the Court of Appeal, that court will be empowered to grant a declaration of incompatibility.

The granting of such a declaration should trigger action by the relevant minister to amend the offending law to ensure compliance.

Hence it seems likely that there will be a flood of cases raising issues related to Convention rights once the Human Rights Act 1988 comes fully into force in they year 2000. Only then will it become possible to carry out a meaningful comparison between the protection of individual rights at common law, and the protection of positive statutory rights under the 1998 Act.

11 Public Order

11.1 Introduction

English law provides for numerous restrictions on the individual's freedom to assemble and associate with others. The purpose of these restrictions is to ensure that public expressions of dissent and protest take place within legal parameters, thus ensuring a balance between the interests of protesters and others who wish to go about their day-to-day business without let or hindrance. Inevitably the imposition of such restrictions can create tensions between those who prioritise public order on the one hand and those who fear excessive state controls on the other.

The demonstration, protest march and public meeting are important political weapons that can result in government policy being changed, for example the abolition of the Poll Tax, the blocking of the anti-fox hunting Bill etc. One of the priorities of government is to maintain public order, and a balance has to be drawn between the right to protest and the existence of legal controls to prevent the breakdown of public order. Historically governments have reacted to threats to social order by introducing measures that restrict the scope of protest action. In the United Kingdom, in the latter part of the twentieth century, public order problems have been raised by violence on football terraces, serious disorder in urban areas, terrorist activities and the actions of 'new age' travellers and 'eco-warriors'. Key developments have included the Police and Criminal Evidence Act 1984, the Public Order Act 1986 and the Criminal Justice and Public Order Act 1994. These Acts taken together represent a significant step towards the codification of the law on public order but there are other very significant measures, and various important common law rulings.

11.2 Key points

Common law

a) *Breach of the peace*

Section 40 of the Public Order Act 1986 specifically retains the common law powers to deal with or prevent a breach of the peace, and s17(5) and (6) of the Police and Criminal Evidence Act 1984 preserve common law powers of entry to deal with breaches of the peace. A precise definition of breach of the peace is difficult to give, but it must involve an element of actual or apprehended violence to person or property. It could further be defined as arising when a person causes harm to, or appears likely to do so, persons or property or acts in a manner the natural consequence of which is to provoke others to violence. A police officer who has either witnessed a breach of the peace, or who has reasonable grounds for believing that a breach of the peace is about to occur, can arrest an offender without warrant: see *R* v *Howell* [1982] QB 416; *R* v *Chief Constable of Devon and Cornwall, ex parte CEGB* [1982] QB 458; *Moss* v *McLachlan* (1984) 149 JP 167. In *Duncan* v *Jones* [1936] 1 KB 218 the power was used to effectively prevent a public meeting. In *Moss* v *McLachlan* (1985) 149 JP 167 flying pickets were turned back on the basis that a breach of the peace was imminent.

b) *Entry into meetings*

The police have the right to be present in public places where there are fears of public disorder. They also have the right to enter private premises where there are reasons to believe a breach of the peace is imminent as a result of a private meeting being held there: see *Thomas* v *Sawkins* [1935] 2 KB 249. Similarly, there is a power to enter private premises to deal with 'domestic' disputes: see *McLeod* v *Commissioner of the Metropolitan Police* [1994] 4 All ER 553.

Statutory powers

a) *Obstruction of the police*

Under the Police Act 1996 s89(1) any person who assaults a police constable in the execution of his duty or (under s89(2)) resists or wilfully obstructs a police constable in the course of his duty is guilty of an offence. Policing inevitably involves the exercise of discretion. In the context of public order the issue is the extent to which the police can lawfully intervene. See *Duncan* v *Jones* [1936] 1 KB 218; *Piddington* v *Bates* [1960] 3 All ER 660.

b) *Obstruction of the highway*

Under the Highways Act 1980 a person is guilty of an offence if he wilfully obstructs the free passage of the highway. To initiate a meeting which results in such an obstruction can result in conviction, even in circumstances where the highway was not completely blocked: see *Arrowsmith* v *Jenkins* [1963] 2 QB 561; *Hirst and Agu* v *Chief Constable for West Yorkshire* [1987] Crim LR 330.

c) *Public Order Act 1986*

The Public Order Act 1986 provides a framework of controls that apply to processions and demonstrations and enacts a range of offences to deal with conduct of varying seriousness.

i) Public order offences

The Public Order Act 1986 abolishes the common law offences of riot, rout, unlawful assembly and affray. It also abolishes the statutory offence of threatening behaviour under the Public Order Act 1936. These it replaces with an expanded range of public order offences – riot, violent disorder, affray, threatening behaviour and disorderly conduct.

Section 1 – riot. The offence of riot is retained for the most serious public order offences.

- Twelve or more persons must be present together and the difficult concept of common purpose is retained. This is to underline the seriousness of violent behaviour when committed collectively.

- A person of reasonable firmness must, as a result of the incident, fear for his personal safety. This hypothetical person need not actually be present at the scene at the time of the riot.
- Each of the persons present using unlawful violence is guilty of an offence. Unlawful violence is defined in s8.
- The consent of the DPP is necessary for a prosecution with underlying policy implications.

Section 2 – violent disorder. The offence of violent disorder is intended to deal with a range of situations from major public disorder to minor group disturbances, eg football hooliganism. It is a lesser offence than riot.

- Note the similarities with riot, ie the use or threat of unlawful violence and the fact that a person of reasonable firmness present at the scene should fear for his personal safety (although again this hypothetical person need not actually be present): see *R* v *Hebron* [1989] Crim LR 839.
- The number of persons present need only be three.
- The consent of the DPP is not necessary for a prosecution.

Section 3 – affray. This redefined offence is directed at those who use or threaten violence towards others as individuals.

- A person of reasonable firmness must fear for their personal safety.
- The offence anticipates the following sort of conduct – fighting outside pubs or football grounds and also on private premises: see *R* v *Davison* [1992] Crim LR 31.
- The jury should be directed to consider what the effect of the appellant's actions would have been on a putative third person, ie the bystander of reasonable firmness. Although there need not actually be any third person present for the offence to be made out, such a direction was necessary because the offence of affray was enacted for the protection of the innocent bystander, as opposed to the person at whom the violence was aimed: see *R* v *Sanchez* (1996) The Times 6 March

Section 4 – threatening behaviour. This section replaces s5 of the Public Order Act 1936.

- The concept of threatening abusive or insulting words or behaviour is retained and words can be verbal or in writing.
- There must be an intention to provoke unlawful violence or a person must believe that unlawful violence will be used against him: see *R* v *Horseferry Road Magistrates Court, ex parte Siadatan* [1990] Crim LR 598.
- Much of the old case law will continue to be relevant: see *Brutus* v *Cozens* [1973] AC 854; *Jordan* v *Burgoyne* [1963] 2 All ER 225.
- Section 154 of the Criminal Justice and Public Order Act 1994 adds a s4A to the Public Order Act 1986. An offence is committed where a defendant, with intent to cause a person harassment, alarm or distress (a) uses threatening, abusive or insulting words or behaviour, or disorderly behaviour, or (b) displays any writing, sign or other visible representation which is threatening, abusive or insulting, thereby causing that person, or another person, harassment, alarm or distress.

Section 5 – this section introduces a new offence of causing harassment, alarm or distress.

- The offence applies to disorderly behaviour and a person who sees or hears the conduct must be likely to be caused harassment, alarm or distress. The objective here is to protect the vulnerable.
- 'Disorderly behaviour', not being defined in the Act, is to be given its ordinary and everyday meaning and whether it was made out is also a question of fact for the court at first instance. In general terms, the expression does not require proof of threatening, abusive or insulting behaviour as these were matters dealt with elsewhere in the 1986 Act: see *Chambers and Edwards* v *DPP* [1995] Crim LR 896
- Defences are: (i) that the accused had no reason to believe that any such person was present; (ii) that the conduct was reasonable; and (iii) that the accused was inside a dwelling and had no reason to believe anyone outside could see or hear them.

Sections 17 to 23 – racial hatred. The sections deal with a variety of circumstances in which racial hatred is likely to be stirred up.

- As with s4, conduct must be threatening, abusive or insulting. The consequence must be the stirring up of racial hatred.
- The same interpretative conditions will apply to 'threatening', or 'abusive' or 'insulting' as with s4: see *Jordan* v *Burgoyne* [1963] 2 QB 744. Racial hatred is defined in s17. See too *Mandla* v *Lee* [1983] 2 AC 548.

Section 155 of the Criminal Justice and Public Order Act 1994 makes publishing or distributing racially offensive material (s19 Public Order Act 1986) an arrestable offence.

ii) Processions and demonstrations

A more comprehensive legal framework is laid down by the Public Order Act 1986 for the control of public processions and public meetings.

Section 11 – this section requires advance notice to be given to the police of public processions. By and large this section is intended to cover planned marches, including commemorative marches and excluding instances where it is not practicable to give notice, ie a spontaneous march.

Section 12 – authorises a senior police officer to impose conditions as to time, place or route on a public procession. There must be belief that serious public disorder or damage to property will result or that the objective is intimidation.

Section 13 – authorises the chief constable to apply to the council for an order prohibiting all marches for three months.

- The ban is a blanket ban and not aimed at specific groups. Clearly the chief constable must believe that serious public disorder would result in the event that the march was allowed to proceed.
- The ban is subject to the consent of the Home Secretary.
- The ban is subject to judicial review: *Kent* v *Metropolitan Police Commissioner* (1981) The Times 15 May.

Section 14 provides that a senior police officer may impose conditions in relation to public assemblies. Sections 70 and 71 of the Criminal Justice and Public Order Act 1994 insert new sections into s14 Public Order Act 1986 concerning the regulation of assemblies in progress. A chief constable can apply to the local authority for an order banning a trespassory assembly on the grounds that it may give rise either to serious disruption to the life of the community, or where the land or a building or monument on it is of historical, architectural, archeological or scientific importance and significant damage to the land, building or monument may occur.

These provisions cover places to which the public has no, or limited, rights of access. The ban is for up to four days and needs the consent of the Secretary of State.

Public assemblies are defined in s16, and the conditions on public assemblies are virtually the same as for public processions.

d) *Public Order Act 1936*

Section 1 of the Act makes it an offence to wear a uniform signifying membership of a political organisation: see *O'Moran* v *DPP* [1975] QB 364.

e) *Picketing*

Pickets can be in breach of both the civil and criminal law. Generally there is no 'right' to picket because it will not be a reasonable use of the highway unless for passing and re-passing. However, under s220 of the Trade Union and Labour Relations (Consolidation) Act 1992, picketing is lawful if it is in contemplation or furtherance of a trade dispute and at or near the strikers' own workplace for the purpose only of peacefully obtaining or communicating information or peacefully persuading any person to work or to abstain from working. This provision provides pickets with immunity in respect of civil actions for trespass or for inducing breach of contract. It follows from this that picketing someone else's place of work is illegal and the employer can obtain an injunction to stop it. In addition pickets find themselves in breach of the Public Order Act 1986 (as above).

f) *Criminal Justice and Public Order Act 1994*

i) Removing trespassers

Section 61 repeals s39 of the Public Order Act 1986 and gives police new powers to remove trespassers on land. Trespass was already criminalised by s39 of the 1986 Act, but it proved difficult to enforce. Section 61 is more tightly drawn and covers cases where permission to be on land has been withdrawn, reduces the number of vehicles required for a dispersal order to be made from 12 to six, extends definition of 'land' to include common land, and gives police powers to confiscate vehicles not willingly removed.

ii) Aggravated trespass

Section 68 – a person commits an offence if he trespasses on land in the open air and, in relation to any lawful activity which people there assembled are doing or are about to engage in, does anything that is intended by him to have the effect of:

- intimidating those persons so as to deter them from engaging in that activity; or
- obstructing that activity; or
- disrupting that activity.

iii) Squatters

Sections 75 and 76 – lawful owners and occupiers of property now have access to quicker and effective remedies against squatters. They can go to court immediately and apply for an interim possession order. If granted, squatters will have 24 hours to leave premises. Failure to do so will be an offence.

iv) Unauthorised campers

Section 77 – local authorities now have the power, where people are for the time being residing in a vehicle or vehicles on a highway or any unoccupied land, or on any occupied land without the occupier's consent, to give a direction that those persons must leave, taking vehicles and property with them. Failure to comply is a criminal offence. Note that s80(1) repeals a provision in the Caravan Sites Act 1968 which required local authorities to provide sites for gypsies. They are still empowered to do so, but are no longer required to.

v) Raves

Sections 63 to 67 – a rave is defined as a gathering in open air of 100 or more persons (whether or not they are trespassers), at which amplified music is played during the night which, by reason of its loudness and time at which it is played, is likely to cause serious distress to inhabitants of the locality. If a police officer reasonably believes that two or more people are planning a rave and that ten or more are waiting for it to begin or attending such a gathering, dispersal orders may be made requiring them to leave. Powers of entry and seizure of vehicles and sound equipment are given. Police officers are also empowered to turn people within a five-mile radius away before sufficient numbers gather.

g) *Protection from Harassment Act 1997*

Under this Act it is a criminal offence to use words or behaviour, on more than one occasion, which puts the victim in fear of violence, either intentionally or in circumstances where a reasonable person would have realised this would be the effect. The maximum penalty upon conviction is five years' imprisonment or an unlimited fine. The Act also provides for a lesser offence of using words or behaviour, on more than one occasion, which could cause the victim to be harassed, alarmed or distressed, either intentionally, or in circumstances where a reasonable person would have realised this would be the effect. The maximum penalty upon conviction is six months' imprisonment or a £5,000 fine. In respect of both offences there is a defence to the effect that the defendant was acting in the interests of national security; to prevent or detect crime; or was otherwise authorised by statute. The lesser offence is also be subject to a defence that the defendant had acted reasonably and necessarily in pursuit of a business trade or profession or other lawful activity. Both offences are 'arrestable' in the sense that police have powers of arrest without warrant as outlined in s24 of the Police and Criminal Evidence Act 1984.

11.3 Recent cases and statutes

DPP v *Jones* [1997] 2 WLR 578 – Queen's Bench Divisional Court held that an assembly could be trespassory contrary to ss14A and 14B of the Public Order Act 1986, even though it was peaceful and did not amount to an obstruction of the highway.

Steel and Others v *United Kingdom* (1998) The Times 1 October – European Court of Human Rights held that arrest and detention for breach of the peace could amount to a breach of art

10 of the European Convention on Human Rights where those arrested where engaged in peaceful protests. An appeal is pending before the House of Lords.

The Human Rights Act 1998 incorporates aspects of the European Convention on Human Rights into domestic law, including art 11, which provides:

'(1) Everyone has the right to freedom of peaceful assembly and to freedom of association with others, including the right to form and to join trade unions for the protection of his interests.

(2) No restrictions shall be placed on the exercise of these rights other than such as are prescribed by law and are necessary in a democratic society in the interests of national security or public safety, for the prevention of disorder or crime, for the protection of health or morals or for the protection of the rights and freedoms of others. This Article shall not prevent the imposition of lawful restrictions on the exercise of these rights by members of the armed forces, of the police or of the administration of the State.'

The Act is unlikely to come into effect before 2001.

The Crime and Disorder Act 1998 adds a number of racially aggravated versions of public order offences under the Public Order Act 1986 Act, specifically s4 (causing fear or provocation of violence), s4A (intentional harassment, alarm or distress) and s5 (harassment, alarm or distress). For these purposes an offence is racially aggravated if (under s28 of the 1998 Act):

'(a) at the time of committing the offence, or immediately before or after doing so, the offender demonstrates towards the victim of the offence hostility based on the victim's membership of, or association with members of, a racial group; or

(b) the offence is motivated (wholly or partly) by hostility towards members of a racial group based on their membership of that group.'

11.4 Analysis of questions

Questions can be problems or essays. Included below are examples of each. A knowledge of the Public Order Act 1986 as amended is essential and a methodical application of the provisions of the statutes to any problem will earn marks. An essay question may require a broader if limited knowledge of the social background to the various statutory provisions. The Criminal Justice and Public Order Act 1994 gives police further powers and must be understood alongside existing provisions.

11.5 Questions

QUESTION ONE

What difference, if any, has the Public Order Act 1986 made to English law?

University of London LLB Examination
(for External Students) Constitutional Law June 1987 Q8

General Comment

A relatively straightforward question concerning the Public Order Act 1986. Students should know the changes introduced by this Act and compare the new provisions with those existing at common law and under the Public Order Act 1936. A question like this is now unlikely to be set, but it is included for revision purposes on the provisions of the 1986 Act.

Skeleton Solution

- Introduction. General provisions of the Public Order Act 1986.
- Abolition of common law riot, rout, unlawful assembly and affray. Introduction of statutory riot, violent disorder and affray.
- Provisions relating to processions. Sections 12 and 13.
- Provisions relating to assemblies. Section 14.
- Provisions relating to racial hatred.
- Causing fear or provocation of violence. Causing harassment, alarm or distress.
- Miscellaneous provisions.

Suggested Solution

The Public Order Act 1986 was passed on 7 November 1986. Some provisions of the Act came into force on 1 January 1987. Most of the rest of the Act came into force on 1 April 1987. The Act firstly repeals certain provisions of the Public Order Act 1936. Second, it abolishes the common law offences of riot, rout, unlawful assembly and affray. Third, it introduces new statutory offences to replace some of the common law offences abolished or statutory offences repealed. Fourth, it amends or repeals other statutory provisions including those concerning racial hatred. Fifth, it introduces new powers in relation to offences committed at or in connection with football matches. Sixth, it introduces miscellaneous provisions in relation to tampering with goods on sale and also mass trespass.

One of the main differences made to the law under the new Act is that the ancient common law offences of riot, rout, unlawful assembly and affray have been abolished and replaced by three statutory offences: riot, violent disorder and affray. The basis of these offences is no longer breach of the peace but fear for personal safety on the part of a person of reasonable firmness present at the scene.

As regards the Public Order Act 1936 this is largely repealed. Section 3 has been repealed and replaced by a new provision of greater scope and effect and has been extended to certain public assemblies. As was already the case under the old 1936 Act, s12 of the 1986 Act gives the police the power to impose conditions on certain processions and under s13 the chief officer of police may in certain circumstances prohibit processions in his district with the consent of his local authority and the Home Secretary. The major difference under the new Act however is that now the organisers of public processions must give advance notice in writing to the police not less than six clear days before the date of any procession which is intended to demonstrate support for or opposition to the views or actions of any person or body of persons; or publicises a cause or campaign; or which marks or commemorates an event.

Section 14 of the 1986 Act (as amended by ss70 and 71 of the Criminal Justice and Public Order Act 1994) provides that a senior police officer may impose conditions in relation to public assemblies if, having regard to the time or place at which and the circumstances in which any public assembly is being held or is intended to be held, he reasonably believes that: (i) it may result in serious public disorder, serious damage to property or serious disruption to the life of the community; or (ii) the purpose of the persons organising it is the intimidation of others with a view to compelling them not to do an act they have a right to do, or to do an act they have a right not to do. The section states that he may give directions imposing on the persons organising or taking part in the assembly such conditions as to the place at which the assembly may be (or continue to be) held, its maximum duration, or the maximum number of persons who may constitute it, as appears to him necessary to prevent such disorder, damage, disruption or intimidation. Section 16 defines 'public assembly' as an assembly of 20 or more persons in a public place which is wholly or partly open to the air. Events such as the 'invasion' of Stonehenge during the summer solstice led the government to conclude that the 1986 Act was lacking in terms of the powers vested in the police to deal with static demonstrations. Hence, under ss14A, B and C (added by the 1994 Act), a chief officer of police is empowered to apply to the relevant local authority for an order prohibiting trespassory assemblies on land to which the public does not normally have a right of access, provided that there are grounds to reasonably believe that the owner of the land has not granted permission for the assembly and that the trespassory assembly may result in either serious disruption to the life of the community, or significant damage to land or buildings of historical, archeological or scientific importance. It is an offence to organise or participate in any such trespassory assembly in the knowledge that a banning order has been granted. *DPP* v *Jones* (1997) confirms that even peaceful non-obstructive gatherings are prohibited if such a ban is in force. Under s14C a police constable has the power to intercept and stop those reasonably believed to be proceeding to a trespassory assembly, and direct them not to proceed to the assembly. Disobedience to an order under this provision is a summary offence in relation to which a constable may exercise a power of arrest without a warrant.

Section 5A of the 1936 Act dealing with racial hatred has been restructured and amended to produce six new offences. Section 17 of the 1986 Act defines racial hatred as hatred against a group of persons in Great Britain defined by reference to colour, race, nationality (including citizenship) or ethnic or national origins. All six offences created by the Act require the consent of the Attorney-General to institute proceedings. All of these offences concern conduct which is threatening, abusive or insulting and which is intended or which is likely, having regard to all the circumstances, to stir up racial hatred. They are: (i) using such words or behaviour or displaying such materials; (ii) publishing or distributing such materials; (iii) presenting or directing a public play which involves such words or behaviour; (iv) distributing, showing or playing a recording of such visual images or sounds; (v) certain participation in a broadcast or cable programme service which includes such images or sounds; and (vi) possessing such material or recordings with a view to its being displayed, published, distributed, broadcast or included in a cable broadcast service.

Section 5 of the 1936 Act has also been repealed, and replaced by two new offences. Section 4 of the 1986 Act creates the offence of causing fear or provocation of violence. A person is guilty of an offence if he uses towards another person threatening, abusive or insulting words or behaviour, or distributes or displays to another person any writing, sign or other visible representation which is threatening, abusive or insulting, with intent to cause that person to believe that immediate unlawful violence will be used against him or another by any person, or to provoke the immediate use of unlawful violence by that person or another, or whereby that person is likely to believe that such violence will be used or it is likely that such violence will be provoked.

Section 5 of the 1986 Act creates the controversial offence of causing harassment, alarm or distress. A person is guilty of an offence if he uses threatening, abusive or insulting words or behaviour, or disorderly behaviour, or displays any writing, sign or other visible representation which is threatening, abusive or insulting, within the hearing or sight of a person likely to be caused harassment, alarm or distress thereby. Section 5 provides for three specific defences. First, that the defendant had no reason to believe that there was anyone within hearing or sight of his or her conduct who was likely to be harassed, alarmed or distressed; second, that he or she was inside a dwelling and had no reason to believe that the conduct would have been seen or heard by anyone outside; third, that his or her conduct was reasonable.

Following the enactment of s154 of the Criminal Justice and Public Order Act 1994 a further offence of causing intentional harassment alarm or distress has been created by adding a s4A to the 1986 Act. Under s4A a person will be guilty of the offence if he, with intent to cause another harassment, alarm, or distress, uses threatening, abusive or insulting words or behaviour or disorderly behaviour, or displays any writing, sign or other visible representation which is threatening, abusive or insulting, thereby causing another person harassment, alarm or distress. The offence can be committed in a public or private places, except where both parties are in private dwellings. A constable may arrest without a warrant anyone he reasonably suspects to be guilty of committing the offence. The offence is likely to be charged in cases of racial harassment, although it is clearly not limited to such activities. The new offence will effectively be an aggravated form of the offence created by s5 of the 1986 Act, ie causing harassment, alarm or distress, and shares many of its features. The Crime and Disorder Act 1998 also introduced racially motivated versions of the offences under ss4 and 5.

The 1986 Act also creates several miscellaneous offences. Under s30 a court by or before which a person is convicted of an offence connected with football may make an exclusion order prohibiting him from entering premises to attend a prescribed football match. Section 38 creates various offences connected with contamination of or interference with goods.

A further area in which the 1986 Act has been found wanting is in relation to so-called 'mass trespass'. Originally dealt with by s39 of the Public Order Act 1986, the matter is now dealt with by ss61 and 62 of the Criminal Justice and Public Order Act 1994. The provisions, which seem to be specifically targeted at the activities of persons leading a nomadic lifestyle ('new age travellers', etc), state that a police constable is empowered to order the removal of trespassers (ie two or more persons) from land where he reasonably believes that: (i) they are present with the common purpose of residing there for any period; and (ii) reasonable steps have been taken by or on behalf of the occupier to ask them to leave; and either (iii) any of the persons has caused damage to the land or property on the land or used threatening or abusive or insulting words or behaviour towards the occupier, his family or agents; or (iv) the trespassers have between them six or more vehicles (a reduction from 12 under the 1986 Act) on the land. For these purposes 'land' does not include land forming part of a highway other than footpaths, bridleways, byways or cycle tracks. Subject to certain statutory defences, failure to comply with a constable's direction under this section is an offence in relation to which a person can be arrested without a warrant, and in relation to which a constable has the power to seize vehicles involved. A person removed from land under these provisions is prohibited from returning for the following three months.

QUESTION TWO

The PRO organisation arrange a procession through the streets of London. They do not ask anyone for permission. The ANTI organisation arrange a counter demonstration, again without seeking official permission. When the two marches converge on the Strand, violence breaks out. Nobody in the PRO march uses force except in self defence. A police constable orders the PRO marchers to stop their procession and to disperse. They continue to march and are arrested. Pleased with their success the ANTI marchers disperse and make their way home. A dozen of them decide to have some 'fun' on the Underground platform. They surround an old lady and begin to chant 'euthanasia, euthanasia'. She is alarmed by this and collapses. The ANTI marchers later discover that she was of an unusually weak disposition and had previously suffered heart attacks. But at the time they panic and run away. One of them is intent on escape and has no intent of causing further trouble. The others take the opportunity of lashing out violently at passers-by.

Which offences, if any, have been committed against the Public Order Act 1986?

Written by the Editors

General Comment

A question which demands a comprehensive knowledge of public order offences but a well prepared student should have no problem if application is logical and thorough. Clearly a good grasp of the Public Order Act 1986 is essential.

Skeleton Solution

- Introduction. Effect of the Public Order Act 1986.
- Powers of the police to impose conditions on processions – s12. Common law powers to prevent a breach of peace.
- Section 1 Riot.
- Section 2 Violent disorder.
- Section 3 Affray.
- Section 4 Provoking violence.
- Section 5 Disorderly conduct.
- Analyse and apply facts to above sections of the Act.

Suggested Solution

Regarding the problem for consideration, the PRO organisation have arranged a procession through the streets of London and have not asked for permission. While there is no requirement under the law that permission has to be obtained to hold a procession, under s11 of the Public Order Act 1986 the organisers of public processions must give advance notice in writing to the police not less than six clear days before the date of any procession which is intended to demonstrate support for or opposition to the views or actions of any person or body of persons; or publicise a cause or campaign; or which marks or commemorates an event. In not giving such notice the procession organisers therefore commit an offence. The same will be true of the organisers of the ANTI procession.

When the two groups converge violence, instigated by the ANTI marchers, breaks out and a police constable orders the PRO marchers to stop their procession and disperse. It is of course a fundamental principle of our law that one cannot be stopped from doing what one is lawfully entitled to do merely because others act unlawfully (*Beatty* v *Gillbanks* (1862)). However, s12 of the 1986 Act gives the police the power to impose conditions on certain processions if a senior police officer, having regard to the time or place at which and the circumstances in which, any public procession is being held or is intended to be held, reasonably believes that (a) it may result in serious public disorder, serious damage to property or serious disruption to the life of the community, or (b) the purpose of the persons organising it is the intimidation of others with a view to compelling them not to do an act they have a right to do, or to do an act they have a right not to do. Further, under s13 the chief officer of police may in certain circumstances prohibit processions in his district.

While the power therefore exists under the Public Order Act for the police to impose conditions on, and even in some circumstances ban, a lawful procession, it is questionable whether the conditions for so doing apply in this particular case. If they do, conditions can be imposed by the most senior police officer at the scene, arguably a constable in uniform: see s12(2). Under s12(7) a constable may arrest without warrant anyone he reasonably suspects to be committing an offence under s12. At common law a police officer has the power to take such steps as are reasonably necessary to prevent a breach of the peace and in so doing is acting in the execution of his duty so that a failure to obey would be an offence under s89(3) Police Act 1996, and if a breach of the peace is occurring or threatened there is a common law right to arrest preserved by the Police and Criminal Evidence Act 1984.

As regards the violence which takes place in the Strand and the actions of the ANTI marchers on the Underground platform, various offences under the Public Order Act 1986 may have been committed.

The basis of these offences is fear for personal safety on the part of a person of reasonable firmness present at the scene. Section 1 redefines the offence of riot. Where 12 or more persons who are present together use or threaten unlawful violence and the conduct of them (taken together) is such as would cause a person of reasonable firmness present at the scene to fear for his personal safety, each of the persons using or threatening unlawful violence for the common purpose is guilty of riot.

The s2 offence of violent disorder has similarities with riot but the three persons (rather than 12) need not be acting for a common purpose. Note *R* v *Hebron* (1989) which established that mere threats suffice to support a conviction.

Section 3 defines the offence of affray. A person is guilty of affray if he uses or threatens unlawful violence towards another and his conduct is such as would cause a person of reasonable firmness present at the scene to fear for his personal safety.

Section 4 of the 1986 Act creates the offence of causing fear or provocation of violence. A person is guilty of an offence if he uses towards another person threatening, abusive or insulting words or behaviour, or distributes or displays to another person any writing, sign or other visible representation which is threatening, abusive or insulting, with intent to cause that person to believe that immediate unlawful violence will be used against him or another by any person, or to provoke the immediate use of unlawful violence by that person or another, or whereby that person is likely to believe that such violence will be used or it is likely that such violence will be provoked.

Section 5 of the 1986 Act creates the controversial offence of causing harassment, alarm or distress. A person is guilty of an offence if he uses threatening, abusive or insulting words or behaviour, or disorderly behaviour, or displays any writing, sign or other visible representation which is threatening, abusive or insulting, within the hearing or sight of a person likely to be caused harassment, alarm or distress thereby. Section 5 provides for three specific defences. First, that the defendant had no reason to believe that there was anyone within hearing or sight of his or her conduct who was likely to be harassed, alarmed or distressed; second, that he or she was inside a dwelling and had no reason to believe that the conduct would have been seen or heard by anyone outside; third, that his or her conduct was reasonable. Additionally, the demonstrators may have committed an offence contrary to s4A to the 1986 Act (added by s154 of the Criminal Justice and Public Order Act) of intentionally causing harassment, alarm or distress.The offence can be committed in a public or private place, except where both parties are in private dwellings. A constable may arrest without a warrant anyone he reasonably suspects to be guilty of committing the offence.

From the facts given in the problem it appears that the actions of the ANTI organisation in the Strand could amount to riot, violent disorder and affray since it appears that the violence was instigated by them. However, the PRO organisation acting only in self defence do not seem to fall within the definitions of ss1 and 2 since they acted only in self defence, ie no *unlawful* violence.

When the ANTI demonstrators gather on the underground platform it seems they simply surround the old lady and chant 'euthanasia, euthanasia'. From the facts given it would seem doubtful whether it would be possible to establish 'use or threats of unlawful violence' so as to sustain charges under ss1, 2 and 3 and s4 also depends upon the threat of 'immediate unlawful violence'. It would therefore seem that the actions in respect of the old lady would have to be prosecuted under s5, causing harassment, alarm or distress. The words 'euthanasia, euthanasia' could be classified as threatening and since an old lady has been singled out for the treatment none of the defences seem appropriate. It will of course be no defence that the ANTI group was not aware of her unusually weak disposition. In *Jordan* v *Burgoyne* (1963), a case dealing with similar provisions in the old s5, Public Order Act 1936, it was made clear that the person using threatening, abusive or insulting words cannot look at their effect on a hypothetical reasonable audience but must take note of the effect on the actual audience addressed.

The ANTI demonstrators then disperse, one on his own, leaving 11 who commit acts of violence on passers by. Since there are then only 11 people no offence of riot can be established but violent disorder and affray charges are available, under ss2 and 3 of the 1986 Act respectively.

QUESTION THREE

'The Public Order Act 1986 represents a failure on the part of Parliament to rationalise the law. Public order law remains a miscellany of disparate rules.'

Discuss.

University of London LLB Examination
(for External Students) Constitutional Law June 1991 Q4

General Comment

A question that requires a good knowledge of the central measures in the Public Order Act 1986, and also a knowledge of the related common law provisions. The theme of the solution is to pick out the salient provisions of the 1986 Act, and demonstrate the extent to which they overlap with other statutory and common law provisions.

Skeleton Solution

- Assemblies, Public Order Act 1986, other statutes, common law.
- Processions, Public Order Act 1986, other statutes, common law.
- Examples of other pieces of legislation and common law powers.
- Explain need for reform.

Suggested Solution

It is well known that under English law individuals are free to meet together in public in such groups and for such purposes as they see fit, subject only to the limitations imposed by the law. There is no right to march or demonstrate, but instead a variety of limitations imposed by common law and statute.

The Public Order Act 1986 (hereinafter referred to as the 1986 Act) represents an attempt to clarify certain points of law relating to public order, and to consolidate and update the law on a number of issues, but as the quotation under consideration suggests, it has only been partially successful in this respect. The problem remains that the term 'public order law' is necessarily vague. To ascertain the law relating to meetings both public and private, and marches on the highway, one still has to consult a variety of pieces of legislation, and some confusing and contradictory statements at common law.

Consider the law relating to public assemblies. Section 14 of the 1986 Act (as amended by ss70 and 71 of the Criminal Justice and Public Order Act 1994) provides that a senior police officer may impose conditions in relation to public assemblies if, having regard to the time or place at which and the circumstances in which any public assembly is being held or is intended to be held, he reasonably believes that: (i) it may result in serious public disorder, serious damage to property or serious disruption to the life of the community; or (ii) the purpose of the persons organising it is the intimidation of others with a view to compelling them not to do an act they have a right to do, or to do an act they have a right not to do. The section states that he may give directions imposing on the persons organising or taking part in the assembly such conditions as to the place at which the assembly may be (or continue to be) held, its maximum duration, or the maximum number of persons who may constitute it, as appears to him necessary to prevent such disorder, damage, disruption or intimidation. Section 16 defines 'public assembly' as an assembly of 20 or more persons in a public place which is wholly or partly open to the air. Events such as the 'invasion' of Stonehenge during the summer solstice led the government to conclude that the 1986 Act was lacking in terms of the powers vested in the police to deal with static demonstrations. Hence, under ss14A, B and C (added by the 1994 Act), a chief officer of police is empowered to apply to the relevant local authority for an order prohibiting trespassory assemblies on land to which the public does not normally have a right of access, provided that there are grounds to reasonably believe that the owner of the land has not granted permission for the assembly and that the trespassory assembly may result in either serious disruption to the life of the community, or significant damage to land or buildings of historical, archeological or scientific importance. It is an offence to organise or participate in any such trespassory assembly in the knowledge that a banning order has been granted. The Crime and Disorder Act 1998 also introduced racially motivated versions of the offences under ss4 and 5. Under s14C a police constable has the power to intercept and stop those reasonably believed to be proceeding to a trespassory assembly, and direct them not to proceed to the assembly. Disobedience to an order under this provision is a summary offence in relation to which a constable may exercise a power of arrest without a warrant.

This may be thought to be a comprehensive measure governing such gatherings. But one would still have to have regard to other measures if the meeting takes place on the highway: see s137(1) Highways Act 1980, under which it is a criminal offence wilfully to obstruct the free passage along a highway. If the highway is obstructed then a constable can arrest those causing the obstruction. Obstruction, in this context, is a very flexible term. Special provisions apply to meetings in certain public places such as Hyde Park Corner or Trafalgar Square which are Crown property. For any meeting to take place the permission of the Secretary of State for the Environment is needed, and he can if he wishes impose restrictions on any meeting for which permission has been granted.

The 1986 Act also seeks to regulate the use of the highway for processions. Advance notice of public processions must be given in certain circumstances. Section 11 provides that proposals to hold a public procession must be notified to the police if it is a procession intended to demonstrate support for or opposition to the views or actions of any person or body of persons; or publicise a cause or campaign; or mark or commemorate an event. Written notice must be given to the police not less than six clear days before the date of the procession, or as soon as is practicable. The organisers commit an offence if they fail to satisfy these requirements or, if in general, the conduct of the procession differs from that indicated in the notice. The powers provided by the Act are directed to preventing serious public disorder rather than dealing with it when it has occurred. The framework of control has two stages. Marches can be allowed subject to conditions (s12) or banned outright (s13).

These provisions are tolerably clear in their scope and effect, but again they are not comprehensive. Other legislation needs to be consulted in certain cases. For example, Under s52 of the Metropolitan Police Act 1839, the Commissioner of Police of the Metropolis may make regulations for preventing obstruction of the streets within the vicinity of Parliament. Any contravention of those regulations is a criminal offence. The police also have the power to stop potential disorderly processions by bringing the possible demonstrators before the magistrates before the demonstration. They may then be bound over to keep the peace. Should they refuse to be bound over then they can be imprisoned for up to six months.

Those partaking in a procession along the highway could be dealt with under the common law if the procession goes beyond what is a reasonable use of the highway, since it may constitute a public nuisance. This offence is rare but it was used in the case of *R* v *Clarke (No 2)* (1964).

There remains the question of the offences that may be committed once disorder breaks out during a public meeting during a procession. The 1986 Act creates a range of new offences that can be used in such situations.

Section 1 redefines the offence of riot. Section 2 creates a new offence of violent disorder. Section 3 redefines the offence of affray. Section 4 largely replaces s5 of the Public Order Act 1936 with the new offence of causing fear or provocation of violence. Finally s5 introduces the controversial offence of causing harassment, alarm or distress.

All of these new offences co-exist, however, with long established offences such as breach of the peace, an offence drawn in such broad terms it allows the police the power to arrest in situations where the legality of their actions may be unclear.

A brief list will give a flavour of the other disparate offences touching upon 'public order law'. The Unlawful Drilling Act 1819, which prohibits assemblies for the purpose of training or drilling in the use of arms or practising military exercises without lawful authority. The Public Meeting Act 1908, makes it an offence to endeavour to break up a public meeting by acting in a disorderly manner for the purpose of preventing the transaction of the business for which the meeting was called together. The Representation of the People Act 1983 s97 makes it an offence to cause a disturbance at an election meeting. The Police Act 1996 s89(1) makes it an offence to assault a police officer in the execution of his duty. Section 89(2) makes it an offence to wilfully obstruct the police in the execution of their duty.

Finally, the Criminal Justice and Public Order Act 1994 adds further offences relating to the removal of trespassers, further powers to ban trespassory assemblies and powers to deal with squatters and 'raves'.

Not only does the 1986 Act co-exist alongside myriad other related offences, the Act itself was used by Parliament as an opportunity to enact measures which in some cases have only a tenuous link with public order. For example s38 creates various offences connected with contamination of or interference with goods.

In short it is submitted that the whole of the law relating to public order should be looked at again with a view to greater consolidation and rationalisation.

Domestic law on this topic is likely to come under greater scrutiny following the incorporation of the European Convention on Human Rights into domestic law by virtue of the Human Rights Act 1998. No date has been set for the Act to come fully into force, but when it does there will, for the first time, be a positive right to public protest as enshrined in art 11.

QUESTION FOUR

Article 11 of the European Convention on Human Rights provides that 'Everyone has the right to peaceful assembly'. How is this human right guaranteed in English Law?

University of London LLB Examination
(for External Students) Constitutional Law June 1996 Q5

General Comment

This is a potentially wide-ranging question and the student should direct his/her attention to the area of assemblies and not be diverted into discussing other areas of public order such as processions. The main statutes to be familiar with are the relevant sections of the Public Order Act 1986 and the Criminal Justice and Public Order Act 1994. In addition, candidates should be aware of the available common law powers to curb an assembly, as well as any statutes that might be utilised for this purpose.

Skeleton Solution

- The issue of 'rights' in English law.
- The impact of the Human Rights Act 1998
- Section 14 Public Order Act (POA) 1986.
- Criminal Justice and Public Order Act (CJPOA) 1994 – trespass, trespassory assemblies, 'raves'.
- Common law powers to control assemblies.
- Highways Act 1980.
- Conclusion.

Suggested Solution

Historically English law has not recognised any positive right to public protest. According to Dicey (Dicey, *Law of the Constitution* (10th edn, 1959)), rights were residual. This meant that the individual was permitted to do something provided it was not forbidden by the law.

All that is about to change. The Human Rights Act 1998 incorporates aspects of the European Convention on Human Rights into domestic law, including art 11, which provides:

'(1) Everyone has the right to freedom of peaceful assembly and to freedom of association with others, including the right to form and to join trade unions for the protection of his interests.

(2) No restrictions shall be placed on the exercise of these rights other than such as are prescribed by law and are necessary in a democratic society in the interests of national security or public safety, for the prevention of disorder or crime, for the protection of health or morals or for the protection of the rights and freedoms of others. This Article shall not prevent the imposition of lawful restrictions on the exercise of these rights by members of the armed forces, of the police or of the administration of the State.'

No date has been set for the Act to come fully into force – it now seems unlikely to happen before early in the year 2001 – but when it does, all the restrictions imposed under statute and common law will have to be read subject to the requirements of art 11.

How does the existing law meet the requirements of art 11? Most of the modern provisions, such as the Public Order Act 1986 attempt to achieve a balance between the interests of those wishing to protest and those wishing to go about their business unhindered or use their property without undue interference.

For example the Public Order Act (POA) 1986 imposes no requirement to obtain permission from the police in order to organise an assembly. A public assembly is defined by s16 POA 1986 as being 'an assembly of 20 or more persons in a public place that is wholly or partly open to the air'. While, however, no permission is needed to organise an assembly it has to be in the words of art 11 a 'peaceful' gathering. If a senior police officer reasonably believes that the assembly will result in serious public disorder, serious damage to property or serious disruption to the life of the community, or the purpose is the intimidation of others (see *Police* v *Reid* (1987), he may impose conditions on the organisers relating to the duration of the assembly and the maximum number of people who may make up the meeting: s14 POA 1986. What constitutes the reasonable belief of the senior police officer (presumably the senior police officer present) as to these factors is not defined in the Act. One may suppose that the belief is either *Wednesbury* reasonableness (*Associated Provincial Picture Houses Ltd* v *Wednesbury Corporation* (1948)), or more likely a combination of subjective/objective reasonableness. That is, did the police officer have an honest and reasonable belief as to the facts and would a police officer in those circumstances have reasonably formed this view? What is certain is that a police officer cannot arbitrarily forbid an assembly.

A much more far-reaching statute in this area is the Criminal Justice and Public Order Act (CJPOA) 1994. This Act was passed in response to a number of public order issues ranging from 'New Age Travellers' to 'rave' parties on disused airfields. Associated with these groups and events is the issue of trespass and trespassory assembly. The POA 1986 attempted to deal with some of these issues by providing a senior police officer (ie the most senior present) with powers to direct trespassers to leave land: s39 POA 1986. These could only be invoked if the police officer believed that two or more persons had entered the land as trespassers with a common purpose of residing there, that they had not heeded reasonable steps, by the occupier, to leave and that they had caused damage to the property on the land or that they had used threatening, abusive or insulting words or behaviour towards the occupier or his agent. The police officer could also direct the trespassers to leave the land if they brought 12 or more vehicles on the land: s39(1)(b).

The above proved inadequate to deal with a number of increasingly popular gatherings in the 1980s and 90s. Section 61 CJPOA 1994 went further than s39 POA 1986. By s61, even in the case of individuals who entered the land by invitation, if the invitation is withdrawn they are then categorised as trespassers and can be asked to leave. Moreover, while s39 talked about damage to property, the CJPOA refers to damage to the land. Damage may presumably be caused by cars driving onto fields and the number of vehicles has been reduced from 12 or more (in s39) to six. The use of the definition of land has now been extended and, for instance, common land and bridleways are included. Gatherings at historical monuments may also be curtailed, a move designed to prevent the gathering of people at the time of the summer solstice at Stonehenge. By s70 CJPOA 1994 the relevant chief police officer may apply to the local council for an order prohibiting for a specified period the holding of all trespassory public assemblies in a specified area, provided the Secretary of State consents. One of the specified areas described in the statute is an area of historical monuments, provided that a case is made out of potential damage to the said structures. Following the ruling of the Divisional Court in *DPP* v *Jones* (1997) it would appear that even though an assembly is peaceful and does not amount to an obstruction of the highway, if there is a s14A order in force, any assembly of 20 or more persons will amount to a trespassory assembly within the terms of s14A. The decision raises directly the question of the extent to which the prohibition on peaceful demonstrations, effected by orders under s14, is actually consistent with the United Kingdom's obligations under art 11 of the European Convention on Human Rights. Under art 11, restrictions on the right to peaceful assembly are only permissible to the extent that they are necessary in a democratic society etc. Does domestic law strike the right balance in this instance between the rights of demonstrators, and the rights of those wishing to pass and repass on the highway without being exposed to demonstrations? It is likely that the House of Lords will consider this appeal in the near future.

Assemblies may also be prohibited if their aim is to disrupt or obstruct a lawful activity by trespassing on land in the open air with that aim in mind. This new offence of 'aggravated trespass' (s68(1)) is designed to include the activities of, for instance, hunt saboteurs.

Finally, the CJPOA has prohibited assemblies in the open air where amplified music is played during the night, provided there is an attendance of 100 or more people: s63. Moreover, the Act gives the police a new power to stop somebody they reasonably, believe is travelling to such an assembly or 'rave'. This power can only be utilised within five miles of the boundary of the assembly: s65.

In addition, English law has extensive common law powers that can, in effect, curtail an assembly. The test is whether there will be a breach of the peace or a reasonable likelihood of breach of the peace at the gathering, rather than what is the intention of the organisers or those attempting to reach the assembly. In *O'Kelly* v *Harvey* (1883), for instance, a meeting of the 'Land League' was ordered to be dispersed by the local justice of the peace as it was in danger of being broken up 'Orangemen' – members of a Protestant organisation hostile to the aspirations of the Land League. The reasoning of this nineteenth-century precedent has been utilised by the police in preventing individuals from attending a gathering whose purpose is per se lawful. In *Moss* v *McLachlan* (1985) the Divisional Court held that the police had reasonable grounds for apprehending a breach of the peace as imminent when they stopped a group of striking miners from going to attend a mass picket. The miners were arrested for obstruction of the police. It is not necessary in such a situation to argue that the meeting is unlawful, but rather whether the natural consequence of the meeting will be a breach of the peace. If, however, the natural consequence of an assembly is not to provoke violence then it would appear that it is legitimate to proceed. *R* v *Morpeth Ward Justices, ex parte Ward and Others*

(1992) appears to indicate that individuals may protest at a meeting but not in a manner likely to provoke violence.

The European Court of Human Rights has confirmed that the concept of breach of the peace is not so vague as to fall foul of art 5 of the Convention, but use of powers of arrest for breach of the peace might amount to a violation of art 10 – right to free speech – if the power is used in respect of peaceful demonstrations: see *Steel and Others* v *United Kingdom* (1998). The recognition by the court that the arrest of those engaged in peaceful protest may involve violations of the Convention again calls into question the legality of the court's ruling in *DPP* v *Jones* (above).

Notwithstanding this, a peaceful assembly may fall foul of other legislation such as the Highways Act 1980. Designed to provide for free passage along the highway it has also been utilised to curb demonstrations and assemblies – from an attempt to halt a demonstration outside a fur shop (*Hirst* v *Chief Constable for West Yorkshire* (1987)) (reversed on appeal) to the arrest for obstruction of the highway of the television presenter Esther Rantzen for stopping pedestrians and asking them to sample bat soup!

In conclusion, the individual may attend a peaceful assembly but the constraints are numerous. Legislation has been passed in response to such phenomenon as New Age Travellers and rave parties. The thrust of legislative changes and judicial rulings has been to confine the right to convene an assembly within strict limitations.

12 Freedom of Expression

12.1 Introduction

English law has traditionally relied on the principle that, as far as freedom of expression is concerned, what is not prohibited is permitted. The common law and legislature have, between them, attempted to strike a balance between the right of their individual to express his opinions, and the right of the individual to be protected from the worst excesses of those views. In addition there is the public interest in the state security and public order. The result is a wide range of specific offences to provide remedies to either individuals or the state when views expressed go beyond what is considered tolerable. The area includes such diverse topics as theatre censorship and state security, contempt of court, obscene publications and the right to privacy. With the enactment of the Human Rights Act 1998 United Kingdom law will see the introduction of a positive right to freedom of expression as enshrined in art 10 of the European Convention on Human Rights. Although the Act was enacted in 1998 it is unlikely that the provisions relating to the protection of fundamental rights will come into effect before early in the year 2001.

12.2 Key points

a) *The protection of the state*

i) Sedition

This common law offence is now largely of historical interest as other offences have largely superseded the need to prosecute for sedition.

The element of incitement to violence has been stressed. *R* v *Caunt* (1948) unreported.

ii) Incitement to disaffection

It is an offence to undermine the loyalty of:

- a police officer: s53 Police Act 1964; or
- a member of the armed forces: Incitement to Disaffection Act 1934. See *R* v *Arrowsmith* [1975] QB 678.

iii) Incitement to racial hatred

- Threats, abuse and insults which are likely to result in unlawful violence are criminal: Public Order Act 1986 s4.
- Threats, abuse or insults which are intended or are likely to stir up racial hatred are

specifically dealt with by ss17–23 Public Order Act 1986. The offences are unlikely to be committed by those who use reasoned argument: *Jordan* v *Burgoyne* [1963] 2 QB 744.

Note the meaning of racial group – a group of persons defined by reference to colour, race, nationality or ethnic or national origins: *Mandla* v *Dowell Lee* [1983] 2 AC 548.

iv) Blasphemy

- Blasphemy is a common law offence committed through the vilification of Christ, the Christian religion, the Bible, or any subject sacred to Christians.
- In *R* v *Lemon* [1979] AC 617 it was held that there was no need for an intention to blaspheme, publication was enough. Publication need not necessarily lead to a breach of the peace.
- In *R* v *Bow Street Magistrates, ex parte Choudbury* (1990) The Times 9 April the Divisional Court refused an application for judicial review of the magistrates' refusal to issue a summons for blasphemy in respect of the Salman Rushdie book *Satanic Verses*.
- The Law Commission Working Paper: *Offences against Religion and Public Worship* (No 79) based its conclusions on the need to promote free speech, the fact that most serious instances of blasphemy could now be prosecuted under other public order offences, the inappropriateness of giving special protection to Christianity in what was now a multi-faith society, and the unfairness that could result from the imposition of strict liability.
- The United Kingdom's blasphemy laws were, indirectly, relied upon by the European Court of Human Rights as justifying the British Board of Film Classification's refusal to grant a certificate to a video entitled *Visions of Ecstasy*: see *Wingrove* v *United Kingdom* Case 19/1995 (1996) The Times 5 December.

v) Criminal libel

Criminal libel covers cases of libel where there is considered to be some threat to the preservation of the peace. Prosecutions are rare and only with the order of a High Court judge: *Goldsmith* v *Pressdram Ltd* [1976] 3 WLR 191.

vi) Freedom of communication and information

- Government has a duty to preserve the security of the state. National security includes not only measures intended to protect the state from espionage but also all matters that are considered subversive. Governments are often seen as using the cloak of national security to 'gag' the communication of information which should be in the public domain.
- What is 'national security'?

  It is not clear exactly what is included in the concept of national security. Courts often accept the word of governments. National security interests have been invoked in a variety of instances, such as: defence of the realm and the prosecution of war (*The Zamora* [1916] 2 AC 77); the disposition of the armed forces (*Chandler* v *DPP* [1964] AC 763); nuclear weapons (*Secretary of State for Defence* v *Guardian Newspapers* [1984] 1 All ER 453); and the activities of intelligence services (*Attorney-General* v *Guardian Newspapers (No 2)* [1988] 3 All ER 545).

- Official Secrets Acts

  Section 1 of the Official Secrets Act 1911 creates offences of espionage. It is not restricted to spying but includes acts of sabotage: *Chandler* v *DPP* [1964] AC 763.

  Section 2 created some 2,000 offences directed at the misuse of information. It was criticised for being used to keep policy making free of outside scrutiny.

  In 1989, s2 was repealed by the Official Secrets Act 1989. The Act creates specific categories of information which is sensitive and should be controlled. These are: (i) security and intelligence; (ii) defence; (iii) international relations; and (iv) criminal investigations. The disclosure must be 'damaging'. This concept operates differently in respect of each of the four categories. There is no public interest defence or a defence of prior publication.

- 'D' Notices

  A form of extra legal censorship which depends on co-operation between governments and the press with the objective of achieving a ban on the publication of matters which are considered likely to jeopardise national security.

- Interception of Communications Act 1985

  Under the Act it is an offence to intercept communications (specifically telephone communications) unless authorised by the Secretary of State who may issue a warrant in the interests of national security or for the purpose of preventing serious crime or for the purpose of safeguarding the economic well being of the United Kingdom. See generally *Malone* v *United Kingdom* (1985) 7 EHRR 14.

- Breach of confidence

  An equitable doctrine to ensure that a person should not take unfair advantage of confidences obtained: *Argyll* v *Argyll* [1967] Ch 302; *Attorney-General* v *Jonathan Cape* [1976] QB 752.

  It is worth noting in this context because of the attempt made by the government in the 'Spycatcher' affair to assert that members of the security services owe a lifelong duty of confidentiality to the Crown: *Attorney-General* v *Guardian Newspapers (No 2)* [1988] 3 All ER 545.

  It seems that the courts are more willing to consider the issue of 'the public interest' and not to depend on the government's view: *Lord Advocate* v *Scotsman Publications* [1990] 1 AC 812.

b) *Obscene publications*

   i) The trade in pornography is lucrative and the state seeks to limit publication to limit 'depravity'. There are statutory and common law offences.

   ii) Obscene Publications Act 1959

   An obscene article is one where the effect '... if taken as a whole, would tend to deprave and corrupt persons who are likely having regard to all the circumstances to read, see or hear the matter contained or embodied in it': s1.

   - Article is defined widely and includes pictures, books and film negatives.
   - The definition of obscene requires the jury to consider whether the article has a tendency to deprave and corrupt and this has caused inconsistency. It is not limited

to sexual matters: *John Calder (Publishers)* v *Powell* [1965] 1 QB 509; *Director of Public Prosecutions* v *A and BC Chewing Gum Ltd* [1968] 1 QB 159.

- Policing the trade in pornography is difficult – 'an attempt to eradicate the ineradicable' (Robert Mark, ex Chief Commissioner for the Metropolis, in *Policing a Perplexed Society* (1977)). See *R* v *Metropolitan Police Commissioner, ex parte Blackburn (No 3)* [1973] QB 241.
- Section 3 confers search, seizure and forfeiture powers.
- Section 4 makes it a defence if the material is 'for the public good on the grounds that it is in the interests of science, literature, art or learning'. Whether publication is for the public good is for the jury to decide.

See *Attorney-General's Reference (No 3 of 1977)* [1978] 3 All ER 1166; *R* v *Penguin Books* [1961] Crim LR 176.

iii) The Obscene Publications Act 1964 allows the police to seize material if the material was 'in possession for gain' thus it can be effective – material can be seized – before publication.

iv) Other legislation

This includes Customs Consolidation Act 1876, the Children and Young Persons (Harmful Publications) Act 1955, the Post Office Act 1953 and the Protection of Children Act 1978.

v) Common law offences

- Conspiracy to corrupt public morals: *Shaw* v *DPP* [1962] AC 220.
- Conspiracy to outrage public decency: *Knuller* v *DPP* [1973] AC 435.

vi) Cinema and theatre

There are general controls over films (Cinemas Act 1985 and Video Recordings Act 1984) and over live performances (Theatres Act 1968).

c) *Contempt of court*

i) Civil contempts

The breach of or disobedience to an order of the court: *Harman* v *Secretary of State for the Home Department* [1982] 2 WLR 338.

ii) Criminal contempts

The objective here is to ensure both the fairness of a trial and also that the judiciary is accorded respect.

iii) Contempt of Court Act 1981

The Act clarified the position regarding newspaper publication of matters of public interest which could prejudice the outcome of court proceedings by the following reforms.

See also *Attorney-General* v *Times Newspapers Ltd* [1974] AC 273, a case which went to the European Court of Human Rights.

- It is an offence 'to interfere with the course of justice in particular legal proceedings regardless of intent' where the proceedings in question are active: s1.

- There is no offence if there was no reason to suspect that proceedings are active (s3) or that publication is a discussion in good faith of public affairs: *Attorney-General* v *English* [1982] 2 WLR 278.
- Section 10 gives limited protection to journalists of their sources unless disclosure is necessary in the interests of justice, national security or for the prevention of disorder or crime: *Secretary of State for Defence* v *Guardian Newspapers Ltd* [1984] 2 WLR 268.
- The prevention of crime exception in s10 encompasses the prevention of crime in general: *Re an Inquiry under the Company Securities (Insider Dealing) Act 1985* [1988] AC 660.

d) *Censorship*

i) Theatres are subject to the laws on obscenity, defamation and incitement to racial hatred.

ii) Cinemas are licensed by the local authority which attaches conditions and recommendations of the British Board of Film Censors are usually followed.

iii) Broadcasting

Both the BBC and IBA are under a duty to provide programmes which comply with good taste and decency and to preserve political impartiality. This last point has sometimes caused political controversy with governments.

e) *Defamation*

i) Defamation is a tort, in respect of which damages can be obtained, that can take one of two forms: if transitory in nature, such as the spoken word or gestures, it is referred to as slander; if in a more permanent form, such as the printed word, or a broadcast, it is referred to as libel. The essence of the tort is that, as a result of things said, done or published by the defendant, the plaintiff has suffered the hatred, ridicule and contempt of others such that would tend to lower him in the estimation of right-thinking members of society.

ii) Defences at common law include: justification, ie that the impugned statement is essentially true; 'fair comment', provided the defendant was expressing his view of a matter of public interest, was not motivated by malice, and that the statement did not contain any significant factual errors; absolute privilege, which attaches to statements made during proceedings in Parliament and statements made during judicial proceedings. Absolute privilege also extends to fair and accurate reports of proceedings in public before any court in the United Kingdom, the European Court of Justice and the European Court of Human Rights: see further s14 Defamation Act 1996. Qualified privilege is a defence to defamation in respect of statements made by a defendant in the course of his performing a legal, social or moral duty, where the statements are directed to another person who has a corresponding interest in receiving the material, and where the defendant is not motivated by malice, ie he believes the statement to be accurate. The defence is also available to those who publish fair and accurate reports of proceedings in Parliament; for the scope of this defence: see now s15 of the Defamation Act 1996.

iii) Section 1 of the Defamation Act 1996 provides that a person has a defence if he shows that: he was not the author, editor or publisher of the statement complained of; he took reasonable care in relation to its publication; he did not know, and had no reason to believe, that what he did caused or contributed to the publication of a defamatory statement.

iv) The 1996 Act also creates a new defence based upon the defendant's offer to make amends. The defence replaces the defence of unintentional defamation created under s4 of the Defamation Act 1952. The defendant must be prepared to make a suitable correction of the statement complained of and a sufficient apology to the aggrieved party; to publish the correction and apology in a manner that is reasonable and practicable in the circumstances; and to pay to the aggrieved party such compensation (if any), and such costs, as may be agreed or determined to be payable. An offer to make amends cannot be made if a defence to the action has already been served.

v) Changes introduced in the Courts and Legal Services Act 1990 empowered the Court of Appeal to overturn 'excessive' awards: see further *John* v *MGN Ltd* (1995) The Times 14 December. Section 8 of the Defamation Act 1996 introduces a new summary procedure for the disposal of defamation actions where there is either 'no realistic prospect of success' for the plaintiff, or no defence.

f) *Prior restraint*

A person whose interests are likely to be affected by the publication of material or the Attorney-General in his role as guardian of the public interest can apply to the court for an injunction restraining such publication. The injunction is interim until such time as a full hearing of the issues can take place: see *Attorney-General* v *Guardian Newspapers (No 1)* [1987] 3 All ER 316; *Attorney-General* v *Newspaper Publishing plc* [1987] 3 All ER 276. Note that some prior constraints are extra- legal, eg D notices.

12.3 Recent cases and statutes

Attorney-General v *Newspaper Publishing plc* [1997] 1 WLR 926 – no contempt of court in publishing restricted documents unless the administration of justice in the relevant proceedings has been wholly frustrated or rendered utterly futile.

Goldsmith v *Bhoyrul* [1997] 4 All ER 268 – political party cannot be defamed.

Reynolds v *Times Newspapers Ltd and Others* [1998] 3 All ER 961 – defamation – implied criticism of politician –whether statements attracting qualified privilege where they were concerned with public conduct of affairs of state.

The Human Rights Act 1998 brings certain provisions of the European Convention on Human Rights into domestic law, including art 10 which provides:

'(1) Everyone has the right to freedom of expression. This right shall include freedom to hold opinions and to receive and impart information and ideas without interference by public authority and regardless of frontiers. This article shall not prevent states from requiring the licensing of broadcasting, television and cinema enterprises.

(2) The exercise of these freedoms, since it carries with it duties and responsibilities, may be subject to such formalities, conditions, restrictions or penalties as are prescribed by law and are necessary in a democratic society, in the interests of national security, territorial integrity or public safety, for the prevention of disorder or crime, for the protection of health or morals, for the protection of the reputation or rights of others, for preventing the disclosure of information received in confidence, or for maintaining the authority and impartiality of the judiciary.'

When the Act comes into effect – in early 2001 – the courts will have to interpret domestic legislation so as to ensure compliance with art 10 in so far as this is possible. It will also become unlawful for any public authority to act in a way that is inconsistent with the Convention rights. Section 12 of the 1998 Act provides in particular that the courts must have regard to the importance of the Convention right to freedom of expression.

12.4 Analysis of questions

London University has not questioned students directly on this topic in recent years. Other examiners may emphasise a particular area, for example state security, with a view to examining students' knowledge on that specific subject. The topic does lend itself to a general essay-type question, eg 'consider to what extent in your view a balance has been achieved between competing interests in the areas of ...', and an examiner could then identify the areas the student should focus on.

In any case a general knowledge of the topic is important in, for example, answering a question on a Bill of Rights.

12.5 Questions

QUESTION ONE

To what extent does the law successfully balance competing interests in the area of press freedom?

Written by the Editors

General Comment

A straightforward question requiring students to review the law on civil and criminal law restraints on press freedom.

Skeleton Solution

- Introduction nature of freedom of speech in the United Kingdom remedies available.
- Prior restraint an evaluation of the effect of prior restraint on the media.
- Defamation
- Breach of confidence its use particularly by government.
- Official Secrets Act 1989.
- Contempt of court.
- The individual and the press remedies and contrasts with the above.

Suggested Solution

Freedom of speech is fundamental to a free society. It is protected by art 10 of the European Convention on Human Rights. As yet the Convention is not directly applicable in UK courts, but this will change when the Human Rights Act 1998 comes fully into force late in the year 2000 or in early 2001. Pending that change, the position in the United Kingdom is that individual members of the state are free to express views and opinions that are not against the numerous laws that restrict freedom of speech and to this extent the law attempts to balance competing rights. The press has a fundamental role to perform in informing the public, not least on government activities. However, individuals have a right not to be offended or abused and the state has a right to prevent the publication of sensitive material that could, for example, jeopardise national security. There is an inherent conflict here and some of the ways in which the law deals with that conflict in relation to press freedom will now be examined. The major restrictions on press freedom are to be found in the laws on defamation, breach of confidence and contempt of court.

It is important at the outset to draw a distinction between prior restraint and subsequent penalties. Blackstone (in his *Commentaries* (1765)) emphasised the importance in a free society of laying no prior restraints on publications, namely 'every free man has an undoubted right to lay what sentiments he pleases before the public; to forbid this is to destroy the freedom of the press', and his sentiments were included in the first amendment to the American constitution. It is arguable that prior restraint has become relatively easy to obtain in Britain either by the person whose interests are affected or by the Attorney-General as 'guardian' of the public interest. The injunction is interim and the applicant has to show that he has an arguable case, and that the balance of convenience is against publishing and damages are not an adequate remedy. That balance of convenience is normally in favour of a ban and some writers (see G Robertson, *Freedom, the Individual and the Law*) argue that this can amount to political interference with free speech. In *Attorney-General* v *BBC* (1987) the government was successful in getting an interim injunction against a series entitled *My Country Right or Wrong* on the grounds that ex-employees of the security services might have breached confidences during interviews.

Injunctions can also be granted to protect commercial interests when the courts balance the public's right to information against the private interest in ensuring that discussion should be prevented. In this context the private interest will be to protect trade secrets whilst the public interest may relate to the effect for example of a drug: *Schering Chemicals* v *Falkman Ltd* (1981). An injunction once granted binds third parties: *Attorney-General* v *Observer Newspapers Ltd* (1988). Whilst the nature of the injunction is limited to the period until trial, it may well be that the information may by then be no longer important.

The press will always be mindful of the restrictions imposed by the law of defamation. The essence of this tort is that, as a result of things said, done, or published by the defendant, the plaintiff has suffered the hatred, ridicule, contempt of others such that would tend to lower him in the estimation of right thinking members of society. Key defences where comment is made on the activities of those in the public eye are that the impugned statement is essentially true; 'fair comment', provided the defendant was expressing his view of a matter of public interest, was not motivated by malice, and that the statement did not contain any significant factual errors; absolute privilege which attaches to statements made during proceedings in Parliament and statements made during judicial proceedings; and qualified privilege – where statements are made by a defendant in the course of his performing a legal, social or moral duty. The latter defence was considered in *Reynolds* v *Times Newspapers Ltd and Others* (1998) where the Prime Minister of Ireland claimed that he had been defamed in an article critical of his alleged involvement in the appointment of a former Irish Attorney-General to the post of President of the Court. The defendant newspaper sought to rely on the defence of qualified privilege at common law. Regarding the defence of qualified privilege, Lord Bingham CJ identified the following three tests that had to be satisfied for the defence to be made out. The 'duty' test. 'Was the publisher under a legal, moral or social duty to those to whom the material was published (which in appropriate cases, as noted above, may be the general public) to publish the material in question?' The 'interest' test. Did those to whom the material was published (which again in appropriate cases may be the general public) have an interest to receive that material?' The 'circumstantial' test. Were the nature, status and source of the material, and the circumstances of the publication, such that the publication should in the public interest be protected in the absence of proof of express malice?

Breach of confidence is a civil matter providing protection where information is given in circumstances of confidence. It can include intimate communications between husband and wife (*Duke of Argyll* v *Duchess of Argyll* (1967)), trade secrets (*Lion Laboratories* v *Evans* (1984)) and often arises from a contract of employment. Claims to confidentiality can be defeated if the claimed confidences relate to criminal activity or if the disclosure serves the public interest. A confidence ceases to be a confidence once it is in the public domain. In *Attorney-General* v *Guardian Newspapers (No 2)* (1988) the House of Lords held that given a government secret was in the public domain – in this case the information was obtainable in Australia and the USA – then the remedy should not be available to prevent British citizens reading it. Nevertheless, the court confirmed the lifelong duty of confidentiality owed by members of the security services. The public interest may continue to be served, however, where the revelations contain substantial allegations of wrongdoing.

Governments are concerned to limit information which is of a sensitive nature in terms of national security but also may be inclined to prevent publication where information is simply politically embarrassing. The use of the discredited s2 of the Official Secrets Act 1911 provides evidence of the preoccupation of governments with secrecy. In *R* v *Aitken* (1974) the government prosecuted under s2 for the publication of information already in the public domain, and in the celebrated case of *R* v *Ponting* (1985) the jury found not guilty a civil servant who had leaked information to an opposition MP which revealed that the government was attempting to deceive Parliament. Section 2 of the Act has been repealed by the Official Secrets Act 1989. Journalists and editors can be imprisoned if they encourage civil servants to make disclosures or publish such disclosures. During the debate, attention focused on whether there should be a public interest defence, but amendments to the Bill were successfully resisted. Under s5 members of the press can be successfully prosecuted if they publish information which they know is protected by the Act and they had reason to believe the publication would be damaging to the interests of the United Kingdom. If information is published from former or serving members of the security service the offence is one of strict liability. It is notable that the court in *Attorney-General* v *Guardian Newspapers (No 2)* (1988) accepted the principle of a public interest defence in breach of confidence actions which the government was anxious not to see in the Official Secrets Act 1989.

It is essential that court proceedings are not disrupted and justice is not impeded through press comment on cases in progress. In *Attorney-General* v *News Group Newspapers Ltd* (1987) an injunction to restrain further publication of allegedly defamatory material was refused because the trial was some months away and a substantial risk to proceedings would not result. Clearly if the press were to publish details of a person's previous convictions shortly before trial, or publish a picture of someone involved in identification evidence, there would be contempt. The Contempt of Court Act 1981 legislation, enacted in the wake of the decision of the European Court of Human Rights in *Sunday Times* v *United Kingdom* (1979) sought to provide a clear logical basis for the operation of the rules on contempt. For liability to arise there must be a 'substantial risk' to proceedings: see s2. Under s5, media comment, made in good faith, where the risk to legal proceedings is incidental, should not result in liability: see *Attorney-General* v *English* (1983). Section 10 of the Act provides for the protection of journalistic sources unless it be established to the satisfaction of the court that disclosure is necessary in the interests of justice or national security or for the prevention of disorder or crime. The courts have tended to order disclosure however eg *Secretary of State for Defence* v *Guardian Newspapers Ltd* (1984), and more recently in *X* v *Morgan Grampian (Publishers) Ltd* (1991).

While there are many remedies available to the government to restrict press freedom, the protections available to individuals are more limited. The action of defamation can be brought but the expense involved is often prohibitive. The private interests of individuals and the lack of a comprehensive law on privacy in this country all too often leave the individual with no remedy: *Re X (A Minor)* (1975). The Press Council considers complaints against newspapers but in practice has little effect against newspapers which invade privacy in the interests of sensationalism.

QUESTION TWO

'Viewed as a liberalising measure, the Official Secrets Act 1989 is something of a disappointment.'

Discuss this view, by reference to the aims and provisions of the Act.

University of London LLB Examination
(for External Students) Constitutional Law June 1995 Q6

General Comment

This question requires detailed knowledge of the terms and the scope of the Official Secrets Act 1989 and the role it played in reforming the 1911 Act. Where the candidate is comfortable with the subject-matter, the structure of the Act should determine the structure of the answer.

Skeleton Solution

- Aim of the 1911 Act.
- Aim of the 1989 Act.
- Categories of person criminalised.
- Categories of act criminalised.
- Absence of a public interest defence.

Suggested Solution

The aim of the Official Secrets Act 1911 was to protect the interests of the state against espionage and other activities which might be useful to an enemy and therefore injurious to state security; and to guard against the unauthorised disclosure of information held by servants of the state in their official capacity, whether or not the information had any direct reference to state security as such.

The 1989 Act grew out of the Franks Committee report which recommended protection of: classified information relating to defence matters and internal security which would cause injury to the nation; information relating to the prosecution of criminal offences; information which had been entrusted to government by individual concerns for tax or social security purposes; and Cabinet documents. The Committee recommended that protection of Official Secrets and information should be by criminal sanctions only where the circumstances required it.

The 1989 Act repealed s2 of the 1911 Act, but introduced sanctions against unauthorised disclosure of a narrower range of information. Section 1 of the 1989 Act protects from disclosure information relating to security and intelligence, but distinguishes between disclosures without lawful authority by security and intelligence staff on the one hand, and civil servants and government contractors on the other hand. It is an offence for any person to disclose any information obtained in the course of employment in the intelligence services. Disclosure by civil servants and government contractors is unlawful where it is 'damaging' to the defence of the nation or international affairs. Sections 2 and 3 make it an offence for a civil servant or government contractor to disclose damaging information in this way. In the case of disclosures made in the area of defence, the material is considered to be damaging where it restricts the capability of the armed forces to carry out their tasks. Disclosure is considered to be damaging with reference either to defence or international affairs where it endangers the interests of the United Kingdom abroad, or where it endangers the safety of British citizens abroad.

Under s4 of the 1989 Act it is an offence for a civil servant or government contractor to disclose any information where it results in the commission of an offence or facilitates an escape from custody or impedes the prevention or detection of criminal offences. It is similarly an offence to disclose information relating to the obtaining of information as a result of any phone-tapping operation or interference with private property where the latter is permitted by the Security Service Act 1989. Therefore, information obtained without a warrant can be disclosed lawfully under s4 but not under s1 of the 1989 Act.

In all circumstances the offence is committed where the information is disclosed without lawful authority. This is similar to s2 of the 1911 Act, which provided that the offence was committed where the disclosure was unauthorised. There is, however, great difficulty in identifying those cases where a Crown agent or employee is permitted to disclose information. There is also difficulty here with reference to disclosures by Cabinet ministers or senior ministers. Under s7 of the Act a disclosure is authorised where it is made in accordance with the official duty of the minister or civil servant in question. An offence may be committed only by the official disclosing the information or where a third party discloses that information and reports it (for example, a newspaper or radio station).

It is no longer an offence to receive information protected against disclosure. However, under s5 of the 1989 Act it is an offence for the recipient to disclose the information without lawful authority knowing or having reasonable cause to believe that it is protected from disclosure. Therefore, it would be an offence were a newspaper to publish protected information under the Act where that information had been leaked without authorisation. In this circumstance there is no public interest defence because the government rejected the inclusion of such a defence in the Act. The newspaper would be liable only if the disclosure were damaging and was made in the knowledge (or having reasonable cause to believe) that it was damaging.

It is this aspect of the 1989 Act which undermines some of the liberalising effect of much of the Act. The failure to provide for leaking in the public interest maintains the culture of official secrecy which many sought to have removed with the introduction of the 1989 Act. In the United Kingdom the constitutional position is far less advanced than in the United States in refusing to hold that there should be a public interest defence in making disclosures which fall foul of the Official Secrets Act 1989.

QUESTION THREE

'The security of the state is one of the most important functions of government.' To what extent does the law relating to national security reflect this importance?

University of London LLB Examination
(for External Students) Constitutional Law June 1991 Q8

General Comment

There is no 'right way' to tackle a question of this nature since its terms are open to such wide interpretation. Establish what you mean by the term national security law and proceed to cite relevant statutory and common law examples.

Skeleton Solution

- Explain difficulties of interpretation.
- Relate leading judicial review cases.
- Note judicial reluctance to question ministers' views.
- Cite various statutory provisions concerned with national security.

Suggested Solution

The question refers to 'the law relating to national security', and asks to what extent that law reflects the importance of the movernment's role in maintaining state security. An initial difficulty in answering such a question lies in ascertaining the area of law the question is referring to. Clearly national security is not a recognised discrete area of law such as contract or criminal law. If anything it is a concept that cuts across many different areas of law that is used to justify, action or inaction on the part of the government of the day.

In proceedings for judicial review of administrative action the courts have, on occasion, refused to interfere with the decision of a minister on the ground that he has cited 'acting in the interests of national security' to justify his actions.

R v *Secretary of State for the Home Department, ex parte Hosenball* (1977), concerned a challenge to the actions of the Secretary of State himself in refusing to give information about the reasons for making a deportation order against an alien. The Divisional Court and the Court of Appeal refused to grant an order of certiorari because the refusal had been based on grounds of national security. Note that if the refusal of reasons had occurred in what Lord Denning MR called an 'ordinary case', that is, one in which national security was not involved, the position would have been different. He stated:

'... if the body concerned, whether it be a minister or advisers, has acted unfairly, then the courts can review their proceedings so as to ensure, as far as may be, that justice is done.'

Similarly, in *Council of Civil Service Unions* v *Minister for the Civil Service* (1985), where the House of Lords had to consider a challenge to the validity of the Prime Minister's oral direction prohibiting civil servants employed at GCHQ from membership of a trade union, Lord Fraser stated that:

'... whatever their source, powers which are defined, either by reference to their object or by reference to procedure for their exercise, or in some other way, and whether the definition is expressed or implied, are in my opinion normally subject to judicial control to ensure that they are not exceeded. By "normally" I mean provided that considerations of national security do not require otherwise.'

In that particular case, the House of Lords held that, had it not been for the issue of national security, (ie the need for the Prime Minister to pre-empt potentially damaging industrial action by unilaterally banning union membership), her actions would have been in breach of natural justice on the ground of her failure to consult the civil servants on an issue relating to their terms and conditions of employment.

The courts have always been careful to maintain the view that they will not accept an argument based on national security as being sufficient in itself to oust their jurisdiction, but in practice they have rarely if ever, rejected it. Some of the dicta in *Chandler* v *DPP* (1964) are instructive on this point. The House of Lords considered the appeal by CND members who claimed that they had not been planning to act in a manner prejudicial to the interests of the State by preventing planes carrying nuclear warheads from taking off. Lord Reid stated:

'Who then is to determine what is and is not prejudicial to the interests of the State? ... I do not subscribe to the view that the Government or a Minister must always or even as a general rule have the last word about that ... It is in my opinion clear that the disposition and armament of the armed forces are, and for centuries have been, within the exclusive discretion of the Crown, and that no one can seek a legal remedy on the ground that such discretion has been wrongly exercised.'

Lord Devlin concurred:

'... there is no rule of the common law that whenever questions of national security are being considered by any court for any purpose, it is what the Crown thinks to be necessary or expedient that counts, and not what is necessary or expedient in fact ... In a case like the present, it may be presumed that it is contrary to the interests of the Crown to have one of its airfields immobilised ... but the presumption is not irrebuttable ... men can exaggerate the extent of their interests, and so can the Crown. The servants of the Crown, like other men animated by the highest motives, are capable of formulating a policy ad hoc so as to prevent the citizen from doing something that the Crown does not want him to do. It is the duty of the courts to be as alert now as they have always been to prevent any abuse of the prerogative. But in the present case there is nothing at all to suggest that the Crown's interests in the proper operation of its airfields is not what it may naturally be presumed to be, or that it was exaggerating the perils of interference with their effectiveness ...'

The judiciary, therefore, cannot be criticised for failing to give sufficient weight to the significance of the government's responsibility in safeguarding national security.

Various statutes also recognise the importance of ministers acting in the interests of national security.

In relation to broadcasting the Home Secretary can prevent television and radio programmes from being broadcast on the ground that damage would be done to national security; see also the operation of the 'D' Notice committee (Defence, Press and Broadcasting Committee).

A further obvious example is provided by the Official Secrets Act 1989. Section 1 imposes a stringent duty on members or retired members of the security and intelligence services and those notified that they are subject to the section. It provides that such a person commits an offence if without lawful authority he discloses any information or document he has received in the course of such work or while such notification is in force.

Certain modern statutes expressly refer to the concept of 'national security' such as the Interception of Communications Act 1985, which was introduced to regulate 'phone tapping'. The Secretary of State may issue a warrant to intercept in this way if it is necessary in the interests of national security.

Similarly, s10 of the Contempt of Court Act 1981 which provides:

'No court may require a person to disclose, nor is any person guilty of contempt of court for refusing to disclose, the source of information contained in a publication for which he is responsible, unless it be established to the satisfaction of the court that disclosure is necessary in the interests of justice or national security or for the prevention of disorder or crime.'

The effect of this provision was considered in *Secretary of State for Defence* v *Guardian Newspapers Ltd* (1984), which concerned the refusal of the Guardian newspaper to reveal the source of leaked documents concerning the arrival of Cruise missiles at RAF Greenham Common. Regarding the construction of s10 of the 1981 Act, the House of Lords held that the disclosure of the document was needed in order to identify the servant of the Crown who in breach of his statutory duty had copied the document and supplied a copy to *The Guardian*. The real issue was that it had in its employment a servant or servants who had access to classified information and who were prepared, for reasons which seemed good to them, to betray the trust which was reposed in them. On that basis it was fully established that the exceptions to s10 applied, and that the Crown was entitled to discovery as an aid to pursuing its rights against its servant.

QUESTION FOUR

'When the security of the State is under threat the rights and freedoms of the individual must give way to the greater interests of society as a whole.'

Discuss in the light of recent changes in the law.

University of London LLB Examination
(for External Students) Constitutional Law June 1990 Q6

General Comment

A relatively easy question requiring students to assess whether the balance between state security and the freedom of the individual is achieved, or whether the state exercises excessive powers.

Skeleton Solution

- Review procedures open to the State where national security is considered to be at risk:
  a) prerogative powers:
  b) Emergency Powers Acts 1920 and 1964;
  c) Public Order Act 1986;
  d) Prevention of Terrorism (Temporary Provisions) Act 1989.
  e) Prevention of Terrorism (Additional Powers) Act 1996
- Conclude with question of justifiability.

Suggested Solution

In the modern world, threats to the security of some or all of the nation, may come in a large variety of forms, often considerably different from those experienced in the past. Principally, the development of systems that allow a complex society to function smoothly also make it vulnerable. From the terrorist's bomb on a plane to security considerations in defence establishments, law makers have been forced, by the circumstances of recent years, to curtail the freedoms that individuals have come to expect. Some prohibitions seldom have been placed 'across the board', but their effect has been felt in many areas of everyday life.

In extremis, it is conceivable that in circumstances of dire emergency, where civil authorities, due to internal or external disruption, abrogate their power in favour of military authorities, such a situation, although unlikely, would amount to the imposition of martial law. This term is something of a misnomer since it is a state where normal civil laws are in suspense in favour of the discretion of senior military commanders. Such a situation would certainly involve the individual's rights giving way to that of society. However, it is clear from such authorities as we have that the courts may still review whether the circumstances justify imposition of this extreme measure and may also exercise judicial review. Thus, in *Egan* v *Macready* (1921), a court felt able to declare that the prerogative purported to be exercised by military authorities had been superseded by statute. Furthermore, if Dicey is to be believed, liability would be incurred by military authorities for any unnecessary harm once civil law was restored. It is, however, more likely that the military would be indemnified by subsequent statute against legal actions arising out of the period of martial law.

A more common occurrence, relatively speaking, is the nation being forced onto a war footing, either where there is no official state of war in existence, or where there is actual hostility. Powers relating to the declaration and conduct of war are primarily matters of prerogative.

Since the prerogative allows for the internment and deportation of enemies and the requisition of their property, as well as the tactical destruction or confiscation of property generally, individual rights and freedoms may be curbed. Such powers were seen at work in the Persian Gulf, where sanctions prohibit the carrying on of all but humanitarian trade with Iraq and Britain retained for the military forces in the Gulf the right of interception of property and vessels. This directly interfered with the trading interests of individuals within this country. The crisis also saw the expulsion of diplomatic and other Iraqi nationals. Most of these prerogatives relate to the conduct of affairs outside the United Kingdom or are exercised against those who are not British subjects. However, in other war situations, citizens might find their commercial and proprietary interests affected by such prerogative powers. Although, as in the case of the *Burmah Oil Co* v *Lord Advocate* (1965), the courts may review such actions and award compensation, indemnification of the Crown, in a similar manner to that effected by the War Damage Act 1965, would be likely to prevent redress from being made. Furthermore, it must be remembered that even where the exercise of prerogative is compensated, the rights of the individual still take a back seat to the immediate requirements of national security and as such are held in suspense until the immediate crisis has passed.

The immediacy of the crisis is largely the yard stick that the courts have used to determine the extent to which the Crown may set aside considerations of individual rights. In interpreting the Defence of the Realm Acts 1914–1915 and the Emergency Powers (Defence) Acts 1939–1940, the judiciary have given considerable weight to the degree of emergency at any given time. Under these statutes, wide discretionary powers are conferred on the Crown, enabling it to make regulations that it deems necessary for the safety of the nation, including the suspension of normal peace time courts. Such an order was not itself made, but regulations relating to the internment of British subjects were viewed by the courts with varying degrees of approval in various stages of the First and Second World Wars.

It is not only in times of war or military threat that wide legislative powers can be adopted by the Crown. In states of emergency the Emergency Powers Acts 1920 and 1964 provide for legislation by Orders in Council when the provision of essential services is disrupted. The breadth of the powers is such that a court might find it difficult to declare such Orders ultra vires. The necessity of positive affirmation by Parliament is intended to provide a constitutional safeguard, but this does not of itself guarantee the rights of individuals, except insofar as the Act prohibits excessive criminal sentencing, forced labour or military conscription and the outlawing of normally legitimate strike actions. However, the increased powers of the police and the stricter regulation of trade union activities has meant that in the last decade other methods have been used to ensure the supply of essential services, in contrast to the frequent use in the 1970s of these provisions.

These modern methods of control reflect what some writers, such as the late Professor De Smith, perceive as a change in the nature of the threats to the security of the state. The 1980s were marked by a sharp increase in public disorder, relating to industrial, political and leisure activities. Furthermore, there has been an increasing sensitivity to the dissemination of information both factually and subjectively generated. Whether such attitudes genuinely reflect a new form of threat to national security or the re-emergence of historical trends, accompanied by deepened insecurity amongst authorities, is open to debate. Nonetheless, in response to the changing situation, there has been a perceptible change in tactics. Instead of the sweeping invocation of emergency powers, the legislature has chosen to put into place more or less permanent structures that may be employed by subordinate authorities at their discretion. Although it is arguable whether violent disorders constitute serious threats to the security of the state, or at least the level of disorder that has prompted such measures, it is principally the police who now have wider powers in given circumstances to curtail the rights of the individual. Additionally, more and more activities are required to be performed only with authorisation and due compliance with regulatory stipulations. To enumerate the panoply of recent legislation that directly or indirectly tackle matters relating to the security of the state would be quite a considerable task. Therefore, our survey must confine itself to certain notable examples of the 'new tactics'.

The difficult area of the retention and security of official secrets and the consequence scrutiny, resulted in new legislation in 1989. It tightens the reign on the free dissemination of information, which will lead to a 'knock-on' effect for free speech. There can be no defence based on 'public interest' – that is to say that publication was done on the basis that the information should be in the public domain because it reveals government corruption and so on. Equally, the broadcasting reforms provide for a system of vetting material that is potentially harmful to the viewer, and as a result is certain to narrow the channels for more controversial forms of entertainment. The Public Order Act 1986, which regulates all manner of potential threats to the Queen's peace, prohibits, by virtue of s5, the use of communications and representations likely to cause harassment, alarm or distress to a person exposed to them. Similarly, material and communications that might induce racial conflict is liable to criminal sanction under ss17–23. To what extent these measures are intended to protect the state, rather than society, is debateable, but certainly the thinking behind such legislation is to prevent inflammatory situations from developing.

The Police and Criminal Evidence Act 1984 and the Public Order Act 1986 confer on the police significant powers with regard to freedom of movement and expression. The former allows for the use of road blocks and searches as a preventative measure, whilst the latter reforms and codifies public order laws imposing more coherent powers for the policing of demonstrations, processions and assemblies. Coupled with these measures are the requirements in most circumstances for due authorisation to organise these activities.

Anti-terrorist legislation involves the vesting of extensive powers in the police to preserve the safety of the State and public order. The Prevention of Terrorism (Temporary Provisions) Act 1989 (renewed by virtue of SI 1996/891), permits the Home Secretary to classify certain organisations as 'proscribed' thus making it an offence to belong, or profess to belong, to such an organisation, to solicit or invite non-financial support for it, or for any person to wear any item of dress or to wear, carry or display any article in a public place in such a way or in such circumstances as to arouse reasonable apprehension that he is a member or supporter of a proscribed organisation.

Under Part II of the Act he can make exclusion orders in respect of any person who is or has been concerned in the commission, preparation or instigation of acts of terrorism. Under s13, as amended by s81 of the Criminal Justice and Public Order Act 1994, a senior officer may authorise the use of powers to stop and search vehicles for articles that could be used in connection with acts of terrorism. A constable may exercise these powers whether or not he has reasonable grounds for suspecting that a stop and search of a person or vehicle may reveal such articles. The Prevention of Terrorism (Additional Powers) Act 1996 further empowers an assistant chief constable, or where appropriate a more senior officer, to apply to the Home Secretary to have a location declared to be a 'specified area' for a period of up to 28 days (renewable). The effect of such a declaration will be that, within the designated area, police officers will have power to stop and search individuals, search non-residential buildings if they have information that terrorist materials are concealed therein, search unaccompanied cargo at ports, and cordon off areas if there is a threat of terrorist activity, or a terrorist incident has occurred.

One must finally observe that other measures relating to the prevention of terrorism give rise to the prevention of the full exercise of certain public rights. Most recently, it has been announced that the free movement and free expression of persons in airport premises is to be restricted by the imposition of imprisonable sanctions for those who enter aircraft without authorisation or make misleading statements about the contents of baggage. Thus, it has been widely observed, a person exercising free speech by joking that he has a bomb in his suitcase might theoretically be convicted by virtue of these measures.

One is faced with a difficulty in these areas of relevance to the question. The security of the state is not seriously at risk by most of the activities that are envisaged by these statutes. The primary use of these laws is to protect society. However, since it is largely viewed by the courts that deciding what matters relate to state security is to be decided by central government, one must assume that the government's views on this matter must be conclusive.

The perceived change in tactics seems to confirm this view, since a shift in reliance on the concept of a transient national emergency to that of building safeguards into the everyday laws of the land must reflect a belief that the problem has changed. This might be an admission of the view that the Queen's peace is no longer prevalent throughout the land, which would indicate a siege mentality that requires individuals to relinquish their rights from day to day as new threats emerge. Alternatively, there might be a view that administrative convenience is better served by placing individual liberty in second place. This change must either signal the belief that the state has become more vulnerable or sensitive or that the democratic safeguards of using 'laws of last resort', which are brought out of the legislative armoury in times of dire emergency, are less important than they were. The fact that the Emergency Powers Act was used five times by the Heath government in the 1970s would appear to confirm the first synopsis. The complexities of the modern state make it more dependent and therefore more vulnerable and the facilities available to those who seek to threaten it have become equally sophisticated. As a result of such progress individual rights are placed between the rock of potential threats and the hard place that are the reinforced walls of the state.

13 Police Powers

13.1 Introduction

This is an important constitutional law topic covering as it does the powers of the police to stop and search an individual on the street and enter his premises. It should be noted that some examination boards cover police powers on their English legal system syllabuses. You should check your particular examination syllabus and past papers to establish whether this is a likely examination topic in your case. The University of Wolverhampton syllabus, for example, examines this topic in constitutional and administrative law.

13.2 Key points

Virtually all police powers are now contained in the Police and Criminal Evidence Act 1984 – commonly referred to as PACE – and the codes of practice accompanying the Act.

You must know the following key sections of the 1984 Act.

a) *Sections 1–3*

These are the stop and search provisions.

They allow an officer to stop and search individuals and vehicles provided:

i) they are in public places, and

ii) the officer has reasonable grounds to suspect that he will find articles relating to:

- burglary
- theft
- joy riding
- obtaining property by deception

or that he will find an offensive weapon.

See *Harris* v *DPP, Fehmi* v *DPP* [1993] 1 All ER 562.

iii) An article searched for under s1 may be seized.

b) *Section 4*

Road checks may be authorised to check whether a vehicle is carrying a person who has committed an offence, or intending to commit an offence, a person unlawfully at large or a witness to an offence. Note, in addition, the powers under s163 Road Traffic Act 1988.

c) *Sections 17–18 and 32*

Police powers to enter at common law are retained to deal with a breach of the peace: s17(6); *Thomas* v *Sawkins* [1935] 2 KB 249; *Lamb* v *DPP* [1990] Crim LR 58.

Police can enter to execute an arrest warrant or to arrest for any arrestable offence, to recapture someone unlawfully at large (*D'Souza* v *Director of Public Prosecutions* [1992] 1 WLR 1073), to save life and limb or to prevent serious damage to property.

Where a person has been arrested for an arrestable offence s18 gives a power of entry and search. The premises searched must be occupied or under the control of the person arrested, and there must be reasonable grounds for believing that there is evidence of the offence or of a connected or similar offence on the premises.

Section 32 confers powers to enter and search premises which the arrested person left immediately prior to the arrest and applies to any offence.

d) *Section 19*

This section gives a general right of seizure provided an officer is lawfully on the premises, ie:

i) he has a search warrant; or

ii) he has entered pursuant to the above sections.

e) *Protected material*

i) Legally privileged material – designed to protect the confidentiality of communications between client and legal adviser. Access cannot be obtained.

ii) Excluded material – defined in s11.

iii) Special procedure material – defined in s14.

Access to these categories of material cannot be obtained by means of an ordinary search warrant. Note that it may be seized if discovered in the course of a lawful search: s19.

f) *Section 24*

This section gives power to arrest anyone without a warrant provided it is an 'arrestable offence' as defined above.

The person making the arrest must inform the arrested person of the fact and reasons for arrest: s28. The reasons must be given as soon as is reasonably practicable: *DPP* v *Hawkins* [1988] 1 WLR 1166; *Lewis* v *Chief Constable of the South Wales Constabulary* [1991] 1 All ER 206. A person making the arrest may use reasonable force against the person arrested.

g) *Section 56*

This section allows anyone who has been arrested and is at a police station the right to inform someone of his arrest as soon as is reasonably practicable.

h) *Section 58*

This gives an arrested person held in custody the right to consult a solicitor privately at any time.

This is an extremely important provision – in particular a person has a right by reason of this section to have his solicitor present before he is interviewed in relation to the offence for which he has been arrested.

i) *Section 76*

This is a most important evidential provision allowing a 'confession' to be given in evidence against an accused even though technically it would be hearsay evidence ie a statement made outside court by a person other than the one giving evidence and put forward to show the truth of what has been said.

Note the wide definition of a confession namely any statement wholly or partly adverse to the maker: s82.

Section 76, however, guards against the risk of confessions brought about by oppression by putting the onus of proof on the prosecution to show that it was not obtained by either:

i) oppression; or

ii) anything done or said which might render it unreliable.

Unless the prosecution can show this, the confession will not be admissable.

j) *Section 78*

This section goes hand in hand with s76 but is much wider because it applies to any evidence – not simply confessions.

It gives the court a discretion to exclude any evidence which, having regard to the circumstances in which it was obtained, would have such an adverse influence on the fairness of the proceedings that the court ought not to admit it.

This section is aimed at giving a court a discretion to exclude evidence obtained in breach of PACE, eg an illegal search under s17 or an interview where access to a solicitor under s58 was denied.

A confession may not be excluded under s76 but may nevertheless be excluded under s78: *R* v *Mason* [1988] 1 WLR 139.

Furthermore, breaches of the Codes of Practice (see following section) may also lead to exclusion of evidence under s78.

k) *The Criminal Justice and Public Order Act 1994*

Under s34 of the Criminal Justice and Public Order Act 1994 Act if a suspect fails to mention any fact relied on in his defence (being something that he could reasonably be expected to have mentioned) either when being questioned after cautioning by a constable, or after having been charged with an offence or officially informed that he might be prosecuted, the court or jury may draw such inferences from the failure as appear proper. Section 36 provides similarly in relation to an arrested person's failure to account for any object in his possession, or any substance or mark on his person, clothing or article in his possession when required to do so by a constable investigating an offence, and s37 applies similarly to an arrested person's failure to account for his presence at a particular location.

A consequence of this change in the law is the amendment to the police caution that has been in use for over 30 years. In place of the previous wording the Code of Practice now requires the following wording:

'You do not have to say anything. But it may harm your defence if you do not mention when questioned something which you later rely on in court. Anything you do say may be given in evidence.'

l) *The Codes of Practice*

The major Code provisions are:

i) once persons are suspected of a crime they should be cautioned;

ii) basic comforts such as breaks for refreshment, proper rest, adequate heating and ventilation should be afforded whilst a person is in custody and being interviewed;

iii) consent to an identification parade is required. If a person is suspected it is wrong to show a witness photographs before asking that witness to pick someone out at an identification parade;

iv) if photographs are shown to a witness a minimum of 12 photographs ought to be shown.

The Codes of Practice were revised and modified with effect from 1 April 1995. Key changes included the following:

Once a person is detained at a police station he has to be informed not only that he has a right to have a solicitor present before he is interviewed but also that the services of a solicitor are free.

Interviews inside police stations should be made in the presence of a solicitor (if the detainee so wishes) but in any event shall be tape-recorded.

Interviews outside police stations (which clearly cannot have the protection of being tape-recorded or have the presence of a solicitor) are not permitted unless the following apply:

i) no decision has been reached as to whether the interviewee is to be arrested; or

ii) the questioning does not relate to the interviewee's involvement or suspected involvement in any crime; or

iii) delay in interviewing would result in:

- interference or harm to any evidence or potential witness;
- the alerting of others suspected of being involved in the crime;
- the hindering of the recovery of stolen property.

Where an ordinary identification parade is impracticable then identification by video is permissible (ie the witness may be shown a video containing the suspect and at least eight other persons of similar appearance to the suspect).

It is important to remember that a breach of the Codes of Practice is likely to result in the court exercising its discretion under s78 of the 1984 Act to exclude the admissibility of any evidence obtained as a result of a breach of a provision of the Code.

13.3 Recent cases

Foulkes v *Chief Constable of Merseyside Police* [1998] 3 All ER 705 – arrest – breach of the peace – power to arrest where breach of the peace apprehended – whether arrest lawful.

Gapper v *Chief Constable of Avon and Somerset Constabulary* [1998] 4 All ER 248 – arrest for being found on enclosed premises – whether power to arrest survived the enactment of PACE

O'Loughlin v *Chief Constable of Essex* (1997) The Times 12 December – statutory power of entry exercised by constable under s17 PACE – reasons to be given.

R v *Chalkley* [1998] 2 All ER 155 – arrest – ulterior motive for arrest – whether arrest lawful.

R v *Chief Constable of the Royal Ulster Constabulary, ex parte Begley* [1997] 4 All ER 833 – whether any common law right to consult privately with a solicitor.

13.4 Analysis of questions

No questions on police powers have been set in recent years by some examination boards (although on the University of London LLB External programme the area is examined in English legal system).

If this area is examined the likely examination question will be a problem solving exercise setting out a series of police actions eg entering premises, searching, seizing evidence, arresting an individual, and asking the candidate to comment on the legality or otherwise of the police actions.

13.5 Questions

QUESTION ONE

PC Black was called to the premises of Smiths (Jewellers) Limited following a report of a theft. When he arrived the owner, James Smith, told him that £450 had been stolen from his safe. There had been no sign of any break in or any damage to the safe itself. Smith told PC Black that he suspected an 'inside job' and named Terry Jones as a likely suspect. Terry Jones had only been employed by Smith for a few weeks and he knew the safe's combination.

PC Black went around to Terry Jones's house intending to arrest him. When he arrived no-one was in but the back door was not locked and PC Black entered the premises. Having established that Terry was not in PC Black proceeded to search the house and in an upstairs wardrobe he found £400 in cash wrapped in a pullover.

Just as he finished his search Terry Jones entered the house. PC Black asked Terry where he had been and whether he knew anything about the break in at Smiths Jewellers. Terry replied that he knew nothing about the theft. He was then searched by PC Black who found another £50 in cash in Terry's jacket pocket. Terry was asked where he got the money from and replied that it had 'nothing to do with' PC Black.

PC Black then arrested Terry and cautioned him. He took him to the police station where he was charged by the custody sergeant with theft.

PC Black then placed Terry in an interview room and asked him to make a statement. Terry asked whether he could speak to his solicitor before he answered any question but was told that was impossible. Terry refused to answer any questions and was kept in the interview room for a further six hours without being given any refreshments or being allowed to use the toilet.

Nevertheless, Terry still refused to answer any questions. However PC Black then told Terry that they were going to arrest and charge his eight months pregnant wife with receiving stolen money. However Terry was told that if he 'held his hands up' to the crime the police would not involve his wife.

Thereupon Terry signed a statement confessing to the theft.

Discuss the validity of PC Black's actions in this matter.

Written by the Editors

General Comment

A question involving knowledge and application of the major aspects of the Police and Criminal Evidence Act 1984.

Skeleton Solution

- Was the entry lawful? Yes, because he had reason to believe Terry was guilty of an arrestable offence and might be at his house.
- Was the search legal? No, because he had no search warrant and had not arrested Terry when he searched the wardrobe.
- Was the search of Terry legal? No, because he had not been arrested when he was searched and it was not a public place therefore ss1–3 PACE not applicable.
- Was the initial questioning of Terry proper? No, because he suspected him immediately yet did not caution Terry before asking him any questions in breach of the Code of Guidance.
- The interview – in breach of Code of Guidance in way interview conducted. Wrong to deny access to solicitor: s58 PACE.
- The confession – oppressive/unreliable within meaning of s76 – *R* v *Fulling* (1987), *R* v *Samuel* (1988).
- Would evidence be admissible? Even though evidence obtained illegally court has discretion to allow its admissability. However strong argument that such illegally obtained evidence would be excluded because of s78.

Suggested Solution

This question demands a discussion of police powers and in particular, the limitations on such power laid down by the provisions of the Police and Criminal Evidence Act 1984 (PACE).

When PC Black went to Terry's house he did so with the intention of arresting him for the theft at the jewellers. Accordingly he had a right to enter the premises in order to arrest Terry – theft is an arrestable offence and Black had reason to believe that Terry would be at home: s17 PACE.

However Black did not have a search warrant. Whilst s18 of PACE allows the search of premises of an arrested person, when the wardrobe was searched Terry had not yet been arrested. The finding of the £400 was as a result of an illegal search; this may well lead a court to exclude evidence of this find pursuant to s78 PACE, a matter I return to later.

Furthermore, the search of Terry was illegal. He had not been arrested when he was searched and he was searched inside his house, that is to say a private place. The power to stop and search only applies to public places (see ss1–3 PACE).

Since Black suspected Terry immediately the Code of Guidance required that he caution Terry before asking him any questions. Accordingly evidence of Terry's refusal to give an explanation as to where he got the £50 from may, once again, be excluded under s78 PACE.

The interview at the station can be attacked on a number of grounds. Firstly s58 PACE gives a right to have a solicitor present on request of an accused. Black's refusal to allow access to a solicitor was a clear breach of s58.

Secondly in making Terry remain in the interview room for such a lengthy period without refreshment or being permitted to use the toilet, Black was in breach of the Code of Guidance.

The above two reasons would make any statement made by Terry liable to be excluded by reason of s78 in any event.

However, the confession is very likely to be excluded by reason of s76 PACE. Whilst this section allows a confession to be admitted in evidence it will not be allowed in unless the prosecution can prove that it was not made by reason of oppression or something said or done to make it unreliable.

Terry would argue that the way he was treated in the interview room amounted to oppression and, in any event, the threat about charging his wife was something said to make the confession unreliable. In *R* v *Fulling* (1987) Lord Lane included 'cruel treatment' under the heading of oppression. The treatment of Terry during the interview does appear to be 'cruel'. Furthermore in *R* v *Samuel* (1988) the refusal of access to a solicitor was deemed to be a matter making a confession unreliable.

It is most probable, therefore, that the confession would be excluded by reason of s76 but, in any event, it may well be excluded under s78. In *R* v *Mason* (1988) it was held that confessions could be caught by both s76 and s78.

I have referred to s78 a great deal in this answer. It provides, in effect, that unfairly obtained evidence may be excluded at the discretion of the court. The point to note here, therefore, is that while much of the evidence against Terry has been illegally obtained the court still has a discretion to admit it. However, equally it can exclude it under s78 which permits exclusion if it appears that, having regard to the way the evidence was obtained, its admission in evidence would have an adverse effect on the fairness of the trial. The tendency of courts is to use s78 in favour of defendants rather than against them ie evidence is normally excluded.

In summary, therefore, most of the evidence against Terry is likely to be excluded and Terry will probably not be convicted of this crime. The finding of the money was pursuant to illegal searches and is likely to be excluded under s78. The confession will be excluded under either s76 or s78.

QUESTION TWO

'The Police and Criminal Evidence Act 1984 achieves a satisfactory balance between the interests of the community and the rights and liberties of suspects.'

Say how far you agree with this statement and support your argument by reference to the provisions of PACE and recent case law.

University of London LLB Examination
(for External Students) English Legal System June 1995 Q8

General Comment

Students hoping for a 'problem-type' question on police powers would be disappointed by this question, which presents a very challenging task in subjecting the relevant law to a critical analysis. Familiarity with the Police and Criminal Evidence Act (PACE) 1984 and the Codes of Practice is essential, and the ability to be selective in highlighting issues and illustrating by reference to cases is also crucial. The effect of the Criminal Justice and Public Order Act (CJPOA) 1994 should be touched on, but clearly the question requires concentration on the effect of PACE 1984 and its interpretation in the courts. Despite the apparent invitation in the question to give a personal view, every effort should be made to present a dispassionate, clinical analysis giving equal weight to both sides of the argument.

Skeleton Solution

- Definition of the conflict of interests between protection of the public and safeguards for suspects.
- The purpose of PACE 1984 and the Codes of Practice.
- An appraisal of whether the purpose was achieved and (in outline only) the reasons for the passage of the Criminal Justice and Public Order Act 1994.
- An outline of suspects' remedies for abuse of police powers.
- A detailed analysis of the effect of a breach of PACE and/or the Codes of Practice on admissibility of evidence.
- The rule on confessions in PACE, s76.
- The exclusionary discretion under PACE, s78.
- Case law conflicts of authority on the interpretation of s78.
- Comparisons with USA law on entrapment and the 'Miranda' principle – a critical conclusion on whether English law ought to adopt the USA approach.

Suggested Solution

Presumably the interests of the community may be defined as protection of the public from criminal activities through the effective detection, investigation and prosecution of criminal offences. The rights and liberties of suspects may be defined as protection against abuse of the powers granted for the purposes of detecting, investigating and prosecuting, including protection against oppressive or inhumane exercise of authority. The purpose behind PACE was to strengthen police powers to combat crime, but at the same time preserve and strengthen the safeguards against abuse of such powers. Whether that purpose was achieved and the proper balance struck remains a highly contentious political issue. The Conservative administration which enacted PACE evidently came to the view (urged by the police) that PACE tilted the balance too far towards the interests of suspects, and hence increased police powers and a modification of the right of silence have occurred as the result of the Criminal Justice and Public Order Act (CJPOA) 1994. Critics from civil liberties organisations argue that PACE did not protect suspects' rights as effectively as the Government contended, and that consequently the CJPOA 1994 represents a further undermining of human rights.

One of the problems for a suspect is that his rights depend on whether the relevant provision under which he was stopped and searched, or arrested, or questioned in police custody, is contained in PACE or one of the Codes of Practice issued by the Home Office under the authority of PACE. Breach of a statutory provision would be treated as a serious matter and likely to give rise to a cause of action in tort, or even form the basis for a criminal prosecution against the police. However, breach of the Codes of Practice is expressly declared by s67(10) of PACE not to give rise to any civil or criminal liability; instead the suspect is expected to complain to the Police Complaints Authority so that, for minor breaches, he would be assured of at least an apology, and for more serious breaches he might be assured that appropriate disciplinary action would be taken. Since the police investigate accusations of police malpractice on behalf of the Authority there is a suspicion that this might not prove an effective remedy.

Even more problematic is the effect of a breach of PACE and/or the Codes of Practice on the admissibility of evidence obtained as a result of such breach. The suspect is assured by s76 of PACE that involuntary confessions made as the result of oppression, and unreliable confessions made as the result of an improper inducement, would be inadmissible at his trial. However, all other evidence, including dubious confessions obtained otherwise than by oppression or improper inducements, might be admissible at the trial judge's discretion depending on the character of the breach of PACE and/or the Codes of Practice and the effect of the admission of such evidence on the fairness of the trial: PACE, s78.

The interpretation of s78 has given rise to conflicts of authority. In *R* v *Samuel* (1988) it was robustly stated that a suspect's right to consult privately with a solicitor under PACE, s58, is of fundamental importance, and that evidence obtained after unreasonable denial of such access should be excluded from the trial under PACE, s78. However, this rule of exclusion was not to apply if the police had adequately informed the suspect of his rights (*R* v *Alladice* (1989)); or if the suspect was a 'hardened criminal' well aware of his rights (*R* v *Dunford* (1990)). These decisions appear to make a mockery of the safeguard Parliament intended all suspects to have when held in police custody at a police station.

Trickery by the police in order to obtain incriminating evidence may be a ground for excluding such evidence under PACE, s78, but the difficulty is that PACE, unlike USA law, does not clearly outlaw various forms of 'entrapment' by the police. The more extreme kinds of trickery involving bad faith on the part of the police have resulted in the exclusion of evidence under PACE, s78 on the ground that they involve flagrant breaches of the Codes of Practice, eg *R* v *Mason* (1988), where the police had lied to the suspect and his solicitor about the evidence they had against him, thereby unfairly influencing the legal advice given to the suspect. Similarly, undercover operations in which police officers questioned suspects without cautioning them or acted as 'agents provocateur' in procuring, inciting or counselling a crime, have resulted in the exclusion of evidence: *R* v *Bryce* (1992) and *R* v *Smurthwaite* (1994). But if the police malpractice takes a less extreme form, and it can be said that the criminal applied himself to the trick rather than the police applying the trick to the criminal, then evidence obtained as a result of the trick may be admissible: *R* v *Christou* (1992). Evidence obtained by bugging a police cell, or even a private house, may also be admissible since PACE and the Codes of Practice appear to be silent on suspects' rights to privacy apart from when consulting with a solicitor: *R* v *Bailey* (1993) and *R* v *Khan (Sultan)* (1996).

It follows that those who support civil liberties' philosophy will not be satisfied unless and until English law adopts the USA 'Miranda' principle of automatically excluding from evidence any material obtained illegally or improperly by the police. Those who subscribe to the view that the paramount need is to protect the public from crime will argue that such a step would be harmful to the interests of the community, and that the discretion allowed to exclude such evidence, together with the existence of disciplinary machinery over the police, provide an appropriate balancing of the competing interests.

14 University of London LLB (External) 1997 Questions and Suggested Solutions

UNIVERSITY OF LONDON
LLB EXAMINATIONS 1997
for External Students
INTERMEDIATE EXAMINATION (Scheme A)
FIRST AND SECOND YEAR EXAMINATIONS (Scheme B)
GRADUATE ENTRY LEVEL I (Route A)
GRADUATE ENTRY FIRST YEAR (Route B)

CONSTITUTIONAL LAW

Tuesday, 4 June: 10.00 am to 1.00 pm

Answer *FOUR* of the following EIGHT questions

1 'Membership of the European Community requires a fundamental reassessment of the traditional theory of parliamentary sovereignty'

Do you agree? To what extent does the case law support such a view?

2 'While an unwritten constitution has the merit of flexibility, this flexibility is purchased at the expense of individual rights.'

Critically assess this statement.

3 To what extent was Walter Bagehot correct in his assertion that the close fusion of the executive and the legislature represents the 'efficient secret' of the constitution?

4 'Constitutionalism, like an elephant, is hard to define but easy to recognise.'

Discuss.

5 'The doctrine of individual and collective responsibility requires greater clarification if members of government are to be confined within the rule of law.'

Discuss.

6 To what extent does English law uphold the requirements of the European Convention on Human Rights?

7 Draft a memorandum to the government, outlining your preferred alternative to the current role and composition of the House of Lords. Explain to the government any constitutional implications of your proposed reforms.

8 Critically assess the constitutional role of judicial review in upholding the sovereignty of Parliament and the rule of law. How effective are the courts in fulfilling this role?

QUESTION ONE

'Membership of the European Community requires a fundamental reassessment of the traditional theory of parliamentary sovereignty'

Do you agree? To what extent does the case law support such a view?

University of London LLB Examination
(for External Students) Constitutional Law June 1997 Q1

General Comment

The question requires an explanation of the traditional theory of parliamentary sovereignty, and an assessment of whether or not that doctrine has undergone any significant changes since 1972. It is important to put the issue in perspective and examine the view of the ECJ on this matter. Candidates should explain how judges have tried to accommodate the changes, and note that the European Communities Act 1972 is itself a manifestation of parliamentary sovereignty.

Skeleton Solution

- What the European Community believes the impact to be.
- Why this is a problem for the UK?
- The wording of s2(4).
- The approach of the courts.
- Whether this amounts to a fundamental change.

Suggested Solution

Membership of the European Community has profound implications for the doctrine of parliamentary sovereignty as it operates within the British constitution. In simple terms the doctrine provides that Parliament at Westminster has unlimited power and is free to make or repeal laws as it sees fit – it is not a body of limited jurisdiction.

In practice this means that a later statute passed by Parliament at Westminster can expressly repeal an earlier one, no matter how significant the earlier Act. On those occasions where a later Act is found to be inconsistent with an earlier one, the courts invoke the doctrine of implied repeal. This is illustrated by *Vauxhall Estates Ltd* v *Liverpool Corporation* (1932). The Corporation of Liverpool proposed a scheme for the improvement of a certain area of the city. The Minister of Health confirmed the scheme in an order that incorporated the provisions of the Acquisition of Land (Assessment of Compensation) Act 1919 and the Housing Act 1925. These two Acts each provided a different scheme of compensation for compulsorily acquired land. Notwithstanding the clear terms of the 1919 Act, the court applied the less favourable terms of the 1925 Act, on the basis that Parliament had exercised its power of overriding the provisions of the 1919 Act (albeit unwittingly) by enacting in the later Act of 1925 a set of provisions totally inconsistent with those of the 1919 Act. *Ellen Street Estates Ltd* v *Minister of Health* (1934) provides a further illustration.

The view of the European Court of Justice as regards the sovereignty of member states is equally clear; ie membership of the European Community involves a pooling of sovereignty by member states. In *Costa* v *ENEL* (1964) it explained that the European Community derived its power and identity from 'a limitation of sovereignty or a transfer of powers from the States to the Community', and concluded that member states had limited their sovereign rights, within certain fields, to create a body of law binding on their nationals and themselves. The Court stressed in particular the point that, if the European Community was to work properly, it would have to ensure that European Community law applied equally and to the same extent within each member state. This necessarily limits the scope of each member's legislature to enact laws inconsistent with European Community law – hence the conflict with the traditional theory of parliamentary sovereignty. Similar statements can be found in the decision of the ECJ in *Re Export Tax on Art Treasures (No 2)* (1972), where it was held that the grant to the European Community by member states of the rights and powers envisaged by the provisions of the Treaty of Rome implied a 'definitive limitation of their sovereign powers' over which no appeal to provisions of international law of any kind whatever could prevail. In effect, as far as the European Court of Justice is concerned, the United Kingdom doctrine of the legislative sovereignty of Parliament is irrelevant where the primacy of European Community law is in issue.

The United Kingdom became a member of the European Community with effect from 1 January 1973, the incorporation of the Treaty of Rome being achieved by the enactment of the European Communities Act 1972. The significance of the 1972 Act is that, from the date it came into force, all existing European Community law became part of domestic law. Following the doctrine of implied repeal this meant that any pre-1972 domestic law could now only have effect to the extent that it was consistent with European Community law – ie the doctrine of implied repeal applied. The real problems, however, arose as to the status of domestic law enacted post-1972 that was found to be in conflict with European Community law. The 1972 Act does not expressly deal with the issue of sovereignty, but provision is made in s2(4) for the resolution of such conflicts, where it is stated that any domestic legislation enacted after 1972 will be 'construed and have effect subject to' European Community law. In other words this provision suggests that the traditional doctrine of implied repeal cannot apply where domestic legislation passed after 1972 is found to be in conflict with existing European Community law.

The courts have responded to this problem by developing a rule of interpretation whereby it is presumed that Parliament, in passing legislation, intends to legislate consistently with Community law. On the basis of *Macarthys Ltd* v *Wendy Smith* (1979), and *Garland* v *British Rail Engineering Ltd* (1983), this approach still allows the United Kingdom Parliament to make it clear in an Act that it intends to legislate contrary to Community law, or that legislation will take effect notwithstanding any provision of Community law to the contrary. It would appear that, to the extent that it was in conflict with European Community law, the United Kingdom legislation would prevail. This 'rule of construction' approach is neither consistent with the traditional United Kingdom doctrine of the sovereignty of Parliament, nor with the Community doctrine of the supremacy of Community law over national law. Although the courts have not had to deal with the problem of a United Kingdom Act of Parliament expressing an intention to legislate contrary to Community law, in the *Factortame* litigation (*R* v *Secretary of State for Transport, ex parte Factortame (No 2)* (1990)), the courts had to consider the validity of domestic legislation that was wholly inconsistent with European Community law, and the House of Lords held that domestic courts had no power to grant interim relief to prevent the operation of a statute passed by Parliament, unless it could be shown that there was some overriding principle of Community law which provided that member states must provide such relief. On reference under art 177 (now art 234), however, the ECJ ruled to the contrary. Following this ruling, the House of Lords held that a litigant could be given interim interlocutory relief to suspend the operation of the offending domestic legislation.

On the one hand, therefore, it could be said that there has been a fundamental change to the doctrine of parliamentary sovereignty simply on the basis there is now a legislative body that can create law to which the judges will, normally, give precedence over domestic law. On the other hand it can be argued that this state of affairs is simply a manifestation of parliamentary sovereignty. The United Kingdom is only a member of the European Community because Parliament passed the European Communities Act 1972. When judges give precedence to European Community law they are simply carrying out Parliament's instructions as contained in s2(4) of that Act. When the *Factortame* case returned to the House of Lords for implementation of the ECJ ruling Lord Bridge expressed the view that Parliament has always loyally accepted the obligation to make appropriate and prompt amendments where the ECJ has found domestic law to be in breach of European Community law, and that there was nothing novel in according supremacy to rules of Community law in those areas to which they applied.

The forfeiture of sovereignty is best described as limited and partial. The European Communities Act 1972 is not entrenched, and Parliament can in theory repeal the Act at any time and thus regain its full supremacy as a sovereign legislature. The longer the United Kingdom remains a member , however, the more difficult it will be to extricate itself in political and economic terms. Joining a single currency will accelerate this process. Ultimately the situation may be reached where legislation to withdraw from the European Community may regarded in the same way as, for example, legislation to make Hong Kong a Crown colony again – theoretically possible, but unlikely.

QUESTION TWO

'While an unwritten constitution has the merit of flexibility, this flexibility is purchased at the expense of individual rights.'

Critically assess this statement.

University of London LLB Examination
(for External Students) Constitutional Law June 1997 Q2

General Comment

The question calls for an explanation of what is meant by a flexible constitution and how this can undermine individual rights. Comparison needs to be drawn with a rigid (written) constitution with entrenched rights. Finally some thought needs to be given to how rights might be better protected under a flexible constitution.

Skeleton Solution

- Explanation of unwritten constitution.
- How does it provide flexibility?
- How does this flexibility undermine individual rights?
- Absence of entrenchment.
- Failure of the common law to develop certain rights.
- Proposals for incorporation of the European Convention on Human Rights.

Suggested Solution

The British constitution is usually classified as flexible in nature. This means that it is not fixed, and can be changed relatively easily. The thrust of the quotation under consideration is, therefore, that any rights provided by such a constitution are, of necessity, vulnerable, because they too can be changed or removed just as easily. The primary reason why the British constitution is classified as unwritten is the absence of any document laying down the basic rules within which the legislature, judiciary and executive must operate. By contrast, the American constitution provides perhaps the best known example of a written constitution. Unlike the British constitution, where, in theory, Parliament is sovereign and can make and unmake laws as it pleases, in the American constitution the legislature has to operate within the limits laid down by the written constitution. It is also subject to the controls exercised by the judiciary, for example where legislation is declared 'unconstitutional' by the Supreme Court. To ensure that they are not at the mercy of any particular political administration, the rights laid down in the American constitution are entrenched, meaning that the constitution can only be altered if two-thirds of Congress and three-quarters of the individual state legislatures agree to a proposed change. Hence any change is likely to be a long drawn out business, with ample opportunity for lobbying and debate.

In the British constitution even the most basic civil rights currently provided for by statute, (essentially the House of Commons) such as the right to vote, can be removed by a simple majority in Parliament in favour of a Bill having such effect. There is no written constitution limiting the power of Parliament, and the role of the judiciary is (in theory) to give effect to the will of Parliament as expressed in primary legislation. Other aspects of constitutional practice are found in conventions, such as ministerial responsibility, collective responsibility, and the 'Salisbury Convention' whereby the House of Lords will not block the passage of legislation passed by the House of Commons that reflects a manifesto commitment upon which the government was elected. Again conventions are flexible, because they emerge, develop and disappear according to current political practice. They are treated like rules but do not have the force of law. Although conventions tend to be concerned with the operation of central government, rather than individual rights, they can have an indirect bearing on the rights of the subject.

In the British constitution individual rights can also be developed by the judges at common law, the theory being that the common law is there to supply the omission of the legislature. Again this has the merit of flexibility, the courts being able to respond to new situations or threats as the case may be, but the decisions of the courts have no special status that offers them protection from subsequent change by the legislature, or even the judges themselves. The doctrine of parliamentary sovereignty means that Parliament can legislate to nullify the effect of any court decision it disagrees with or finds inconvenient. The enactment of the War Damage Act 1965 reversing the effect of the House of Lords' decision in *Burmah Oil* v *Lord Advocate* (1965) is a well-known example of this power being used. Neither should it be assumed that the courts are necessarily always willing to recognise the existence of rights at common law. In *Malone* v *Metropolitan Police Commissioner* (1979) the court refused to grant the plaintiff a declaration that his right to privacy was being violated by the police tapping his telephone line – the fact that such a right was enshrined in art 8 of the European Convention on Human Rights did not persuade the court that the common law provided such a right. Similarly, in *DPP* v *Jones* (1997), the court refused to accept that any assembly on the highway was lawful provided it was peaceful and did not amount to an obstruction, and went on to observe that a right to do something only exists if it cannot be stopped: the fact that it would not be stopped did not create a right to do it. Hence the traditional view that, save where rights are provided by statute, in the British constitution the notion of individual rights has always been an essentially a negative one – a citizen is free to do as he pleases provided there is no positive legal limitation on his doing so.

The Labour government elected in May 1997 committed itself to the incorporation of the European Convention on Human Rights into English law, and a Human Rights Act received the Royal Assent in 1998. When fully implemented the Human Rights Act 1998 will allow any 'victim' to bring an action, or apply for judicial review, against a public body, claiming a remedy because his or her Convention rights have been violated. If a court finds that there has been a violation it will be able to grant a declaration of incompatibility to the effect that a particular statutory provision offends against the Convention. It will then be for the appropriate minister to introduce amending legislation by means of a 'fast track' method. This compromise is interesting because it does not affect in anyway the notion of parliamentary sovereignty, nor does it affect the flexibility of the constitution. Instead it assumes that political pressure will ensure the passage of the necessary amending legislation. Similarly, ministers will still be free to introduce into the House of Commons legislation that contravenes the Convention, but will be required to make a statement to this effect. Again, the political repercussions of such a move are such that compliance with the Convention can probably be achieved without recourse to any major constitutional reforms.

QUESTION THREE

To what extent was Walter Bagehot correct in his assertion that the close fusion of the executive and the legislature represents the 'efficient secret' of the constitution?

University of London LLB Examination
(for External Students) Constitutional Law June 1997 Q3

General Comment

Essentially a question dealing with the separation of powers, but one that requires examination of a particular aspect, the relationship between the executive and the legislature. In particular consideration is required of the extent to which there is an overlap in the membership of these two branches of the constitution and the extent to which the legislature is able to perform its task of controlling and scrutinising the executive. The effectiveness of ministerial responsibility, select committees, parliamentary debates and questions needs to be considered.

Skeleton Solution

- Identify the executive.
- Identify the legislature.
- Outline the doctrine of the separation of powers.
- How are the executive and legislature fused?
- Effectiveness of control mechanisms.

Suggested Solution

The executive comprises the Prime Minister, the Cabinet, others holding ministerial office, as well as the civil service and other administrative agencies. The legislature comprises the House of Commons, the House of Lords and, in a technical sense, the Privy Council.

The doctrine of the separation of powers provides that the three functions of government, namely legislative, executive and judicial, should be kept separate. The basis for this is the belief that concentrating more than one function in any one organ of government presents a threat to individual liberty (ie power should not be concentrated in one sector of government). It also holds that each branch of government should, to some extent, be able to limit the power exercised by the others. Hence, under the constitution of the United States, the separation of powers manifests itself in a system of checks and balances whereby, for example, the Supreme Court can declare legislation to be 'unconstitutional'. Although the doctrine is not written into the British constitution, there being no written constitution to provide for this, it is undoubtedly the case that the separation of powers is, to some extent, a feature of the British constitution. For example, the judiciary has the power to declare actions of the executive (ie government ministers) unlawful: see *R* v *Secretary of State for the Home Department, ex parte Fire Brigades Union and Others* (1995). A key difference, however, between the British constitution and that of the United States is that, unlike Congress, Parliament at Westminster has (subject to the self-imposed restraints of EU membership) a legally unchallengeable right to make whatever laws it thinks right. The courts cannot declare an Act of Parliament to be unconstitutional, or in any way invalid. The most that the courts can do is grant interim relief in respect of legislation that appears to contravene Community law.

As Bagehot suggests the relationship between the legislature and executive is more complex. They are clearly not entirely separate branches of government. By convention the Prime Minister is now expected to be a member of the House of Common, as are his key ministers. Indeed, this overlap is recognised in statute by s52(1) of the House of Commons Disqualification Act 1975, which limits the number of ministers who may sit in the House of Commons to 95. Secondly, there is an overlap in terms of functions. Members of the executive do legislate from time to time. An Act passed by Parliament will often empower the relevant minister to deal with detailed issues by means of statutory instrument. Ministers also have residual prerogative powers to legislate without the consent of Parliament by means of Orders in Council. By contrast, under the United States constitution, neither the President nor members of his Cabinet can sit or vote in Congress. They have no direct power to initiate Bills, although the President can recommend legislation in his message to Congress. The President can veto legislation but can be overridden by a two-thirds vote in both Houses. Treaties are negotiated by the President, but must be approved by a two-thirds majority of the Senate.

Given, therefore, that the British constitution fails to conform to the classical notion of the doctrine of separation of powers as regards the relationship between the executive and the judiciary, in what sense can the relationship be described as 'efficient'? First there is the theory that the executive is accountable to the legislature (ie the House of Commons). The executive not only proposes the legislative programme to be considered by Parliament, but the responsible minister has to pilot the Bill through the House of Commons. This means that he has to maintain majority support in the legislature in order to ensure the passage of the legislation. If the government of the day were to lose a vote on a key piece of legislation, such as a Finance Bill, the convention is that it should resign, forcing a general election. Hence, in the most extreme case, the legislature can bring a government down. On a more day-to-day basis, having ministers in the House of Commons means that they can answer questions on the days when time is allocated for questions to ministers. They can also take part in debates, and can be asked to appear before select committees. The efficiency of the relationship between the executive and the legislature depends, however, on the extent to which these mechanisms work. Question Time in the House of Commons is seen by many critics as being merely ceremonial. Ministers will have been briefed on likely questions, and most take it as an opportunity to engage in political posturing, or the manufacture of media 'soundbites'. This is particularly the case with Prime Minister's questions. Debates in the House of Commons will often be poorly attended, many MPs turning up simply to vote according to party allegiance. Select committees have perhaps been more successful in bringing ministers to account, although the rules are not entirely clear in terms of when a minister must appear or what questions he must answer.

Two issues are perhaps fundamental. Short of passing a resolution of 'no confidence' in a government, the legislature can only really perform its task of trying to control the executive if the doctrine of ministerial responsibility is upheld. Increasingly it would appear that the convention of ministerial resignation when things go wrong at a departmental level is disappearing. The Scott Report (inquiry into the 'Arms to Iraq' affair) revealed that the doctrine of ministerial responsibility had not operated effectively to ensure that the House of Commons was kept aware of changes in government policy regarding arms sales. Further, the usual mechanisms for enforcing ministerial responsibility, such as parliamentary questions and hearings of select committees, had not adduced accurate answers, with the result that members of the House were misled. Following a debate on the Scott Report in the House of Commons the Public Service Committee of the House of Commons launched an inquiry into ministerial responsibility, and in its report of 1996 concluded that ministerial responsibility in the modern constitution was less based on a convention of resignation in the wake of departmental failings, and more on keeping Parliament fully and accurately informed, of responding to questions asked in Parliament, whether as parliamentary questions or in front of select committees, and resigning if found to have knowingly mislead the House, ie where it was the minister's decision to lie.

The second issue is the size of a government's majority in the House of Commons. In simple terms a government with a large majority can normally be confident of getting its legislative programme through. A government with a slender majority has to pay far more attention to the views of individual MPs, to head off rebellions that might result in defeat. Where a government has a large majority the role of the executive is more significant as regards its scrutiny of ministerial performance, rather than in challenging government policy.

In conclusion it would seem that Bagehot's observation is essentially correct, but does suggest a degree of complacency. The fusion of the executive and legislature in the British constitution does produce efficiencies, particularly in relation to accountability, but care has to be taken to assess whether those accountability mechanisms are in good working order.

QUESTION FOUR

'Constitutionalism, like an elephant, is hard to define but easy to recognise.'

Discuss.

University of London LLB Examination
(for External Students) Constitutional Law June 1997 Q4

General Comment

This is not a question about the constitution in any general sense, or indeed the sources of the constitution as such. Essentially it is concerned with an examination of government according to law. Hence an examination of the rule of law is required, and the mechanisms that exist to ensure it operates properly.

Skeleton Solution

- Explanation of constitutionalism.
- The nature of constitutional rules.
- The meaning of the rule of law.
- The extent to which the British constitution conforms to this.
- Constitutionalism as a substantive concept.
- The role of the judiciary.
- The importance of non-legal constraints on political action.

Suggested Solution

Constitutionalism is hard to define in any precise sense. In general terms it could be described as government according to the rules of the constitution. This notion can perhaps be developed further by an examination of constitutionalism in terms of form and procedure on the one hand, and an examination of constitutionalism in terms of substantive content, on the other.

In its narrow sense constitutionalism assumes that there are some constitutional rules within which the organs of government must operate. These rules might be found in a written document referred to as 'the constitution' (as is the case with most written constitutions), or by reference to the custom and practice of the organs of government, as is the case with a largely unwritten constitution.

Secondly, constitutionalism assumes that these rules, whether written or unwritten will be obeyed as if they were binding, in other words as if they have the force of law. The essence of the rule of law is that even those who govern should be subject to some higher law and should govern in accordance with that higher law. In his *Law of the Constitution* Dicey identified three aspects of the rule of law that can be equated with the concept of constitutionalism. First, that individuals should not be subject to arbitrary decision making – government should be according to known laws. Second, that the law should apply to all equally. Third, that the rights of the individual are determined by and are dependent upon the ordinary law of the land as developed by the ordinary courts adjudicating in particular cases.

To what extent does the British constitution adhere to this narrow concept of constitutionalism? As regards Parliament itself, it does not. Parliament is sovereign and can pass such laws as it thinks fit. It is effectively a law unto itself. An Act of Parliament could not be challenged in the courts on the basis that the correct procedure in Parliament had not been followed. Any discrepancies in the parliamentary process would be a matter for Parliament itself to deal with: see *Pickin* v *British Railways Board* (1974). As regards administrative agencies such as ministers, tribunals and local authorities, the narrow concept of constitutionalism is much easier to enforce. If a procedural requirement laid down in a statute is not complied with the resulting administrative action can normally be challenged in the courts by way of an application for judicial review. Not all areas of ministerial activity are governed by statute, however. Whether or not a minister should resign in the event of some failure on his part, or that of his department, is governed by convention. The courts will pronounce on the existence of constitutional conventions, but will not enforce them, as they do not form part of the law of the land: see *Re Amendment of the Constitution of Canada* (1982).

Thus constitutionalism can, in the narrow sense, be taken to mean 'playing by the rules'. It is submitted, however, that constitutionalism also bears a wider meaning, in that it can relate to the substance of the decisions taken by those in power. Even if all the procedural rules relating to the enactment of legislation were followed there would still be some laws that would be regarded as unfair or invalid in the sense that they offended against natural justice, or violated certain basic rights regarded as inalienable. Examples might be legislation denying women the right to vote, or legislation permitting the persecution of a racial or religious minority. These would be valid laws in the procedural sense, but could nevertheless be described as 'unconstitutional' because they offend against the norms of fairness that pertain in most liberal, pluralistic, democracies. The examples given are necessarily extreme, in order to make the point. In reality it may be far more difficult to discern whether or not legislation is unconstitutional in the wider sense. A useful indicator may be public and press reaction. The legislation that introduced the Community Charge, or 'Poll Tax', was met with sustained criticism from many quarters, and resulted in riots, civil disobedience and non-observance. These are all clues that suggest that the government of the day may have gone too far. No matter how big a majority a government might have in the House of Commons, it must still be mindful of how the public at large is going to react to a change in the law.

Whilst judges cannot declare primary legislation to be invalid as such, they can strike down delegated legislation on the basis that it is ultra vires. Failure to conform to the standards of constitutionalism is not one of the grounds of judicial review as such, but judges will declare delegated legislation invalid on the grounds that, if put into effect, it will have unacceptable consequences. Hence in *R* v *Secretary of State for Social Security, ex parte Joint Council for the Welfare of Immigrants* (1996), the Court of Appeal held that regulations, removing from asylum seekers any entitlement to income benefit, were invalid because they meant that asylum seekers would effectively be unable to exercise their rights of appeal. Simon Brown LJ described the regulations as 'uncompromisingly draconian' and likely to result in a life for asylum seekers that was 'so destitute that no civilised nation could contemplate it'. The courts will also quash an exercise of executive discretion if they feel that it causes a result which is unfair: see for example *Congreve* v *Home Office* (1976) – minister using a regulatory power in order to raise revenue.

In those areas not governed by statute, whether or not action is regarded as unconstitutional will depend on popular opinion and press comment. For example, failure to resign after losing a vote of 'no confidence' in the House of Commons; appointing individuals who are not Members of Parliament to key ministerial posts; lying to House of Commons; or forcing through significant constitutional changes, such as the introduction of proportional representation, or a single European currency, in the absence of any clear electoral mandate. Notwithstanding that a government, or individual ministers, may have the power to do all of these things (by which is meant there is not positive law against doing these things), many would still describe such actions as unconstitutional, in the sense that they lack political legitimacy. In this sense we do know unconstitutional action when we see it, even if a definition that would satisfy lawyers remains elusive.

QUESTION FIVE

'The doctrine of individual and collective responsibility requires greater clarification if members of government are to be confined within the rule of law.'

Discuss.

University of London LLB Examination
(for External Students) Constitutional Law June 1997 Q5

General Comment

The question clearly calls for an explanation of the doctrines of collective and ministerial responsibility, and the concept of the rule of law, but the link between responsible government and the rule of law must be explored as well. The impact of recent developments such as the Nolan Committee recommendations, and the Scott Report also needs to be considered.

Skeleton Solution

- What is collective responsibility?
- What is ministerial responsibility?
- What is meant by the rule of law?
- What is the relationship between these doctrines?
- Are there clear rules?
- What dangers exist?
- What attempts have been made at clarification?

Suggested Solution

There are two main constitutional conventions that govern the activities of government ministers, namely collective responsibility and individual ministerial responsibility. The convention of collective responsibility is traditionally evidenced by two separate conventions: that the Government must resign if it loses the support of the House of Commons; and that the Government must speak with one voice. In practice this means that ministers must support each other in public, and support agreed Cabinet policy. Individual ministerial responsibility has, traditionally, two aspects: (i) the individual responsibility of ministers to Parliament for decisions taken in their departments, whether by themselves or by their civil servants; and (ii) responsibility for the conduct of private life, to the extent that it might impinge upon a minister's ability to discharge his or her functions effectively.

What is the relationship between these doctrines of responsibility and the rule of law? The traditional view of the rule of law is that the law should be certain (as opposed to arbitrary), and that no one should be above the law, in the sense that all should be equally subject to the rule of law. The difficulty in confining the doctrines of responsible government within the concept of the rule of law lies, initially at least, in the fact that the doctrines are not rooted in law at all, but in convention. Conventions are the custom and practice of government that pertain in those areas where no statute law or common law applies. Conventions often reflect 'efficient' constitutional practice and are borne out of pragmatism, for example the convention that a government should resign if it loses a vote of 'no confidence' in the House of Commons. If a government were to ignore this convention it could remain in office, but it would not be in power, as it would have lost the ability to determine the legislative programme of the House of Commons, hence the need to request a dissolution of Parliament. On the other hand, even though conventions are not, in the technical sense, laws, one should look at the way in which ministers regard them. If conventions are observed as if they are laws, then there is a strong argument that, in a sense, conventions come within the scope of the rule of law.

Given that responsible government is, therefore, largely a matter of convention, as opposed to law, much depends on how certain these conventions are. As regards collective responsibility the position is tolerably clear. Constitutional practice indicates that ministers do resign when they cannot agree with their colleagues. Michael Heseltine's resignation over the Westland affair is an example. Where, however, the disagreements threaten to split the Cabinet there is the possibility that there might be an 'agreement to differ'. In 1932 the Liberal members of the National Government only agreed to remain on condition that they were allowed to speak and vote against it on the question of the imposition of tariffs. In 1975, the Labour Cabinet agreed to differ on the question of the United Kingdom's continued membership of the EEC. It could be argued that a new convention is emerging to the effect that collective responsibility applies except where the Prime Minister of the day allows it to be relaxed. This, however, is such a flexible notion that most would say it goes against the argument that collective responsibility is actually governed by any rules, and therefore confined by the rule of law. Perhaps the more pertinent question to ask is whether or not the doctrine of collective responsibility needs to be clarified any further. There is much to be said for a flexible doctrine that can adapt to the political situation facing any particular government, for example disagreement amongst ministers over the decision to join a single European currency. This is all the more so where the opposition appears split on the same issue.

How clear are the conventions relating ministerial responsibility? In theory, ministers are responsible to Parliament for their own actions, omissions and mistakes as well as for those of the officials in their departments. In its classical form, the convention is that criticism should be directed at the minister rather than at any civil servant who may be at fault, and that in cases where there has been serious mismanagement of a department's affairs, it is the minister who resigns. This convention reflects the theory that individual civil servants are meant to remain anonymous, so as to promote the objectivity and efficiency, of the Civil Service. The Crichel Down affair is an oft-cited example of this convention in operation. In more modern times one might point to the resignation of Lord Carrington over the invasion of the Falkland Islands by the Argentinians. Increasingly, however, ministers have adopted the view that they should not be criticised for shortcomings of which they are not aware, and which they could not reasonably have been expected to discover, or which do not occur as a foreseeable result of their own actions. This is allied to the changes in ministerial responsibility resulting from the transfer of departmental functions to the Next Steps agencies. Increasingly ministers criticised for departmental failings are drawing a distinction between their policies and the execution of those policies by agency staff. Provided the minister sacks the head of the relevant agency when something goes seriously wrong he will feel that he has discharged his ministerial responsibility: see the action taken by Michael Howard as Home Secretary in sacking the chief executive of the Prison Service following a number of escapes from Parkhurst Prison. The weaknesses in the doctrine of ministerial responsibility were further exposed by the 'Arms to Iraq' affair. The Scott Report indicated that guidelines on arms exports had been relaxed, so as to permit the export of militarily useful equipment to countries such as Iraq; that this information had been withheld from Parliament; and that the government had appeared to be willing to rely on public interest immunity certificates being granted to suppress the evidence concerning the changes to the guidelines with the possibility that innocent persons might have been convicted of breaching them. Sir Richard Scott concluded that the doctrine of ministerial responsibility had not operated effectively to ensure that the House of Commons was kept aware of changes in government policy regarding arms sales, and that the usual mechanisms for enforcing ministerial responsibility, such as parliamentary questions and hearings of select committees, had not adduced accurate answers. In a subsequent report, the Public Service Committee of the House of Commons concluded that ministerial responsibility in the modern constitution was not based on a convention of resignation in the wake of departmental failings, but on one of keeping Parliament fully and accurately informed. In short a minister should really only resign if found to have knowingly lied to Parliament. This emphasises that ministerial responsibility has evolved, to some extent, from being a doctrine concerned with responsibility for departments, to being one concerned with effective accountability in the House of Commons.

As regards the personal conduct of ministers, or those closely connected to them, there is no hard and fast convention regarding resignation. Everything depends on the extent to which they are able to command the respect of colleagues and the public at large. Extra-marital activities that suggest subterfuge and deceit generally lead to resignation because they cast doubt upon the honesty of a minister. If it is a minister whose son is discovered trading in illegal substances however, there would appear to be no reason to resign provided there has been no attempt at a cover-up.

All of this suggests that the doctrine of individual ministerial responsibility is more difficult to reconcile with the notion of the rule of law, because there is so little clarity regarding when a minister should resign or how he should conduct himself. As a response to this, and in the wake of the Nolan Committee Report on Standards in Public Life, the Code of Practice, known as *Questions of Procedure for Ministers*, has been revised. Essentially it is an attempt to codify the rules relating to ministerial behaviour. Amongst other things it provides that ministers must give accurate and truthful information to Parliament, correcting any inadvertent error at the earliest opportunity, and makes clear that ministers who knowingly mislead Parliament will be expected to offer their resignation to the Prime Minister.

The revised Code provides greater clarity, therefore, but does not answer criticisms regarding the extent to which such matters are confined by the rule of law, as the Code does not have the status of law. It is enforced by the Prime Minister, and the sanctions are a matter for him. Overall, given the extent to which political expediency plays a part in determining the behaviour of ministers, it is difficult to see what tighter legal controls could achieve.

QUESTION SIX

To what extent does English law uphold the requirements of the European Convention on Human Rights?

University of London LLB Examination
(for External Students) Constitutional Law June 1997 Q6

General Comment

This question requires an examination of the status of the European Convention on Human Rights in English law. When the question was originally set it would have required an examination of the significance of non-incorporation. With the enactment of the Human Rights Act 1998 a different emphasis would now be required. Examples of the extent to which the courts have been prepared to take the Convention into account as a persuasive source of law can be included, but an examination of the effect of the Human Rights Act is required.

Skeleton Solution

- Overview of the present position.
- History of non-incorporation.
- Use as a persuasive source of law.
- Extent to which the common law upholds rights.

- How compliance with ECJ rulings is ensured.
- Effect of Human Rights Act.

Suggested Solution

Until such time as the Human Rights Act 1998 becomes fully operative (expected to be late 2000 or early 2001) it could be argued that, in theory, English law does not uphold the European Convention on Human Rights in any direct sense. The Convention is an international treaty to which the United Kingdom is a signatory. The Convention therefore creates international obligations imposed on the United Kingdom as regards other sovereign states. It became part of domestic law with the enactment of the Human Rights Act 1998 but, as mentioned, is not yet fully in force.

In the past the English courts have applied the Convention to resolve ambiguities in domestic legislation, invoking the rule of statutory interpretation that it is presumed that Parliament would not have legislated in contravention of those obligations without clearly flagging that fact. Beyond this, however, the courts have been reluctant to give effect to the Convention in any sense in which it might be said to override domestic law. In *Uppal* v *Home Office* (1978) the court rejected the argument that deportation would be a breach of the right to respect for family life under art 8 of the Convention, holding that obligations in international law which were not enforceable as part of English law could not be the subject of declaratory judgments. A request for a declaration that art 8 had been violated by police tapping telephone calls was also famously rejected by the court in *Malone* v *Metropolitan Police Commissioner* (1979). The House of Lords made clear in *R* v *Secretary of State for the Home Department, ex parte Brind* (1991), that a public body, in exercising its discretion, was not bound, in law, to take the Convention into account. In arriving at this conclusion the House of Lords recognised that to have accepted such a contention would have amounted to the incorporation of the Convention via the 'back door'.

Simply because the courts have not been willing to give precedence to the Convention, or rely on it to create new rights, does not mean, however, that English law has not uphold any of the Convention rights. The courts have noted that in many cases the common law provides the same protection as the Convention, and it is for that reason that the Convention has not been taken into account. For example, in *Derbyshire County Council* v *Times Newspapers Ltd and Others* (1993), the House of Lords, in holding that a local authority could not use the law of defamation against a newspaper that had been critical of its conduct in certain financial matters, observed that recourse to art 10 of the Convention was unnecessary as the common law was consistent with the Convention. Similarly, in *Rantzen* v *Mirror Group Newspapers (1986) Ltd* (1993), the Court of Appeal expressed the view that art 10 reflected the rules of the common law in relation to freedom of expression.

Where United Kingdom law has more clearly upheld the requirements of the Convention is in those areas where a case has been brought against the United Kingdom in the European Court of Human Rights and the Court has found United Kingdom to be at odds with the Convention. In each case (save those involving derogations etc) the United Kingdom government has taken steps to ensure that domestic law has been altered to meet the requirements of the Convention. For example, the *Malone* case led to the introduction of legal rules on telephone-taping: the Interception of Communications Act 1985. Similarly, *Sunday Times* v *UK* (1979) led to the reform of the law of contempt found in the Contempt of Court Act 1981. Other changes have been made in respect of corporal punishment, and the rights of homosexuals in Northern Ireland. In this sense it can be said that, over a period of time, as more reforms have been introduced in the wake of European Court of Human Rights rulings, English law has increasingly come to uphold the rights protected by the Convention.

Once the Human Rights Act 1998 becomes fully operative United Kingdom law will provide a much more effective means of upholding Convention rights. Individuals will be able to bring proceedings against a public body in the appropriate court or tribunal. A court or tribunal called upon to do so, must interpret primary legislation and subordinate legislation in a way which is compatible with the Convention rights – this duty will apply whether the legislation was enacted before or after the coming into force of the Human Rights Act 1998. In reaching its decision s2(1) of the 1998 Act makes it clear that any court or tribunal determining a question arising in connection with a Convention right *must* take into account: any judgment, decision, declaration or advisory opinion of the European Court of Human Rights. If domestic law cannot be interpreted so as to achieve compliance with the Convention the higher courts will be able to grant a declaration of incompatibility. The assumption is that if such a declaration is made a minister may, if he considers that there are compelling reasons for so doing, make orders to amend the relevant legislation to the extent that considers necessary to remove the incompatibility: see s10(1) and (2).

QUESTION SEVEN

Draft a memorandum to the government, outlining your preferred alternative to the current role and composition of the House of Lords. Explain to the government any constitutional implications of your proposed reforms.

University of London LLB Examination
(for External Students) Constitutional Law June 1997 Q7

General Comment

This is a topical question, which requires some knowledge of the current debate about the future of the House of Lords. It does not ask the candidate to simply explain the workings of the House of Lords. Note that the emphasis is on one reform proposal, so it would be inappropriate to consider a whole range of unconnected options. An essential part of the answer is the assessment of the constitutional impact of reforms, particularly in relation to the powers and status of the House of Commons. Interestingly the question does not seem to permit candidates the option of supporting the status quo.

Skeleton Solution

- Explanation of the political debate.
- Outline of reform ideas.
- Role of hereditary peers.
- Reform of life peerages.
- Appointment process.
- Delaying powers.
- Salisbury convention.
- Examination of the constitutional implications.

- The need for a second chamber.
- Limits on the powers of the House of Commons.

Suggested Solution

The House of Lords, in its present form, is something of a political anachronism and needs reform. The following changes are recommended.

Membership of the House of Lords

At present the composition of the House of Lords is still largely based on the hereditary principle. Peers are entitled to sit in the House of Lords, take part in debates, and vote on legislation simply by virtue of the titles held by their families. As of October 1996 the House of Lords comprised approximately 1207 members, of whom 626 were hereditary peers. Of those hereditary peers, 318 were supporters of the Conservative Party whilst only 15 took the Labour whip. Hence there is a clear imbalance in terms of party support. The continued existence of hereditary peers offends against basic democratic principles, given that they are not elected and are therefore unaccountable. There is also the possibility that a Labour government, elected with a large majority (or even a majority of the popular vote) might find itself thwarted in attempting to pursue its legislative programme by opposition from the disproportionate number of Conservative hereditary peers turning up to vote in the House of Lords (the so-called 'backwoodsmen'). The first recommendation of this paper, therefore, is that legislation be prepared that would: (a) remove from hereditary peers the right to vote in the House of Lords; and (b) end the hereditary principle by providing that no child of any hereditary peer will, in future, automatically become a member of the House of Lords simply by virtue of succession.

The constitutional implications of this change are that there will immediately be a much fairer balance of power between the parties in the House of Lords. Hereditary peers with valuable experience will still be able to contribute to debates for as long as they remain members of the House. As hereditary peers die out, the number of people entitled to attend the House of Lords will drop dramatically, and in due course the membership will be made up almost entirely of life peers, and those who become members by virtue of their office.

This change will raise further questions as to the number of life peers and the manner in which they should be appointed. At present life peers are appointed by the Queen, on the advice of the Prime Minister. By convention those appointed will reflect a range of political views, although there is a clear tendency for the party in office to favour its own supporters. The serious constitutional danger is that a Prime Minister could use his power of appointment to flood the second chamber with supporters, and thus ensure that any opposition to his legislative programme would be overcome. The second recommendation of this paper is, therefore, that: (a) the House of Lords should be renamed, possibly as the 'Upper Chamber'; and (b) that life peerages as they now exist should also be abolished.

A Commission on Appointments to the Upper House should be created, chaired by a High Court judge, with members from across the political spectrum. The Commission could consider nominations for appointment and make recommendations to the Prime Minister. In turn the Prime Minister would be given a statutory power to appoint suitably qualified individuals as 'Members of the Upper House'. This power would be placed on a statutory basis, with clear guidelines on the need to ensure a political balance in the upper house. The power could then be subject to judicial review as a safeguard against abuse. In addition, membership of the

'Upper House' should be for five years in the first instance, a Prime Minister having the power to renew membership for a further five years thereafter if he sees fit. The advantage of this system is that, given that a general election will be held at least every five years, there will be an opportunity for a newly elected government, if not a new Prime Minister, to make appointments reflecting the national mood and preferences. It may also help to ensure that those who wish to be re-appointed demonstrate that they can make a positive contribution to the working of the second chamber. Although more democratic, an elected second chamber is not recommended at present, as this would have as much legislative legitimacy as the House of Commons (if not more, if proportional representation is used), and disputes between the two Houses would be more serious than they are at present.

The role of the House of Lords

The House of Lords at present serves an essential role as a delaying and revising chamber. Where legislation is rushed through the House of Commons, sometimes with the use of a time-allocation order, it can receive more detailed scrutiny in the Lords. At the beginning of a parliamentary session, when there would otherwise be little for the second chamber to do, non-controversial Bills can be introduced into the House of Lords, so that they need not be reconsidered again by that chamber when they have completed the legislative process in the House of Commons. By virtue of the Parliament Acts 1911 and 1949, the House of Lords also acts as an essential brake on the otherwise sovereign power of the House of Commons to enact any law it wishes. Where controversial legislation is put forward, this delaying power provides further time for consideration, lobbying and reform. In particular the House of Lords can veto any Bill to extend the life of a Parliament beyond five years, and thus prevent an unpopular government from postponing a general election. For these reasons no significant change in the powers of the second chamber is proposed. One area that might be looked at, however, is the Salisbury convention, whereby the House of Lords will not veto legislation for which a government has an electoral mandate. In order to diffuse allegations that an unelected second chamber, however appointed, should not have the power to thwart the will of the electorate, it is recommended that the Salisbury convention should be enacted in statute. The Speaker of the House of Commons should be empowered to determine whether or not a Bill embodies a manifesto commitment for which the government has a mandate, and his determination should be immune from legal challenge. It would then be clear that no question of the second chamber preventing the passage of such legislation could arise.

In conclusion it should be noted that, whilst these recommendations are modest, and could be criticised on the grounds that they do not amount to a thorough reform of the second chamber, the history of attempts at reform over the last 60 years indicates that there is a limit to what can be achieved in the lifetime of any one Parliament. These proposals at least have the advantage of appealing to the popular sentiment against hereditary peerages, and are aimed at making the second chamber more responsive and constructive.

QUESTION EIGHT

Critically assess the constitutional role of judicial review in upholding the sovereignty of Parliament and the rule of law. How effective are the courts in fulfilling this role?

University of London LLB Examination
(for External Students) Constitutional Law June 1997 Q8

General Comment

This question calls for an explanation of the constitutional basis for judicial review and the distribution of powers within the constitution. Candidates need to explain the dual role of the courts when exercising judicial review powers, namely giving effect to the intention of Parliament (the parliamentary sovereignty issue), and ensuring that the executive acts within the limits of its powers (the rule of law issue). Bear in mind that a critical assessment is called for, so candidates should not just describe what happens but should offer a view as to whether the courts are discharging these functions satisfactorily, supported by examples.

Skeleton Solution

- The theoretical basis for judicial review.
- How the courts uphold the sovereignty of Parliament.
- Possible exceptions.
- Upholding the rule of law.
- The ultra vires doctrine.
- Examples.
- Critique of the role of the courts.

Suggested Solution

The High Court has a common law jurisdiction to review the legality of actions taken by inferior bodies, or bodies of limited jurisdiction. Arguably the only institutions which do not have limited jurisdiction are Parliament and the Crown, hence judicial review today extends to the whole range of executive and administrative agencies, from tribunals, local authorities and quangos to government ministers. Parliament frequently enacts enabling legislation creating administrative bodies, or enacts legislation that places duties on, and gives powers to, existing administrative agencies. In the event that an application for judicial review is made on the basis that an administrative agency has failed to comply with an enabling Act, it will be the task of the reviewing court to determine what Parliament intended when the legislation in question was enacted. In a sense the courts would describe themselves as enforcing the ultra vires principle (i.e. ensuring that administrative agencies act within the limits of their delegated powers and perform their statutory duties), but in reality they are making sure that the intention of Parliament is reflected in the way in which the administrative body exercises its powers.

Equally, when a court exercises its power of judicial review, it is seeking to ensure that the rule of law is upheld. The ultra vires principle holds that any action taken by an administrative agency that results in it exceeding its powers will be unlawful and invalid. In other words administrative bodies must act within the limits of the powers given to them, and in that sense are subject to the rule of law as imposed by means of judicial review. The courts can therefore ensure that there are known limits to the powers of administrative agencies, rather than them having arbitrary powers over individuals. The courts can also uphold the rule of law by ensuring that the law applies equally to all. Indeed the significance of judicial review lies in the fact that it is a process by which the ordinary citizen can, in principle, challenge the legality of any action in the public law sphere, even that taken by a minister of the Crown. Ultimately, on the assumption that Parliament never intends any inferior body to exceed the limits of its powers, upholding the sovereignty of Parliament and the rule of law are the same thing. The courts will declare administrative action ultra vires because it is beyond what is permitted by an enabling Act. The court will have determined the limits of power by examining the statute in question. The court can justify its actions by claiming to be giving effect to the sovereign wishes of Parliament as expressed in the Act.

So much for the constitutional theory, how well does it work in practice? First, judicial review can only be effective if an application is made. There may be many ultra vires decisions that go unchallenged because those affected are ignorant, impecunious, or simply accept the actions of administrators unquestioningly. Second, the courts may decline to intervene because what is being challenged is a policy issue, the legality of which the courts cannot comment upon. Hence in *R* v *Cambridge District Health Authority, ex parte B* (1995) the court held that it would not review the budgeting decision taken by a health authority refusing to provide treatment due to lack of resources. The courts will also decline to intervene if they characterise an impugned decision as involving principally a question of fact. In *Puhlhofer* v *Hillingdon London Borough Council* (1986) the House of Lords held that it was for a local housing authority to determine whether applicants had been provided with 'suitable accommodation'. A closer reading of the judgments will reveal, however, that the House of Lords was concerned that if it allowed the application for judicial review to proceed local authorities might face a huge increase in the number of judicial review cases. An application for judicial review may also be unsuccessful if the court determines that the decision in question falls into the 'non-justiciable' category. The speeches in *Council of Civil Service Unions* v *Minister for the Civil Service* (1984) identify those matters traditionally considered to fall outside the scope of justiciability, including the conduct of foreign affairs, disposition of troops, appointment of ministers and so forth. Courts are particularly reluctant to intervene where a minister claims to have acted to protect national security. In *R* v *Secretary of State for the Home Department, ex parte Cheblak* (1991) Lord Donaldson MR argued that where the courts declined to review a decision of a minister on the grounds of national security, the constitutional safeguard was supplied by ministerial responsibility to Parliament. The Scott Report perhaps casts doubt upon this view. Finally, decisions such as *R* v *Secretary of State for the Environment, ex parte Nottinghamshire County Council* (1986) suggest that the courts will be reluctant to declare administrative action ultra vires if it has been expressly approved by the House of Commons.

Hence, whilst in principle judicial review is a powerful weapon that the courts can use to uphold the rule of law, and therefore parliamentary sovereignty, it is of no use whatsoever if they decline to exercise it. In essence there will be no means of mounting any legal challenge to these decisions, thus placing them, in effect, above the law. Conversely it can be argued that there are occasions where the court actually subvert the notion of parliamentary sovereignty by way of judicial review. In *Anisminic* v *Foreign Compensation Commission* (1969) (a case that would have been pursued by way of judicial review had it occurred now), the plaintiffs sought a declaration that the Commission had acted ultra vires in denying them the correct level of compensation. The statute in question provided that no determination of the Commission was to be called into question in any court of law. Despite the clear wording of the statute the House of Lords allowed a legal challenge to the Commission's decision, on the basis that the statute only prohibited challenges to intra vires (ie valid) determinations. As the House of Lords had decided that the determination was ultra vires it was not protected by the statute. The decision was quite contrary to the intention of Parliament. The aim of the Act was to prevent any legal challenges to the decisions of the Commission because it only had a finite amount of money to distribute. If it had distributed money and then had its decisions successfully challenged in the courts it could have found itself having to pay out more compensation, having already distributed the fund. The case is perhaps an example of the courts upholding the rule of law (ie that no body should be above the law) in preference to the doctrine of parliamentary sovereignty. There are also many cases were the courts have struck down delegated legislation on the basis that Parliament cannot have intended ministers to have had the power to introduce such extreme measures, only for Parliament to quickly pass amending legislation making it clear that it did intend just that result: see for example *R* v *Secretary of State for Social Security, ex parte Joint Council for the Welfare of Immigrants* (1996). In such cases the courts could argue that the legislation simply did not state Parliament's intentions clearly enough, but the reality is that the courts are not averse to throwing out a constitutional challenge to the legislature when it suits them to do so.

In conclusion it should be noted that, on the one hand, the courts deal with only a tiny fraction of the disputes between the citizen and the state. The majority of disputes are dealt with by tribunals and administrative appeal procedures. On the other hand judicial review has developed over the last 50 years to become a powerful weapon against unlawful executive action. The effectiveness of judicial review depends on the willingness of the judiciary to be assertive and creative in their application of the ultra vires doctrine.

Law Update 2001

Law Update 2002 edition – due February 2002

An annual review of the most recent developments in specific legal subject areas, useful for law students at degree and professional levels, others with law elements in their courses and also practitioners seeking a quick update.

Published around February every year, the Law Update summarises the major legal developments during the course of the previous year. In conjunction with Old Bailey Press textbooks it gives the student a significant advantage when revising for examinations.

Contents
Administrative Law • Civil and Criminal Procedure • Company Law • Conflict of Laws • Constitutional Law • Contract Law • Conveyancing • Criminal Law • Criminology • English Legal System • Equity and Trusts • European Union Law • Evidence • Family Law • Jurisprudence • Land Law • Law of International Trade • Public International Law • Revenue Law • Succession • Tort

For further information on contents or to place an order, please contact:

Mail Order
Old Bailey Press
200 Greyhound Road
London
W14 9RY

Telephone No: 020 7381 7407
Fax No: 020 7386 0952
Website: www.oldbaileypress.co.uk

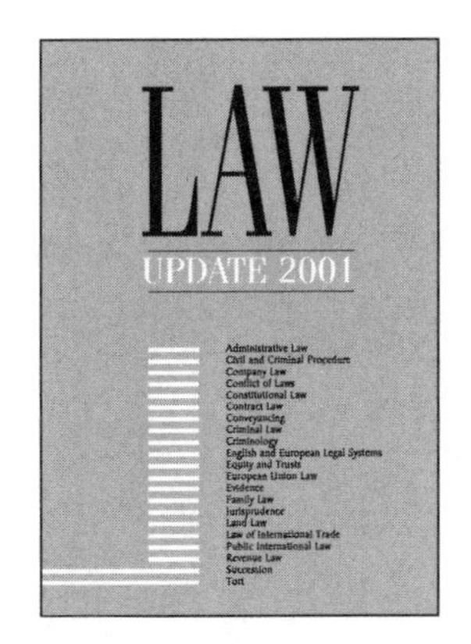

ISBN 1 85836 385 3
Soft cover 246 x 175 mm
408 pages £9.95
Published March 2001

Old Bailey Press

The Old Bailey Press integrated student law library is tailor-made to help you at every stage of your studies from the preliminaries of each subject through to the final examination. The series of Textbooks, Revision WorkBooks, 150 Leading Cases/Casebooks and Cracknell's Statutes are interrelated to provide you with a comprehensive set of study materials.

You can buy Old Bailey Press books from your University Bookshop, your local Bookshop, direct using this form, or you can order a free catalogue of our titles from the address shown overleaf.

The following subjects each have a Textbook, 150 Leading Cases/Casebook, Revision WorkBook and Cracknell's Statutes unless otherwise stated.

Administrative Law
Commercial Law
Company Law
Conflict of Laws
Constitutional Law
Conveyancing (Textbook and Casebook)
Criminal Law
Criminology (Textbook and Sourcebook)
English and European Legal Systems
Equity and Trusts
Evidence
Family Law
Jurisprudence: The Philosophy of Law (Textbook, Sourcebook and Revision WorkBook)
Land: The Law of Real Property
Law of International Trade
Law of the European Union
Legal Skills and System
Obligations: Contract Law
Obligations: The Law of Tort
Public International Law
Revenue Law (Textbook, Sourcebook and Revision WorkBook)
Succession

Mail order prices:

Textbook	£14.95
150 Leading Cases/Casebook	£9.95
Revision WorkBook	£7.95
Cracknell's Statutes	£9.95
Suggested Solutions 1998–1999	£6.95
Law Update 2001	£9.95

To complete your order, please fill in the form below:

Module	Books required	Quantity	Price	Cost
		Postage		
		TOTAL		

For Europe, add 15% postage and packing (£20 maximum).
For the rest of the world, add 40% for airmail.

ORDERING

By telephone to Mail Order at 020 7381 7407, with your credit card to hand.

By fax to 020 7386 0952 (giving your credit card details).

Website: www.oldbaileypress.co.uk

By post to: Mail Order, Old Bailey Press, 200 Greyhound Road, London W14 9RY.

When ordering by post, please enclose full payment by cheque or banker's draft, or complete the credit card details below. You may also order a free catalogue of our complete range of titles from this address.

We aim to despatch your books within 3 working days of receiving your order.

Name

Address

Postcode Telephone

Total value of order, including postage: £

I enclose a cheque/banker's draft for the above sum, or

charge my ☐ Access/Mastercard ☐ Visa ☐ American Express

Card number

☐☐☐☐ ☐☐☐☐ ☐☐☐☐ ☐☐☐☐

Expiry date ☐☐☐☐

Signature: .... Date: ....